JIRA 4 Essentials

Track bugs, issues, and manage your software
development projects with JIRA

Patrick Li

BIRMINGHAM - MUMBAI

JIRA 4 Essentials

First published: May 2011

Production Reference: 1160511

Published by Packt Publishing Ltd.
32 Lincoln Road
Olton
Birmingham, B27 6PA, UK.

ISBN 978-1-849681-72-8

www.packtpub.com

Cover Image by Artie Ng (artherng@yahoo.com.au)

Credits

Author
Patrick Li

Reviewers
Matthew B. Doar

Stafford Vaughan

Marcin Zręda

Acquisition Editor
Amey Kanse

Development Editor
Alina Lewis

Technical Editor
Kavita Iyer

Copy Editor
Neha Shetty

Project Coordinator
Vishal Bodwani

Proofreader
Josh Toth

Indexers
Monica Ajmera Mehta

Rekha Nair

Graphics
Geetanjali Sawant

Production Coordinators
Alwin Roy

Arvindkumar Gupta

Cover Work
Alwin Roy

Arvindkumar Gupta

About the Author

Patrick Li is a senior engineer at AppFusions, the leading Atlassian partner specializing in delivering Enterprise 2.0 solutions for clients in the United States, UK, Australia, and Hong Kong.

He has worked in the Atlassian ecosystem for over four years, developing solutions for Atlassian products and providing expert consulting services. He is one of the top contributors to the Atlassian community, providing answers and suggestions on the Atlassian user forum.

He has extensive experience in designing and deploying Atlassian solutions from the ground up, as well as customizing existing deployments for clients across verticals like Healthcare, Software Engineering, Financial Services, and Government Agencies.

I would like to thank my family, especially my wife Katherine, who has been very supportive during all this time. I would also like to thank everyone who has edited and reviewed the book.

About the Reviewers

Matt Doar first discovered JIRA while writing *Practical Development Environments* (O'Reilly, 2005). Since then, his company **Consulting Toolsmiths** has helped dozens of organizations to use JIRA the way they want to. He is also the author of a number of significant plugins in the Atlassian Plugin Exchange.

Before that, he was a software toolsmith and developer for a number of networking companies in Northern California. He has a Ph.D. in Computer Science from the University of Cambridge.

> I'd like to thank my dear children Elizabeth, Jacob, and Lucas for all their questions and my beloved wife Katherine for her patience with my answers. I think it's for my family that God has established the work of my hands (Psalm 90:17).

Stafford Vaughan started using JIRA in 2005 after getting a Software Engineering degree in Australia and joining CustomWare, Atlassian's leading services partner. He is a founding author of Atlassian's official JIRA training course materials. During his four years as the Atlassian Training Manager, Stafford worked with many Fortune 500 companies, government entities, and universities, including NASA, Intel, Stanford University, The Pentagon, Wells Fargo, and The United Nations. Stafford currently lives in San Francisco and provides training for organizations in and around Silicon Valley.

Marcin Zręda specializes in business analysis and quality assurance. He has many years of experience as a programmer and designer. He is the author of many articles on JIRA and the owner of the `testandtry.com` blog. Has implemented JIRA for many departments that have more than 600 employees. He is currently directing the department of business analysis in a large international company.

www.PacktPub.com

Support files, eBooks, discount offers and more

You might want to visit www.PacktPub.com for support files and downloads related to your book.

Did you know that Packt offers eBook versions of every book published, with PDF and ePub files available? You can upgrade to the eBook version at www.PacktPub.com and as a print book customer, you are entitled to a discount on the eBook copy. Get in touch with us at service@packtpub.com for more details.

At www.PacktPub.com, you can also read a collection of free technical articles, sign up for a range of free newsletters and receive exclusive discounts and offers on Packt books and eBooks.

http://PacktLib.PacktPub.com

Do you need instant solutions to your IT questions? PacktLib is Packt's online digital book library. Here, you can access, read and search across Packt's entire library of books.

Why Subscribe?

- Fully searchable across every book published by Packt
- Copy and paste, print and bookmark content
- On demand and accessible via web browser

Free Access for Packt account holders

If you have an account with Packt at www.PacktPub.com, you can use this to access PacktLib today and view nine entirely free books. Simply use your login credentials for immediate access.

Instant Updates on New Packt Books

Get notified! Find out when new books are published by following @PacktEnterprise on Twitter, or the *Packt Enterprise* Facebook page.

Table of Contents

Preface

This book will introduce you to Atlassian JIRA, the world's most popular issue tracking software. JIRA provides issue and project tracking for software development teams to improve code quality and the speed of development.

This book will show you how to plan and design your own JIRA implementation. You will learn how to customize JIRA to adapt it to your organization and add value to your business. Chapters are structured to guide you through all the key aspects of JIRA. You will have created a practical implementation by the end of the book, working on it throughout as you learn about JIRA.

You will start by setting up your own JIRA and being introduced to all the key features in subsequent chapters. With each chapter, you will learn important concepts such as business processes, workflows, e-mails, and notifications, and you will have the opportunity to put your newly acquired knowledge into practice by following a live JIRA sample implementation.

Packed with real-life examples and step-by-step instructions, this book will help you become a JIRA expert.

This book is an in-depth guide to all the essential aspects of Atlassian JIRA

What this book covers

Chapter 1, *Getting Started with JIRA*, serves as starting point of the book and aims to guide you to set up a local copy of JIRA application that will be used throughout the book. By the end of the chapter, you should have a running JIRA application.

Chapter 2, *Project Management*, covers how to set up projects and project-related administration tasks in JIRA. The concept of schemes will also be introduced, as it is the core concept in JIRA administration.

Chapter 3, Issue Management, covers everything related to issue creation and operations that can be performed on an issue (excluding workflow transitions). Furthermore, this chapter will gently touch on various aspects of issues, as they are the focal point of JIRA. This chapter will also serve as an opportunity to show and allow you to set up dummy data that will be used by the sample project.

Chapter 4, Field Management, covers how JIRA collects data through the use of fields and how to expand on this ability through the use of custom fields. The chapter will then continue on with various behaviors that can be configured for fields.

Chapter 5, Screen Management, builds on top of the preceding chapter and explores the concept of screens and how users can create and manage their own screens. This chapter will tie in all the previous chapters to show the power behind JIRA's screen design capabilities.

Chapter 6, Workflow and Business Process, explores the most powerful feature offered by JIRA, workflows. The concept of issue life cycle will be introduced and various aspects of workflows explained. This chapter will also explore the relationship between workflows and other various JIRA aspects previously covered, such as screens. The concept of JIRA extensions will also be briefly touched in the sample project, using some popular free extensions.

Chapter 7, E-mail and Notification, focuses on how to get automatic e-mail notifications from JIRA and explores the different settings that can be applied. This is a very important and powerful feature of JIRA and also a critical part of the example project for this book. This chapter will also tie in the workflow chapter and explain in detail how JIRA manages its notification mechanism.

Chapter 8, Securing your JIRA, focuses on the different security control features offered by JIRA. As this topic affects all aspects of JIRA, all previous topics will be touched on, explaining how security can be applied to each.

Chapter 9, Searching, Reporting, and Analysis, will focuses on how data captured in JIRA can be retrieved to provide various types of reporting features.

Chapter 10, General Administration, covers other administration features offered by JIRA. These features often do not form the backbone of a JIRA installation but can be very useful when used properly.

What you need for this book

The installation package used in this book will be the Windows Installer standalone distribution, which you can get directly from Atlassian at http://www.atlassian.com/software/jira/JIRADownloadCenter.jspa.

At the time of writing, the latest version of JIRA is 4.2.

You will also need several additional softwares including Java SDK which you can get from http://java.sun.com/javase/downloads and MySQL which you can get from http://dev.mysql.com/downloads.

Who this book is for

If you want to get started with JIRA, then this is the perfect book for you.

You will need to be familiar with basic computer operations, specifically the system on which you will use JIRA, and software project management.

Conventions

In this book, you will find a number of styles of text that distinguish between different kinds of information. Here are some examples of these styles, and an explanation of their meaning.

Code words in text are shown as follows: "We can include other contexts through the use of the include directive."

A block of code is set as follows:

```
<Connector port="8443" maxHttpHeaderSize="8192" SSLEnabled="true"
maxThreads="150" minSpareThreads="25" maxSpareThreads="75"
enableLookups="false" disableUploadTimeout="true"
```

Any command-line input or output is written as follows:

```
service.bat install JIRA
```

New terms and **important words** are shown in bold. Words that you see on the screen, in menus or dialog boxes for example, appear in the text like this: "To access the ZIP option, click on the **Show all** link to the right-hand side."

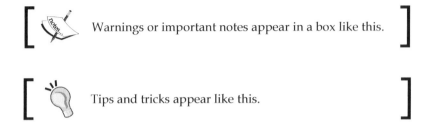

Warnings or important notes appear in a box like this.

Tips and tricks appear like this.

Reader feedback

Feedback from our readers is always welcome. Let us know what you think about this book—what you liked or may have disliked. Reader feedback is important for us to develop titles that you really get the most out of.

To send us general feedback, simply send an e-mail to feedback@packtpub.com, and mention the book title via the subject of your message.

If there is a book that you need and would like to see us publish, please send us a note in the **SUGGEST A TITLE** form on www.packtpub.com or e-mail suggest@ packtpub.com.

If there is a topic that you have expertise in and you are interested in either writing or contributing to a book, see our author guide on www.packtpub.com/authors.

Customer support

Now that you are the proud owner of a Packt book, we have a number of things to help you to get the most from your purchase.

Downloading the example code

You can download the example code files for all Packt books you have purchased from your account at http://www.PacktPub.com. If you purchased this book elsewhere, you can visit http://www.PacktPub.com/support and register to have the files e-mailed directly to you.

Errata

Although we have taken every care to ensure the accuracy of our content, mistakes do happen. If you find a mistake in one of our books—maybe a mistake in the text or the code—we would be grateful if you would report this to us. By doing so, you can save other readers from frustration and help us improve subsequent versions of this book. If you find any errata, please report them by visiting http://www.packtpub.com/support, selecting your book, clicking on the **errata submission form** link, and entering the details of your errata. Once your errata are verified, your submission will be accepted and the errata will be uploaded on our website, or added to any list of existing errata, under the Errata section of that title. Any existing errata can be viewed by selecting your title from http://www.packtpub.com/support.

Piracy

Piracy of copyright material on the Internet is an ongoing problem across all media. At Packt, we take the protection of our copyright and licenses very seriously. If you come across any illegal copies of our works, in any form, on the Internet, please provide us with the location address or website name immediately so that we can pursue a remedy.

Please contact us at copyright@packtpub.com with a link to the suspected pirated material.

We appreciate your help in protecting our authors, and our ability to bring you valuable content.

Questions

You can contact us at questions@packtpub.com if you are having a problem with any aspect of the book, and we will do our best to address it.

1
Getting started with JIRA

When Atlassian first started, they made the decision to create a software that would be inexpensive, fun for the user, and would take minutes to install. Thanks to this philosophy, the installation process of JIRA is relatively simple and straightforward. In this chapter, we will start with a high-level view of JIRA, looking at each of the components that make up the overall application. We will then examine the various deployment options we have, including application servers, databases, and distribution choices. Finally, we will get our hands dirty by installing our very own JIRA application from scratch.

By the end of this chapter, you will have learned about:

- The overall architecture of JIRA
- Platforms and applications supported by JIRA
- Installing JIRA and all of the required software
- Configuring database connections

JIRA architecture

Installing JIRA is simple and straightforward. However, it is important for you to understand the components that make up the overall architecture of JIRA and the installation options available. This will help you make an informed decision and be better prepared for future maintenance and troubleshooting.

High-level architecture

Atlassian provides a comprehensive overview of the JIRA architecture at `http://confluence.atlassian.com/display/JIRA/JIRA+Architectural+Overview`. However, for day-to-day administration and usage of JIRA, we do not need to go into details; the information provided can be overwhelming at first glance. For this reason, we have summarized a high level overview that highlights the most important components in the architecture.

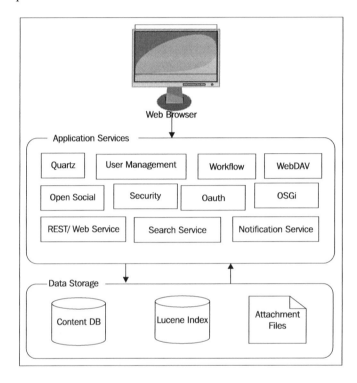

Browsers

JIRA is a web application, so there is no need for users to install anything on their machine. All they need is a web browser that is compatible with JIRA. Since version 4.1, JIRA has undergone some major changes to its user interface. New JIRA interface is now more interactive and dynamic. However, this means a newer version of web browsers will be required to take full advantage of all the functions provided with the new UI. Internet Explorer 6, for example, is no longer fully compatible.

The following table summarizes the browser requirements for JIRA.

Browsers	Compatibility
Microsoft Internet Explorer	8.0, 7.0
	6.0 (all main functions are compatible, some visual effects will be missing)
Mozilla Firefox	3.0, 3.5, 3.6
Safari	4
Google Chrome	Not officially supported but functionally compatible

Application services

The application services layer contains all the functions and services provided by JIRA. These services include various business functions such as workflow and notification, which will be discussed in depth in *Chapter 6* and *Chapter 7*, respectively. Other services, such as REST/Web Service, provide integration points to other applications, and OSGi service provides the base plugin framework to extend JIRA's functionalities.

Data storage

The data storage layer stores persistent data in several places within JIRA. Most business data such as issues and projects are stored in a relational database. Contents such as uploaded attachments and search indexes are stored on the file system. The underlying relational database used is transparent to the users and you can migrate from one database to another with ease.

JIRA installation directory

This is the directory where you install JIRA. It contains all the executable files and configuration files of the application. JIRA does not modify contents of files in this directory during runtime, nor does it store any data inside; the directory is used primarily for execution. For the remainder of the book, we will be referring to this directory as `JIRA_INSTALL`.

JIRA home directory

This directory contains key data files that are specific to each JIRA instance. There is a one–to-one relationship between JIRA and this directory. This means each JIRA instance must and can have only one JIRA Home, and each JIRA Home can serve only one JIRA instance. In the old days, this directory was sometimes called the data directory. It has now been standardized as the JIRA Home. It is for this reason that for the rest of the book we will be referring to this directory as JIRA_HOME.

It is recommended that JIRA Home is be created separately from the JIRA installation. This separation of data and application makes tasks such as maintenance and future upgrades an easier process.

Within JIRA Home, there are several subdirectories that contain vital data.

Directory	Description
data	This directory contains data that are not stored in the database. For example, uploaded attachment files.
export	This directory contains automated backup archives created by JIRA. This is different from a manual export executed by a user; manual exports require the user to specify where to store the archive.
import	This directory contains backups that can be imported. JIRA will only load backup files from this directory.
log	This directory contains JIRA logs.
plugins	This directory is where plugins that are installed. Plugins will be discussed further in later chapters.
caches	This directory contains cache data that JIRA uses to improve its performance at runtime. For example, search indexes are stored in this directory.
tmp	This directory contains temporary files created at runtime, such as file uploads.

When JIRA is running, this directory is locked, when JIRA shuts down, it will be unlocked. This locking mechanism prevents multiple JIRA instances from reading/ writing to the same JIRA Home directory and causing data corruption.

Installation options

JIRA is a Java-based web application developed using many open standards and libraries. Hence it is able to run on many operating systems, relational databases, and application servers. We will take a closer look at each of the components and options you have, and help you to make an informed decision.

Standalone and WAR-EAR distributions

First of all, we need to decide on the distribution. JIRA comes in two distributions:

- Standalone bundled with Apache Tomcat
- WAR-EAR

Fundamentally, there are no differences between the two distributions. The standalone distribution comes with Apache Tomcat, which means you do not have to spend time on deployment efforts that are usually required by Java web applications. The standalone distribution also comes with an embedded in-memory database that can be used for evaluation purposes.

If you would like to deploy JIRA onto an existing application server, such as IBM WebSphere, the WAR-EAR distribution is for you. Due to the differences that exist between different application servers, when you download the WAR-EAR distribution, you are required to build the final deployment artifact with the provided build script file for your application server. Once the artifact is built, you can deploy JIRA just like any other Java web application.

Operating systems

JIRA supports most of the major operating systems, so the choice of which operating system to run JIRA on becomes a matter of expertise, comfort, and in most cases, existing organization IT infrastructure and requirements.

The operating systems supported by Atlassian are Windows, Linux, and MacOS. With Windows, Atlassian provides a wizard-driven installation package that simplifies the installation process (only available for standalone distribution). Other than that, there are minimal differences when it comes to installing, configuring, and maintaining JIRA on the different operating systems.

If you do not have any preferences and would like to keep the initial cost down, Linux is a good choice.

Databases

JIRA stores all its data in a relational database. While you can run JIRA with an in-memory database such as HSQLDB, it is prone to data corruption. For this reason, it is important that you use an enterprise database for production systems.

Most relational databases available in the market today are supported by JIRA, and there are no differences when you install and configure JIRA. Just like operating systems, your choice of database will come down to your IT staff's expertise, experience, and established corporate standards. If you are running Windows as your operating system, you probably want to go with Microsoft SQL Server. On the other hand, if you are running Linux, then you should consider Oracle (if you already have a license), MySQL, or PostgreSQL.

The following is a table summarizing the list of databases that are currently supported by JIRA. It is worth mentioning that both MySQL and PostgreSQL are open source products, so they are excellent options if you are looking to minimize your initial investments.

Databases	Support status
MySQL	MySQL 5.x
PostgreSQL	PostgreSQL 8.2 and later
Microsoft SQL Server	SQL Server 2008
	SQL Server 2005
Oracle	Oracle 11g
	Oracle 10g
HSQLDB	Bundled with standalone distribution

Application Servers

As we saw earlier, JIRA requires a JavaEE compatible application server. With the WAR-EAR distribution, you can deploy JIRA onto any supported application server. With the standalone distribution, Apache Tomcat comes bundled and you do not need to do anything extra for deployment.

All the application servers support both Windows and Linux, so unlike databases, you are not affected by which operating system you are running. Apache Tomcat is an open source product and comes bundled with JIRA in standalone. If you do have any preferences, Tomcat will be your best option as it is the least demanding.

The following is a table summarizing the list of supported application servers. Please note that JBoss is no longer supported.

Application servers	Support status
Apache Tomcat	Tomcat 5.5.27 – 5.5.29
	Tomcat 6.0.20
Oracle WebLogic	WebLogic 9.2
IBM WebSphere	WebSphere 6.1.0.27
JBoss	Not supported.

Installing JIRA

Now that we have a good understanding of the overall architecture of JIRA and the various installation options, we are ready to install our own JIRA deployment.

In the following exercise, we will be installing and configuring a fresh JIRA instance that will be ready for production. We will be basing our installation on a Windows platform. If you are planning to use a different platform, please refer to the vendor documentation on installing the required softwares for your platform.

In this exercise, we will:

1. Install a fresh instance of JIRA.
2. Configure JIRA to an enterprise relational database.
3. Configure JIRA as a service so it will start automatically with the system.

We will continue to use this JIRA instance in our subsequent chapters and exercises as we build up our help desk implementation.

For our implementation, we will be using:

- JIRA standalone distribution 4.2
- MySQL 5
- Java Development Kit 6
- Microsoft Windows XP

Installing Java

JIRA requires Java Development Kit (JDK) version 6 update 10 or higher to run. It is important to note that some systems come with Java Runtime Environment (JRE), which is different and insufficient to run JIRA. If you already have a JDK installed, you can skip this section.

To install JDK onto your system, simply carry out the following steps:

1. Download the latest JDK from `http://java.sun.com/javase/downloads`.

 At the time of writing, the latest version is JDK 6 Update 21.

2. Double-click on the downloaded installation file to start the installation wizard.

3. Select where you would like to install Java, or you can simply accept the default values. The location where you install JDK will be referred to as JAVA_HOME for the rest of the book.

4. Create a new environmental variable named JAVA_HOME with the value of where you installed Java.

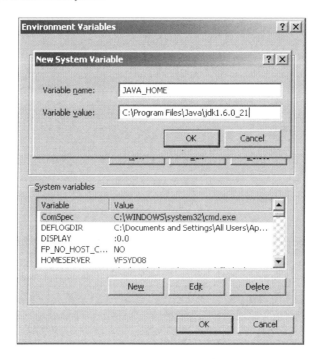

6. Test the installation by typing the following command in a new
    command prompt:

    ```
    java version
    ```

    This will display the version of Java installed.

Installing MySQL

The next step is to prepare an enterprise database for our JIRA installation.

To install MySQL, simply follow the steps below:

1. Download MySQL from: `http://dev.mysql.com/downloads`.

    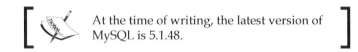

    > At the time of writing, the latest version of
    > MySQL is 5.1.48.

2. Double-click on the downloaded installation file to start the installation
    wizard.

3. Click on **Next** on the welcome screen.

4. Select the **Typical** setup option on the next screen. If you are an experienced
    database administrator, you can choose to customize your installation.
    Otherwise, just accept the default values for all subsequent screens.

5. Once the installation is completed, make sure you check the **Configure
    MySQL Server now** option and click on **Finish**. This will bring up the
    MySQL configuration wizard.

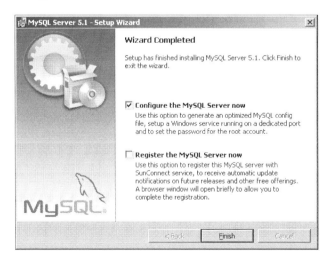

7. From the MySQL configuration wizard, select **Standard Configuration**.

8. Check both the **Install As Windows Service** and **Include Bin Directory in Windows PATH** options on the next screen. This will make MySQL startup when the system starts up and also allow you to run the MySQL command line tools directly.

9. Configure the MySQL root user password. The username will be root.

10. Click on **Execute** on the next screen and MySQL will start applying the configuration options.

Configuring MySQL

Now that we have MySQL installed, it is time to create a database for JIRA.

1. Start a new command prompt.

2. Issue the command below to connect to MySQL:

   ```
   mysql -u root -p
   ```

3. When prompted for password, enter the password you chose during configuration. This will bring up the interactive shell for MySQL.

4. Issue the command below to create a database:

   ```
   create database jiradb character set utf8;
   ```

5. Here we are creating a database called `jiradb`. You can name the database to anything you like. As we will see later in this chapter, this name will be referenced when we connect JIRA to MySQL. We have also set the database to use UTF8 character encoding, as this is a requirement for JIRA. You need to ensure that the database is using the InnoDB storage engine to avoid data corruption.

6. Issue the following command:

    ```
    grant all on jiradb.* to 'jirauser'@'localhost' identified by
    'jirauser';
    ```

7. Here we are doing several things. First, we have created a user called `jirauser` and assigned the password `jirauser` to the user. You can, change the username and password to something else.

8. We have also granted all privileges to the user for the database `jiradb` we have just created so the user can perform database operations such as create/drop tables, and insert/delete data. If you have named your database to something other than jiradb in step 3, make sure you change the command so it uses your database name.

9. This allows us to control the fact that only authorized users (specified in the preceding command) are able to access the JIRA database to ensure data security and integrity.

10. To verify our setup, exit the current interactive session by issuing the following command:

    ```
    quit;
    ```

11. Start a new interactive session with our newly created user:

    ```
    mysql -u jirauser -p
    ```

12. You will be prompted for jirauser's password, which we have set up in our previous command as jirauser.

13. Issue the command:

    ```
    show databases;
    ```

14. This will list all the databases that are currently accessible by the logged in user. You should see **jiradb** amongst the list of databases.

15. Examine the jiradb database by issuing the following commands:

    ```
    use jiradb;
    show tables;
    ```

16. The first command connects us to the `jiradb` database, so all of our subsequent commands will be executed against the correct database.

17. The second command lists all the tables that exist in the `jiradb` database. Right now, the list should be empty since tables have been created for JIRA now, but don't worry—as soon as we connect to JIRA, all the tables will automatically be created.

Installing JIRA

With the JDK and database prepared, we can now move on to install JIRA.

Configuring JIRA application properties

1. Download Atlassian JIRA from `http://www.atlassian.com/software/jira/JIRADownloadCenter.jspa`.

   The Atlassian website will detect the operating system you are using and automatically suggest the installation package for you to download. If you intend to install JIRA on a different operating system than the one you are currently on, make sure you select the correct operating system package.

3. As mentioned earlier, with Windows, there is a Windows installer package and self-extracting ZIP package. For the purpose of our exercise, we will be using the self-extracting option as this will provide us with an insight of the steps usually hidden by installation programs To access the ZIP option, click on the **Show all** link to the right-hand side.

4. Unzip the downloaded file to your intended `JIRA_INSTALL` directory.

5. Open `JIRA_INSTALL\atlassian-jira\WEB-INF\classes\jira-application.properties` file in a text editor.

6. Locate the following line:

   `#jira.home =`

7. Fill in the full path to your `JIRA_HOME` directory and save the file.

   `jira.home = C:/JIRA_HOME`

8. Make sure that you remove the # at the front and use forward slashes (/) instead of backward slashes (\).

Configuring JIRA application settings (optional)

With the standalone distribution, we can also configure some of the applications server settings such as context path and port number. This is useful, for example, if you have multiple web servers running on the same machine, they can co-exist by listening on different port numbers. If JIRA is the only application running on your machine, then you may choose not to make any changes. For our exercise, we will set a context path for our JIRA.

To configure the settings, locate and open the `server.xml` file in a text editor. The file can be found in the `JIRA_INSTALL/conf` directory.

```
<Server port="8005" shutdown="SHUTDOWN">
... ... ... ...
<Connector port="8080" protocol="HTTP/1.1">
... ... ... ...
<Context path="/jira" docBase="${catalina.home}/atlassian-jira"
reloadable="false" useHttpOnly="true">
```

Let's examine the relevant contents in this file.

Line 1: This line specifies the port for command to shutdown JIRA/Tomcat. By default, it is port 8005. If you already have an application that is running on that port (usually another Tomcat instance), you can change this to a different port.

Line 2: This line specifies which port JIRA/Tomcat will be running on. By default, it is port 8080. If you already have an application that is running on that port, or if the port is unavailable for some reason, you can change it to another available port.

Line 3: This line allows you to specify the context that JIRA will be running under. By default, the value is empty, which means JIRA will be accessible through the URL of `http://hostname:portnumber`. If you decide to specify a value for the context, like in our example here, JIRA will be accessible through the URL of `http://hostname:portnumber/jira`.

Configuring HTTPS

By default, JIRA runs with standard, non-encrypted HTTP protocol. This is acceptable if you are running JIRA in a secured environment such as an internal network. However, if you plan to open up access to JIRA over the Internet, you will need to tighten up security by encrypting sensitive data such as usernames and passwords that are being sent, by enabling HTTPS (HTTP over SSL).

For a standalone installation, we will need to perform the following tasks:

- Obtain and install a certification
- Enable HTTPS on our application server (Tomcat)
- Redirect traffic to HTTPS

First, we need to get a digital certificate. This can be from a Certification Authority such as VeriSign (CA certificate), or a self-signed certificate generated by you. CA certificate will not only encrypt data for you, but also identify your copy of JIRA to users. A self-signed certificate is useful when you do not have a valid CA certificate and you are only interested in setting up HTTPS for encryption. Since a self-signed certificate is not signed by a Certification Authority, it is unable to identify your site to the public and users will be prompted with a warning that the site is untrusted when they first visit it. However, for evaluation purposes, a self-signed certificate will suffice until you can get a proper CA certificate.

For the purpose of this exercise, we will create a self-signed certificate to illustrate the complete process. If you have a CA certificate, you can skip the following step.

Java comes with a handy tool for certificate management called keytool, which can be found in the JAVA_HOME\lib directory. To generate a self-signed certificate, run the following commands from a command prompt.

```
keytool -genkey -alias tomcat -keyalg RSA
keytool -export -alias tomcat -file file.cer
```

This will create a key store (if one does not already exist) and export the self-signed certificate (file.cer). When you run the first command, you will be asked to set the password for the keystore and Tomcat. You need to use the same password for both. The default password is "changeit". You can specify a different password of your choice, but you then have to let JIRA/Tomcat know, as we will see later.

Now we have our certificate ready, we need to import it into our trust store for Tomcat to use. Again, we will use the keytool application from Java.

```
keytool -import -alias tomcat -file file.cer JAVA_HOME\jre\lib\security\
cacerts
```

This will import the certificate into our Trust Store, which can be used by JIRA/Tomcat to set up HTTPS.

To enable HTTPS on Tomcat, open the server.xml file in a text editor from the JIRA_INSTALL/conf directory. Locate the following configuration snippet:

```
<Connector port="8443" maxHttpHeaderSize="8192" SSLEnabled="true"
maxThreads="150" minSpareThreads="25" maxSpareThreads="75"
enableLookups="false" disableUploadTimeout="true"
acceptCount="100" scheme="https" secure="true"
clientAuth="false" sslProtocol="TLS" useBodyEncodingForURI="true"/>
```

This enables HTTPS for JIRA/Tomcat on port 8443. If you have selected a different password for your keystore, you will have to add the following line to the end of the preceding snippet, before the closing tag.

```
keystorePass="<password value>"
```

The last step is to set up JIRA so it will automatically redirect from a non-HTTP request to a HTTPS request. Find and open the file web.xml in the JIRA_INSTALL/ atlassian-jira/WEB-INF directory, and add the following snippet to the end of the file, before the closing </web-app> tag.

```
<security-constraint>
    <web-resource-collection>
        <web-resource-name>all-except-attachments</web-resource-name>
        <url-pattern>*.js</url-pattern>
        <url-pattern>*.jsp</url-pattern>
        <url-pattern>*.jspa</url-pattern>
        <url-pattern>*.css</url-pattern>
        <url-pattern>/browse/*</url-pattern>
    </web-resource-collection>
    <user-data-constraint>
        <transport-guarantee>CONFIDENTIAL</transport-guarantee>
    </user-data-constraint>
</security-constraint>
```

Downloading the example code

You can download the example code files for all Packt books you have purchased from your account at http://www.PacktPub.com. If you purchased this book elsewhere, you can visit http://www.PacktPub.com/support and register to have the files e-mailed directly to you.

Now when you access JIRA with a normal HTTP URL such as http://localhost:8080/jira, you will be automatically redirected to its HTTPS equivalent, https://localhost:8443/jira.

Installing database drivers (optional)

Normally, database drivers need to be installed manually for applications to be able to connect to databases. Depending on the database you are using, JIRA may require drivers that are different from the ones that come bundled with some application servers.

Database	Driver requirement
MySQL	JDBC Connector/J 5.1
PostgreSQL	PostgreSQL Driver 8.4.x
Microsoft SQL Server	JTDS 1.2.3
Oracle	Oracle 11.2.x

If you are using PostgreSQL or MySQL, as in our case, then you are lucky as the standalone distribution comes with the drivers for both. However, if you are using a different database such Oracle, you will need to obtain the driver from the vendor (usually downloadable from vendor's website). It is important that you get the driver for your specific database version; otherwise you will experience unexpected behaviors during and/or after installation.

To install a database driver (if you are not using MySQL), simply follow the steps below:

1. Obtain the database driver from the vendor.
2. Copy the driver (usually a JAR file) into your `JIRA_INSTALL/lib` directory.
3. Restart JIRA so the driver can be properly loaded.

Configuring the database connection manual

With the standalone distribution, there are two options to configure database connections. The first option is to configure the setting manually, while the second option is to use an Atlassian-provided GUI tool. Since the second option is not available for WAR-EAR installations, we will be using the first manual option. This will also provide the base knowledge that will be very valuable for future maintenance and troubleshooting.

The first step is to let our application server (Tomcat) know which database to select and how to connect to it. To do so, locate and open the `server.xml` file in a text editor. The file can be found in the `JIRA_INSTALL/conf` directory.

```
<Context path="" docBase="${catalina.home}/atlassian-jira"
        reloadable="false" useHttpOnly="true">
    <Resource name="jdbc/JiraDS" auth="Container"
            type="javax.sql.DataSource"
            driverClassName="com.mysql.jdbc.Driver"
            url="jdbc:mysql://localhost:3306/jiradb?useUnicode=
            true&amp;characterEncoding=UTF8"
            username="jirauser"
            password="jirauser"
            minEvictableIdleTimeMillis="4000" - DELETE
            timeBetweenEvictionRunsMillis="5000" - DELETE
            maxActive="20"
            validationQuery="select 1"/>
```

Let's examine the relevant contents in this file.

Line 1: This line defines the database driver class. For MySQL, the class is `com.mysql.jdbc.Driver`. Other databases will have different driver classes.

Line 2: This line defines the connection URL to the database. The URL is database-specific, so databases other than MySQL will have a slightly different syntax. Note how we add `jiradb` as part of the URL. This tells JIRA to connect to a database with the name `jiradb`, which we created earlier. If you named your database differently, make sure you change the name in the code. For MySQL, it is important to note the two additional attributes used here, `useUnicode=true` and `characterEncoding=UTF8`. This tells JIRA to use UTF8 encoding when writing data to the database.

Line 3 and 4: These two lines specify the username and password which JIRA will use to connect to the database. Replace the credentials to the ones you have setup.

Line 5 and 6: These two lines are used by the in-memory database. Since we are not using an in memory database, they need to be deleted. Otherwise we will experience performance issues.

Line 7: This line contains a simple statement to verify our database connectivity.

The second step is to tell JIRA which database we are using. To do so, locate and open the `entityengine.xml` file in a text editor. The file can be found in the `JIRA_INSTALL/atlassian-jira/WEB-INF/classes` directory.

```
<datasource name="defaultDS" field-type-name="mysql"
    schema-name="PUBLIC" - DELETE
        helper-class="org.ofbiz.core.entity.GenericHelperDAO"
        check-on-start="true"
        use-foreign-keys="false"
```

Let's examine the relevant contents in this file.

Line 1: This line tells JIRA what type of database we are using. In our case, we are using MySQL, so we put in the value `mysql`.

Line 2: This line tells JIRA about the database schema information. Since MySQL does not use this, we need to delete this line.

Configuring the database connection (GUI)

That's all that is required to configure JIRA's database connectivity. Since we have configured this the manual way, it is time for us to take a look at the second option with the GUI interface. We can also use this opportunity to validate our configuration settings.

The tool is called **JIRA Configuration Tool**, a utility application that comes bundled with JIRA. You can find the application in the JIRA_INSTALL/bin directory, called config.bat. Double-click on the file to start the application.

Click on the **Database** tab once the application starts up. You should be able to see all the configuration options are populated with the settings we have just configured.

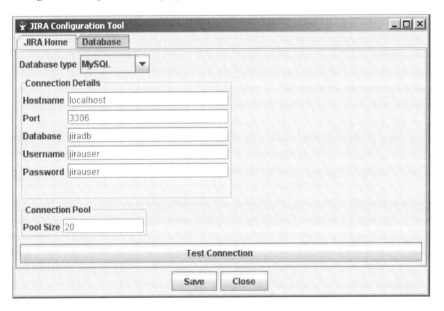

To verify that our settings are correct, make sure that the database is running and click on the **Test Connection** button. If everything is correct, we should see a confirmation message as shown in the following screenshot. From now on, you can use this utility application to update database configurations for JIRA, and you will know what files are being touched when changes occur.

Configuring JIRA as a Windows service

Under Windows, JIRA can be configured to run as a Windows service, thus starting up automatically when the operating system reboots in events such as hardware upgrades and system patching.

To configure JIRA as a Windows service, simply follow the steps below:

1. Start a new command prompt and browse to the JIRA_INSTALL/bin directory.

2. Run the following command:

   ```
   service.bat install JIRA
   ```

3. This will install JIRA as a Windows service. The name of the service will be **Atlassian JIRA**, followed by the name you supplied after the install command. So in our example, the name of the service will be **Atlassian JIRA JIRA**.

4. Verify the configuration by going to **Settings | Administrative Tools | Services**.

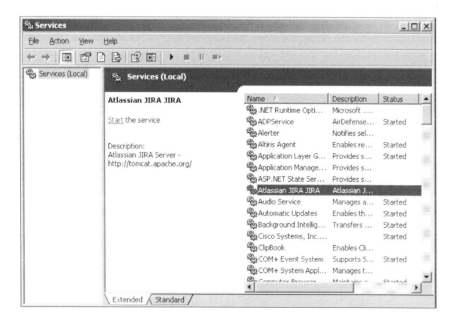

You can now start/stop/restart JIRA from the Windows services panel. You can also set JIRA to start automatically.

Starting JIRA

Once the server is up and running, you can access JIRA from your Internet browser. The URL to your JIRA is `http://hostname:portnumber/contextPath`. In our example, the URL is `http://localhost:8080/jira`. You should be welcomed with the **JIRA Setup Wizard**. On some servers, the firewall will block the default port 8080. If this is the case, you will need to either change the port number to one that is not blocked (for example, 80) or configure your firewall to allow HTTP traffic through port 8080.

On the first page of the wizard, you need to specify a few properties for your JIRA instance.

Property	Description
Application Title	Title given to your JIRA.
Mode	Public will allow user signup.
	Private will disable user signup and only allow administrators to create users.
Base URL	The URL used to access your JIRA. This will be used for links generated by JIRA.
Index	The directory where JIRA will keep its search index files. You can leave it as default and JIRA will create an index directory within `JIRA_HOME`, or you can specify another directory.
	It is recommended that you leave it as the default.
File Attachments	The directory where JIRA will store its attachment files. You can leave it as the default and JIRA will create an attachments directory within `JIRA_HOME`, or you can specify another directory.
	It is recommended that you leave it as the default.
Backup	Whether you would like JIRA to perform automated backups on your data.
License Key	A valid license key for your JIRA. This can be either a full license or evaluation license.
Language	The default language setting for JIRA.

You will need to provide a valid license key for your JIRA instance. If you have already obtained a license from Atlassian, you can cut and paste it into the **License Key** text box. If you do not have a license, you can generate an evaluation license by clicking on the Generate an Evaluation Key link at the bottom. An evaluation license allows you to use JIRA with its full features for three months. Once you have filled in the required properties, click on **Next** to move onto page two.

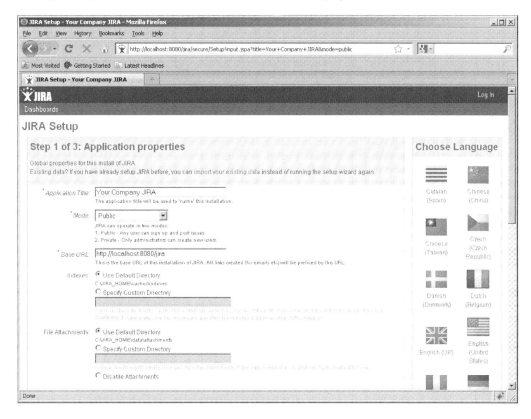

On the second screen, you will be setting up the administrator account for JIRA. It is important that you keep the account details somewhere safe and do not lose the password. Since JIRA only stores the hashed value of the password instead of the actual password itself, you will not be able to retrieve it. However, there are methods for you to reset the password if you do lose it, as we will see in later chapters. Fill in the administrator account details and click on **Next** to move on to the last step.

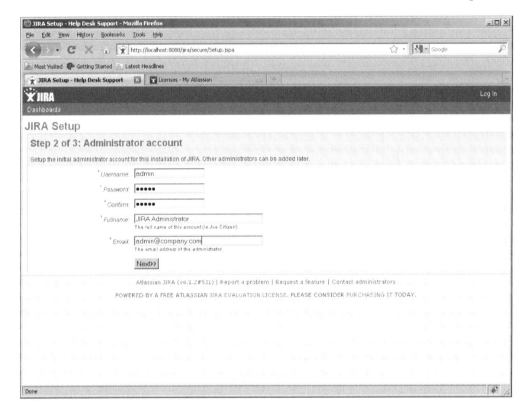

On the final screen, you can set up your e-mail server details. JIRA will be using the information configured here to send out notification e-mails. As we will see in *Chapter 7*, notification is a very powerful feature in JIRA and one of the primary methods for JIRA to communicate with the users. If you do not have your e-mail server information handy, do not worry, we can skip this step now by clicking on **Disable Email Notifications**. JIRA allows you to change your e-mail server settings at any time; we will cover the settings in *Chapter 7* when we delve deeper into JIRA's notification system. After you have filled in the e-mail server details, click on **Finish** to complete the setup wizard.

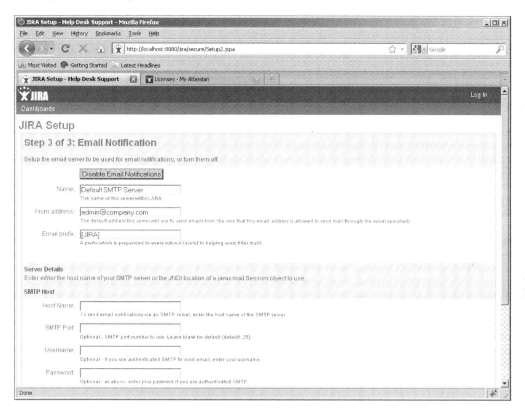

Congratulations! You have successfully completed your JIRA setup. Click on **log in to JIRA** and log in with the administrator account we have just set up, and you are now using your own copy of JIRA!

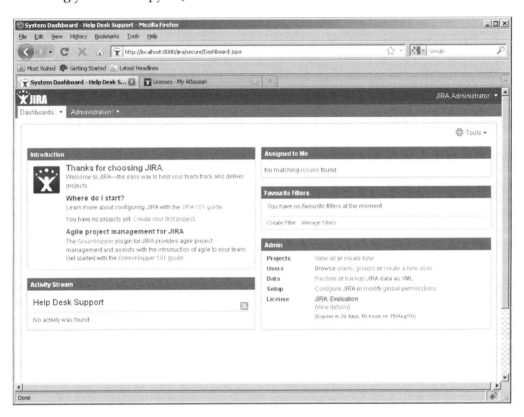

Summary

JIRA is a powerful and yet simple application, as reflected by its straightforward installation procedures. You have a wide variety of options to choose how you would like to install and configure your copy. You can mix and match different aspects such as operating system, database, and application server to best suit your requirements. The best part is that you can have a setup that comprises entirely of open source software that will bring down your cost and provide you with a reliable infrastructure at the same time.

Now that we have a working instance of JIRA, we will start to explore various aspects of JIRA in the following chapters, starting with projects, the first key component in any JIRA installation.

2
Project Management

JIRA was originally designed to be a bug-tracking system to manage software development projects. It has now evolved into a highly-flexible system that can adapt to areas out of software issue tracking.

By the end of this chapter, you will have learned:

- How JIRA structures contents
- About JIRA projects and how to create them
- How to manage and configure a project
- Components and versions
- How to utilize schemes

JIRA hierarchy

Like most other information systems, JIRA organizes its data in a hierarchical structure. At the lowest level, we have fields, which are used to hold information. Then we have issues, which are like units of task to be performed. All issues will belong to one project, which defines the context of the issue. Finally, we have project categories which logically group similar projects together. We will discuss each of these levels in the following sections.

Project category

A project category is a logical grouping of projects of a similar nature. The category itself does not contain any information. It simply helps administrators to group any number of projects together. Project categories are optional. Projects do not have to belong to a category in JIRA.

One way to look at project categories would be to compare a category to a department within an organization. Each team within the department will have their own project. Since tasks are often carried out by each individual team, issues and tasks are logged against the project and not the project category.

Projects

In JIRA, a project is a collection of issues. Projects provide background context for issues by lettings users know where issues should be raised. A project also defines various "rules" and "boundaries" for its issues, such as who will have permission to view the issues and notification recipients when changes are made against an issue.

It is important to remember that projects are not limited to software development projects that need to deliver a product. Some obvious examples of a project include:

- Company department or team
- Software development projects
- Products or systems

Some less obvious examples of a project may include a risks register to log and track risks

Issues

Issues represent tasks to be performed. From a functional perspective, an issue is the base unit for JIRA. Users create issues and assign them to other people to be worked on. Project team members can generate reports on issues to see how everything is tracking. In a sense, you can say JIRA is "issue-centric".

We will be looking at issues in more details in *Chapter 3, Issue Management*. For now, you with only need to remember three things:

- An issue has to belong to one (and only one) project
- There can be many different types of issue
- An issue contains many fields that hold values about the issue

Fields

Fields are the most basic unit of data in JIRA. They hold data for issues and give meaning to them. Fields in JIRA can be broadly categorized into two distinctive categories, namely system fields and custom fields. They come in many different forms such as text fields, drop-down lists, and user pickers. Fields and their related topics are discussed in more depth in *Chapter 4, Field Management*. There are three main points to made about fields:

1. Fields hold values for issues.
2. Fields can have properties such as hidden and/or mandatory.
3. Fields can have view and structure (text field, drop-down list).

JIRA projects

JIRA provides two distinctive interfaces for projects. One interface is used by users for day-to-day operations, such as to browse project contents, called Project Browser. The second interface is used by administrators to manage project configuration settings, called Project Administration. We will first cover Project Browser and then extend our discussion how administrators can manage projects in JIRA.

Project browser

Most people spend time browsing the contents of the project rather than managing their configurations. To browse the content of a project, carry out the following steps:

1. Click on the drop-down arrow for Projects on the top navigation bar. This option will only be available if you have created at least one project.
2. Click on **View All Projects** in the drop-down menu.

3. Select the project you wish to browse from the list of projects. This will bring up the Project Browser.

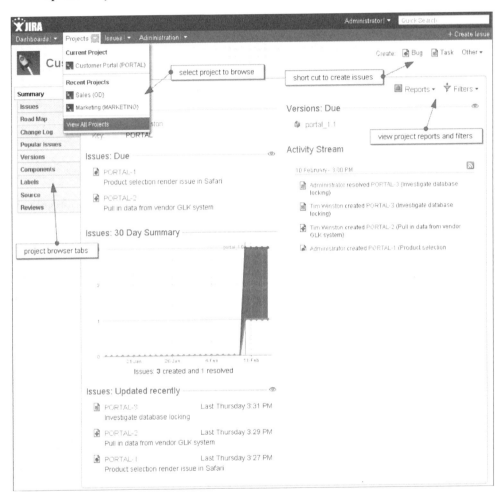

The Project Browser acts as the portal for the selected project. The browser is broken up into several sections controlled by the tabs to the left-hand side. Each section shows different information on the project, which helps users get a better insight on the activities that are going on inside the project. The following table lists all the available browser sections and their purpose.

Browser tab	Description
Summary	Displays a quick overview of the project.
Issues	Display a breakdown of issues in the project grouped by attributes such as priority and status.
Road Map	Displays all unreleased versions for the project.
Change Log	Displays all released versions for the project.
Popular Issues	Displays a list of unresolved issues, ordered by popularity (votes).
Versions	Displays the summary of unreleased versions of the project. This tab is only available when versions are configured.
Components	Displays the summary of components and their related issues. This tab is only available when components are configured for the project.
Labels	Displays all available labels in the project. Labels can be assigned to issues as tags.
Source	Displays change sets from Atlassian FishEye.
Reviews	Displays code reviews from Atlassian Crucible.

Summary tab

The **Summary** tab provides you with a one-page view into the project you are working with. It provides you with a quick glance of the project with key information, including:

- Project description.

- Unresolved issues that are due to be completed.

- Unreleased versions due to be released.

- Recently updated issues.

- Recent activities performed on issues in this project.

- Summary graph showing issues created versus issues resolved.

- The **Summary** tab is also where you will be able to generate project reports and run search filters. Both reports and filters are covered in *Chapter 9*.

Issues tab

The **Issues** tab provides users with a nice view of issues within the project. Issues are broken down and grouped by several key factors, such as priority and assignee, giving users a quick overview on the project's state. For example, the **Unresolved: By Assignee** lets you know how many open issues are being assigned to each user, allowing the project team to plan their resource allocation better.

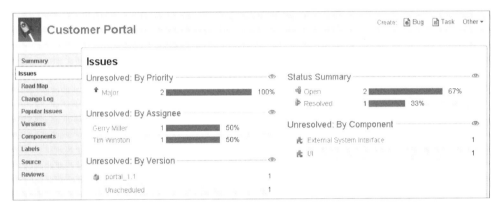

Road Map tab

The **Road Map** tab breaks down issues based on versions they belong to. If you have set up versions in JIRA, this tab will show you upcoming unreleased versions and issues that need to be completed before the version can be completed.

Change Log tab

Similar to the **Road Map** tab, the **Change Log** tab breaks down issues based on versions. The difference is that the **Change Log** tab shows versions that have already been released. This is very useful when you have to go back and check what has been achieved and completed for each of the past versions, providing you with a log of changes.

Versions/Components tabs

The **Versions** and **Components** tabs list all the available versions and components that have been configured for this project, respectively. We will cover versions and components later in this chapter.

Source/Reviews tabs

The **Source** and **Reviews** tabs require you to have the Altassian FishEye and Crucible applications installed, respectively. Once installed, the tabs will pull in data from the applications and display them. If you do not have the required applications installed and configured, the tabs prompt you to install the applications. Installing and configuring both FishEye and Crucible is beyond the scope of this book.

Project management

JIRA segregates the responsibilities of creating and removing projects as well as administering the settings and contents of projects. This allows management operations such as project creation to be centrally controlled by the JIRA administrator, but remove the day-to-day management burden by delegating this to each project's project administrator. In this section, we will first look at how the JIRA administrator can centrally manage all the projects, and later look at how project administrators can manage their own projects.

The JIRA administrator, such as the admin user we created when we installed JIRA, has access to JIRA's central project management page where you can create a new project, delete existing projects, and update their settings.

1. Log in to JIRA as a JIRA administrator.
2. Click the **Administration** link on the top navigation bar. This will bring up the **Projects** page, which will list all the projects in JIRA.

The Projects page will list all the projects you have permission to manage. Since you are the JIRA administrator, all projects will be listed (if you are not, then you will only see projects that you are the project administrator for).

Creating projects

You need to be a JIRA Administrator because you can only create projects from the JIRA administration console page. To create a new project, carry out the following steps:

1. Browse to the **Projects** page.

2. Click on the **Add Project** link.

3. Fill in the add project form by specifying the project details. Please note that the value for the project **Key** cannot be changed once the project has been created.

4. Click on the **Add** button to create the new project.

On this page, you will need to fill in a form with information about your new project. The following table explains each of the fields.

Field	Description
Name	A unique name for the project.
Key	A unique identity key for the project. This key cannot be changed once the project is created. The project key will become the first part of the issue key (for example, HD-12). We will discuss **issues** in the next chapter.
Project Lead	The lead of the project. Each project can only have one lead.
Project Avatar	An image to represent the project.
URL	An optional URL value for the project, for example, to the Help Desk portal.
Default Assignee	The person to whom issues will be assigned by default, if unspecified.
Description	A short description of the project.
Notification Scheme	Notification rules for who will receive notification e-mails when certain events take place for the project.
Permissions Scheme	Permission rules for various access levels.
Issue Security Scheme	Special security rules on who can view issues in this project.

Once you have created a project, you will be taken directly to the project's administration page. From this page, you will be able to edit, delete, and browse issues within the project.

Editing projects

Most of the project details specified at project creation time can be updated at a later time. For example, you can change the name of the project or select a different avatar. To edit an existing project, carry out the following steps:

1. Browse to the **Projects** page.
2. Click on the **Edit** link for the project you wish to update. This will bring up the **Edit Project** page, which will look very similar to the **Create A New Project** page.
3. Update the details of the project.
4. Click on the **Update** button.

You will notice that some options are not available on the **Edit Project** page, such as notification schemes and project key. This is because some of the options such as project key cannot be changed once it is set. Moreover, other options, such as notification scheme, are updated directly from the **Project Administration** page. We will look at these options when we discuss them further in later chapters.

Deleting projects

You can permanently delete a project from JIRA. To delete an existing project, follow the steps below:

1. Browse to the JIRA **administration console** page.
2. Click on **Projects** from the left navigation panel.
3. Click on **Delete Project**.
4. Confirm that you wish to delete the project by clicking on the **Delete** button.

After the project has been deleted, all of its contents will be permanently removed from JIRA-this includes issues and configuration settings such as versions and components. This process is NOT reversible.

Project administration

While it is the JIRA administrator's responsibility to create new projects and manage their settings, it is ideally each project administrator's responsibility to maintain his/her own projects.

Each project has an administration page that allows project administrators to make adjustments to the project. For example, you can change the project's name, select what issue types will be available for the project, and manage a list of components within the project. You need to be a project administrator in order to access this. We will discuss groups, roles, and permissions in *Chapter 8*.

1. Click on the **Administration** link from the top panel. From the **Projects** page, you will see all the projects you can administer listed.
2. Select the project or click on the **View** link; this will take you to the **Project Administration** page.

3. From the **Project Administration** page, you will be able to perform the following key operations:

    ° Update project details, such as project name and description

    ° Configure project roles

    ° Set various schemes used by the project

    ° Manage the list of available components

    ° Manage the list of available versions

4. As you can see, the project administrator has the responsibility of keeping project details up-to-date, controlling permissions within the project through project roles, and maintaining project configuration settings. We already saw how you can update project details and we will discuss permissions in *Chapter 8*. In the following sections, we will take a look at components and versions.

Components

Components can be thought as subsections that make up the full project. In a software development project, components would be various modules that the final product comprises. For example, in a software development project, components might include User Interface and Network Connectivity as components, while a project setup to handle support components might be made up of various systems supported by the team.

Components are project-specific in JIRA. This means components from one project cannot be used in a different project. This allows project administrators to maintain the list of components.

Each issue can have zero or more components, and this information is stored in a system field called Component(s). Unlike other fields like **Summary**, **Components** provide several additional features other than holding information. You will be able to assign leads to your components and default assignees for issues with a given component.

Since components are specific to projects, components are managed on a project level from the **Project Administration** page.

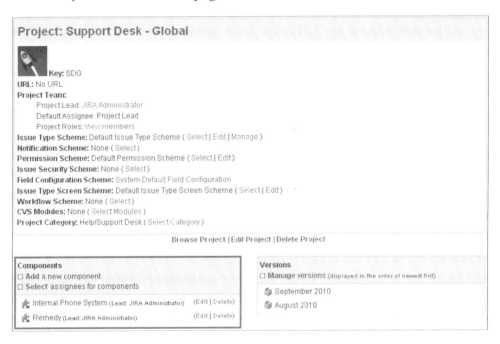

The highlighted area in the preceding screenshot is the component panel which lists all the components for the project.

Creating components

When a project is initially created, there will be no components set up for the project. For you to start using components in a project, as the project administrator, you will have to manually create them. To create new components, carry out the following steps:

1. Browse to the **Project Administration** page.
2. Click on the **Add a new component link** from the **Components** panel.
3. Provide a unique name for the component.
4. Optionally, provide a meaningful description and lead for the component.
5. Click on **Add** to create the new component.

   Component names need to be unique and case insensitive. So component1 and cOmPonent1 are the same in JIRA. Component lead is optional; not all components need a lead specified. Component leads are used in areas such as determining default assignees when an issue is created and setting up e-mail notifications.

Editing components

After a while, you may want to update the components created. While component names are not often changed, the component lead will change from time to time. For example, people will move in and out of teams and projects. When this happens, we need to make sure that the lead of our components are kept up-to-date.

To edit a component, carry out the following steps:

1. Click on **Edit** for the component to be updated from the Components panel. This will bring up the **Edit Component** page, which looks identical to the **Add a Component** page.
2. Update the details for the component.
3. Click on **Update** to save the changes.

Deleting components

Unused components can be removed from a project permanently. However, attention must be paid when deleting a component that is being used by existing issues. The good news is that JIRA automatically detects this and helps you to decide how to migrate these issues. For this reason, it is sometimes a better approach to rename the unused component to something else like "unused component".

To delete a component, carry out the following steps:

1. Click on **Delete** for the component to be deleted from the **Components** panel. You will be prompted to confirm your decision to delete the component. If the component is being used by one or more issues, JIRA will prompt you to set a new component value for these issues.

2. Select the new component for the existing issues. Once deleted, those issues will be automatically updated to the new component.

3. Click on **Delete** again to delete the component.

As shown in the preceding screenshot, JIRA will help you to identify if the component to be deleted is in use and assist you to migrate those issues to a new component.

Selecting the default assignee

As explained in earlier section, one of the useful features of components is the ability to assign a default assignee to each individual component. This means that when a user creates an issue and does not select an assignee, JIRA will be able to automatically assign the issue based on the component selected. This is a very powerful feature where in an organization, members of various teams often do not know each other, so when it comes to assigning issues at creation time, it is difficult to decide who to assign it to. With this feature, it can be set up so that the lead of the component becomes the default assignee and the issues raised can then be delegated to other members of the team.

For example, in our Help Desk project, each of our supported systems has a system expert, which is represented as the lead of the respective component. When the business user logs a ticket and selects a component, the ticket will go directly to the lead. This setup is also flexible enough so that if the user knows who to best assign the ticket to, he or she can directly assign the ticket to the member of the team and the automatic assignment will not take place.

To set the default assignee for a component, carry out the following steps:

1. Click the **Select assignees for components** link from the components panel.

2. Select the default assignee options for each of the listed components in the table.

3. Click on **Update** to save the settings.

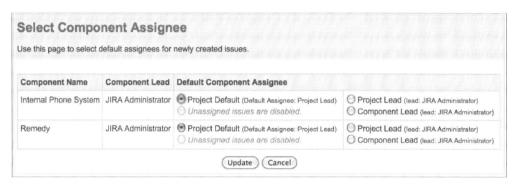

If the issue has more than one component with the default assignee, the assignee for the first component in alphabetical order will be used.

Versions

Versions describe schedules for a project. It is much easier to apply versions to a software development project, where each version in JIRA will usually represent a version of the software that is scheduled to be released on a specific date. Issues such as new features will be raised against a version which will indicate when they will be completed and released. However, the usage of versions is not limited to software development projects. As we will see in our exercise later in this chapter, there are other creative uses to this feature in JIRA.

As with components, versions are specific to projects, so they are managed at the project level from the **Project Administration** page.

Creating versions

Similar to components, project administrators will need to manage and create versions for their projects to use. To create a new version, follow these steps:

1. Click on the **Manage versions** link from the **Versions** panel.
2. Provide a unique name and a short description for the new version.
3. Click on the calendar icon to select a date for the Release Date. This helps JIRA track if a version is on time or behind schedule.
4. Select a schedule for the version (if this is not the first version being added). A schedule helps to order versions in a chronological order. The first version will have the value of **Before First Version**.
5. Click on **Add** to create the new version.

Editing versions

Version details can be updated at anytime. In most cases, this will happen as a result of release schedule change when a version needs to have its planned release date pushed back. To edit a version, follow the steps below.

1. Go to the **Manage Version** page.

2. From the listed versions, click on the **Edit Details** link for the version you wish to edit.

3. Update the version details, including **Name**, **Description**, **Release Date**, and **Schedule**.

4. Click on **Update** to save the changes.

Deleting versions

If an existing version is no longer required, you can remove it permanently from the project. However, just like components, you need to pay attention when removing versions that are in use. To delete a version, carry out the following steps:

1. Go to the **Manage Version** page.

2. From the listed versions, click on the **Delete** link for the version you wish to delete.

3. Select the new version for the existing issues. Once deleted, those issues will be automatically updated to the new version. You can also choose to remove version from the issues

4. Click on Delete again to delete the version.

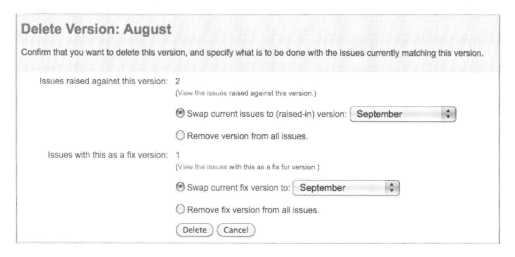

As shown in the preceding screenshot, JIRA will help you detect if the version being removed is in use by issues and help you migrate those issues to a new version, if necessary.

Project configurations

Other than components and versions, there are many configuration settings which you can apply to a project, affecting how JIRA will behave. Settings such as permission and notification rules follow the same paradigm as how projects are managed in JIRA. They are all maintained globally, while controlled at the project level. This means JIRA administrators can create permission setting rules and project administrators can select which set of rules are to apply for their projects. We will discuss each of these configurations, such as permissions, in their own separate chapters. We will first take a look at three of the less complicated settings, issue types, priorities, and resolutions.

Issue types

As we saw earlier, issues in JIRA can represent many things, ranging from software development tasks to support tickets. Issue type is what differentiates one issue from another.

Each issue has an issue type, which is represented by the issue type field. This lets you know what type of issue it is and determines what other fields will be displayed for this issue.

JIRA comes with a set of default issue types, as shown in the following table:

Issue type	Description
Bug	A problem that impairs or prevents the functions of the product.
Improvement	An enhancement to an existing feature.
New Feature	A new feature of the product.
Task	A task that needs to be done.

The default issue types are great for simple software development projects, but they do not necessarily meet the needs of others. Since it is impossible to create a system that can address everyone's needs, JIRA lets you create your own issue types and assign them to projects. For example, for a Help Desk project, you might want to create a custom issue type called **ticket**. You can create this custom issue type and assign it to the Help Desk project and users will be able to log **Tickets**, instead of **Bugs**, in the system.

Issue types are managed through the **Manage Issue Types** page. You can access the page by performing the following steps:

1. Browse to the **Administration Console** page.
2. Click on **Issue Types** from the left panel.

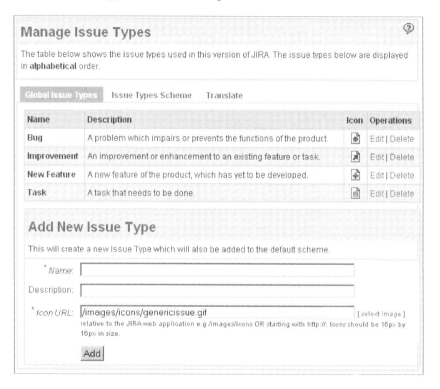

Creating issue types

To create a new issue type, carry out the following steps:

1. Browse to the **Manage Issue Types** page.
2. Type a unique name and a general description for the new issue type.
3. Type in a general description for the issue type.
4. Click on the **select image** link to bring up the **Icon selection** page.
5. Select an image icon.
6. Click on **Add** to create the new issue type.

Editing issue types

To edit an existing issue type, follow these steps:

1. Browse to the **Manage Issue Types** page.
2. Click on the **Edit** link for the issue type you wish to edit. This will bring up the **Edit Issue Type** page.
3. Update the field values for the issue type.
4. Click on the **Update** button to save the changes.

Deleting issue types

To delete an existing issue type, follow these steps:

1. Browse to the **View Priorities** page.
2. Click on the **Delete** link for the issue type you wish to delete. If there are existing issues with the issue type you are trying to delete, you will be asked to select a new issue type for those issues.
3. Select the new issue type for the existing issues. Once deleted, those issues will be automatically updated to the new issue type.
4. Click on the **Delete** button to delete the issue type.

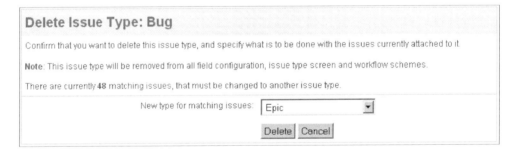

Priorities

Priority represents the importance of an issue. Priority values are global across JIRA. This means that all projects and issues will have the same set of priorities to choose from. Since it is a global-level setting in JIRA, you will need to be a JIRA Administrator to make changes.

JIRA comes with a set of predefined priorities when installed, illustrated by the following table.

Priority	Description
Blocker	Highest priority. Takes precedence over all others.
Critical	Issue is causing a problem and requires urgent attention.
Major	Has a significant impact.
Minor	Has a relatively minor impact.
Trivial	Lowest priority.

The default priorities that come with JIRA are usually sufficient. However, you can create new priorities, edit existing priorities, delete priorities, and re-arrange the order of priorities if there is a need to do so. Since priorities are global and affect all projects in JIRA, careful planning is required before making changes to the established priority list, to avoid confusion.

Priorities are managed through the **View Priorities** page. You can access this page by following these steps:

1. Log in as a JIRA Administrator.

2. Browse to the administration console page by clicking the **Administration** link from the top navigation bar.

3. Click on **Priorities** from the left panel.

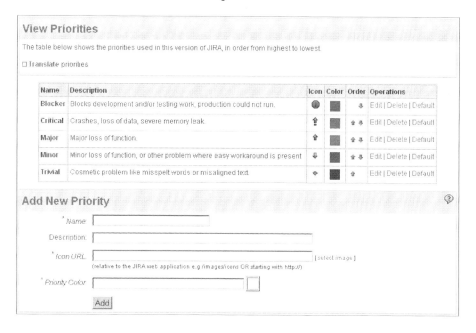

Creating priorities

To create a new priority, carry out the following steps:

1. Browse to the **View Priorities** page.
2. Type a unique name for the priority.
3. Type a brief description and a brief description for this priority explaining its purpose and usage.
4. Select an image icon for the priority. The icon needs to be 16 pixels by 16 pixels.
5. Select a color for the image icon.
6. Click on the **Add** button to create the new priority.

Once created, the new priority will appear in the table of priorities.

Editing priorities

To edit an existing priority, carry out the following steps:

1. Browse to the **View Priorities** page.
2. Click on the **Edit** link for the priority you wish to edit. This will bring up the **Edit Priority: <name>** page.
3. Update the field values for the priority.
4. Click on the **Update** button to save the changes.

Deleting priorities

To delete an existing priority, follow these steps:

1. Browse to the **View Priorities** page.
2. Click on the **Delete** link for the priority you wish to delete. On this page, you will be asked to select a new priority for issues that use the priority to be deleted.
3. Select the new priority for the existing issues. Once deleted, those issues will be automatically updated to the new priority.
4. Click on the **Delete** button to delete the priority.

Arranging priorities

When a user creates an issue, the priorities will be displayed in the order that is presented in the **View Priorities** page. You can re-arrange the order so they reflect their importance more accordingly. This is particularly useful when you start adding your own priorities to the list.

To rearrange priorities, carry out the following steps:

1. Browse to the **View Priorities** page.

2. Click on the up and down arrows in the table to move priorities up and down through the list. The orders are saved as they are being moved.

Resolutions

A resolution is another system field that comes with JIRA. It represents how an issue is resolved (completed). When an issue reaches a certain stage in its life cycle, usually when it is resolved, a resolution value is assigned. This value tells the user how the issue is resolved, for example, if it is completed successfully, or if it is simply a false alarm and does not require any further actions. We will discuss issue life cycle in detail in *Chapter 6, Workflow and Business Process*. Resolutions also play an important role when users generate reports on the project, which we will discuss in *Chapter 9*.

Resolution	Description
Fixed	A fix for this issue has been implemented.
Won't Fix	This issue will not be fixed; it may no longer be relevant.
Duplicate	This issue is a duplicate of an existing issue.
Incomplete	There is not enough information to work on this issue.
Cannot Reproduce	This issue could not be reproduced at this time, or not enough information was available to reproduce the issue. If more information becomes available, please reopen the issue.

Like priorities, resolutions are also global settings, thus it is important to make sure care is taken when making changes to the resolution list, so we do not confuse the users by introducing resolutions with identical or ambiguous meanings. Unlike priority, resolution values are usually selected when the issue is being resolved. Depending on the workflow, this is usually done by the group that is being assigned the issue and is members of the project, in our case, the Help Desk team. For this reason, there would be a much smaller user group that needs to be informed of the correct usage of available resolutions. In any case, the best approach is still to come up with sensible resolutions names and descriptions to minimize confusion, and try to keep the list as concise as possible.

1. Log in as a JIRA Administrator.

2. Browse to the administration console page by clicking the **Administration** link from the top navigation bar.

3. Click on **Resolutions** from the left panel.

View Resolutions

The table below shows the resolutions used in this version of JIRA, in order they are displayed to the user.

☐ Translate resolutions
☐ Clear defaults

Name	Description	Order	Operations
Fixed (Default)	A fix for this issue is checked into the tree and tested.	⬇	Edit | Delete
Won't Fix	The problem described is an issue which will never be fixed.	⬆ ⬇	Edit | Delete | Default
Duplicate	The problem is a duplicate of an existing issue.	⬆ ⬇	Edit | Delete | Default
Incomplete	The problem is not completely described.	⬆ ⬇	Edit | Delete | Default
Cannot Reproduce	All attempts at reproducing this issue failed, or not enough information was available to reproduce the issue. Reading the code produces no clues as to why this behavior would occur. If more information appears later, please reopen the issue.	⬆	Edit | Delete | Default

Add New Resolution

Name: _____

Description: _____

[Add]

Creating resolutions

To create a new resolution, carry out the following steps:

1. Browse to the **View Resolutions** page.
2. Type a unique name and a brief description for the resolution.
3. Type a brief description for this priority explaining its purpose and usage.
4. Click on the **Add** button to create the new resolution.

Once created, the new resolution will appear in the table of resolutions.

Editing resolutions

To edit an existing resolution, carry out the following steps:

1. Browse to the **View Resolutions** page.
2. Click on the **Edit** link for the resolution you wish to edit. This will bring up the **Edit Resolution** page.
3. Update the field values for the resolution.
4. Click on **Update** button to save the changes.

Deleting resolutions

To delete an existing resolution, carry out the following steps:

1. Browse to the **View Resolutions** page.
2. Click on the **Delete** link for the resolution you wish to delete. This will bring up the **Delete Resolution** page. On this page, you will be asked to select a new resolution for issues that used the resolution to be deleted.
3. Select the new resolution for the existing issues. Once deleted, those issues will be automatically updated to the new resolution.
4. Click on the **Delete** button to delete the resolution.

Arranging resolutions

Similar to priorities, the resolutions will be displayed in the order that is presented in the **View Resolutions** page, and you can rearrange the order of resolutions.

To rearrange resolutions, carry out the following steps:

1. Browse to the **View Resolutions** page.
2. Click the up and down arrows in the resolutions table to move them up and down through the list. The orders are saved as they are being moved.

Schemes

JIRA uses the notion of schemes to manage its configuration options. A scheme can be thought of as a template or collection of configurations. Once we have created a set of configurations such as permissions, we can save that as a scheme (known as Permission Scheme) and this can be reused and applied to multiple projects. In this sense, we can say that those projects have the same behaviors.

In the following pages, we will explore JIRA's scheme types.

Issue type scheme

Issue type schemes are templates for a group of issue types. When a new issue type is created in JIRA, it is added to the **Default Issue Type Scheme**. This means the new issue type will be available to all projects by default. This will become a problem when we start to have specialized projects such as Help Desk and issue types such as **Bug** become inappropriate.

To overcome this problem, JIRA lets us group a set of issue types together. We can also re-arrange the order of the issue types within the group so that they appear in the drop-down list in a logical manner to the users. In effect, we are creating an issue type scheme, a template for issue types and their order, which can be reused and applied to one or more projects.

We will be creating a new issue type scheme for our example of JIRA implementation later in the chapter.

Creating issue type scheme

Now that we have created our new issue types, when we create a new issue in our Help Desk project, we will see both ticket and incident as options. However, the default issue types such as Bug and Improvement are still selectable options, and by leaving them there, we are running the risk of confusing the users and allowing mistakes to be made. What we really want is to limit the issue types to only ticket and incident for the Help Desk project. This is where issue type schemes come in.

To create a new issue type scheme, carry out the following steps:

1. Browse to the administration console page.
2. Click on **Issue Types** from the left panel.
3. Click on the **Issue Type Scheme** tab.

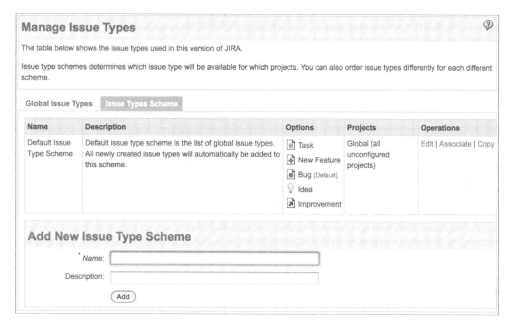

4. Type a meaningful name for our new scheme such as **Help Desk Issue Type Scheme**.
5. Type a short description of the scheme that is informative, allowing other administrators to easily know when to use this scheme.
6. Click on **Add** to create the new scheme.

Notification scheme

JIRA can generate e-mail notifications based on events that happen during an issue's life cycle. For example, when an issue is created, an "issue created" event is fired and this will trigger an e-mail notification. For each event that exists in JIRA, we can set who the recipients will be and those users will receive e-mail notifications when the event is fired. Notification schemes are discussed further in *Chapter 7, E-mail and Notification.*

Permission scheme

Permission schemes outline the permission settings in JIRA. JIRA provides fine-grained permission settings that allow administrators to control who should have access to projects, issues, and can perform actions on them. Similar to notification schemes, JIRA has a list of permissions, such as create issue and edit issue, which can have a list of users specified to control access. Permission schemes are discussed further in *Chapter 8, Securing your JIRA.*

Issue security scheme

Issue security schemes are another security mechanism offered by JIRA. Unlike permission schemes, which affect projects on a broad level, issue security schemes let users select the security level of individual issues to control who has access to view the issues. Issue security schemes are discussed further in *Chapter 8, Securing your JIRA.*

Field configuration scheme

As explained earlier, fields can have properties. They can be mandatory and/or hidden fields. These behaviors can be grouped together in a scheme and applied to a project. Field configuration scheme is discussed further in *Chapter 4, Field Management.*

Screen scheme

JIRA allows you to customize the screens to view, create, and edit issues by organizing what fields are to be displayed and their orderings. Screen schemes capture customization and save them as template schemes so that you will be able to reuse them later. Screen schemes are discussed further in *Chapter 5, Screen Management.*

Issue type screen scheme

Issue type screen schemes tie in issue type schemes and screen type schemes together to add a new dimension for project administrators to configure screen layouts for projects and issue types. You will be able to set up screen layouts for different issue types within a single project. Issue type screen schemes are discussed further in *Chapter 5, Screen Management*.

Workflow scheme

Workflow schemes are of workflows associated with specific issue types. This brings together workflows and issue types to allow different types of issues to have their own workflow configurations within the same project. Workflows and workflow schemes are discussed in detail in *Chapter 6, Workflow and Business Process*.

Help Desk project

Now we have seen all the key aspects that make up a project, let's revisit what we have learned so far and put them to practice. In this exercise, we will be setting up a project for our support teams. In order to do this, we need:

1. A new project category for all support teams
2. A new project for our help desk support team
3. Customized issue types designed for help desk support
4. A new issue type scheme to control the types of issues a user can create
5. New priorities
6. New resolutions
7. Components for the systems supported by the team
8. Versions to better manage issues created by users

Creating a new project category

Let's start by creating a project category. We will create a category for all of our internal support teams and their respective JIRA support projects.

Please note this procedure is optional, as JIRA does not require a project to belong to a project category.

1. Log into JIRA as a JIRA Administrator.
2. Click on **Administration** to bring up the administration console page.

3. Click on **Project Categories**.

4. Fill in the fields as shown in the following screenshot.

5. Click on **Add** to create the new project category.

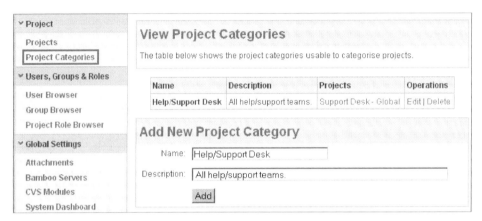

Creating a new project

Now that we have a project category created, let's create a project for our help desk support team. To create a new project, carry out the following steps:

1. Click on **Administration** to bring up the administration console page.

2. Click on **Projects**.

3. Click on **Add Project** to bring up the **Add a New Project** page.

4. Name the new project Support Desk - Global.

5. Give the new project a key SDG.

6. Select the admin user as the Project Lead.

7. Accept the default values for the other fields and click on Add to create the new project.

8. Click on **Add** to create the new project.

Creating new priorities

For our Support Desk system, we will be adding a new priority of **Urgent**, which will sit above **Critical** and below **Blocker**. The name of priorities alone can sometimes be confusing as people may not know the difference of importance between critical and urgent, so the ordering of the priorities becomes crucial when helping users decide what priority to assign to their issues

1. Browse to the **View Priorities** page.

2. Type **Urgent** for the **Name** field.

3. Type a brief description for this priority explaining its purpose and usage.

4. Type in `/images/icons/serious_warning_16.gif` as the Icon URL.

5. Type **#ff9900** as the color for the priority.

6. Click on the **Add** button to create the new priority.

7. Use the up arrows to move the **Urgent** priority up the list so it sits between **Critical** and **Blocker**.

Creating new resolutions

We will also need to create a new resolution for our Support Desk project. We want to have the ability to specify whether an issue is to be deferred until a later stage due to current circumstances.

1. Browse to the **View Resolutions** page.

2. Type **Deferred** for the **Name** field.

3. Type a brief description for this resolution, explaining its purpose and usage.

4. Click on the **Add** button to create the new priority.

Creating issue types

Since our project is for a support desk team, the default issue types that come with JIRA are not appropriate for this purpose. For this reason, let's create our own issue types and associate them with the project. For this exercise, we will create two new issue types: **incident** and **ticket**.

The first step to set up issue type association is to create the issue types we need. To create issue types, carry out the following steps:

1. Browse to the **Manage Issue Types** page.

2. Type in **Ticket** for the **Name** field.

3. Type in a general description for ticket.

4. Click on the **select image** link to bring up the **Icon selection** page.

5. For ticket issue type, let's select the unused **documentation** icon.

6. Click on **Add** to create the new ticket issue type.

You should now see the new ticket issue type in the table. Now let's add the incident issue type.

1. Type in **Incident** for the **Name** field.
2. Type in a general description for **Incident**.
3. Click on the **select image** link to bring up the **Icon selection** page.
4. For the ticket issue type, let's select the unused **exclamation** icon.
5. Click on **Add** to create the new **Incident** issue type.

You should see both the **Ticket** and **Incident** issue types. Now that we have our new issue types, let's try to log a ticket!

1. Click on the drop-down arrow of **Issues** from the top navigation bar.
2. Click on **Create Issue** from the drop-down list.
3. Click on the **Issue Type** drop-down list and you should see a the list of the available issue types, as shown in the following screenshot:

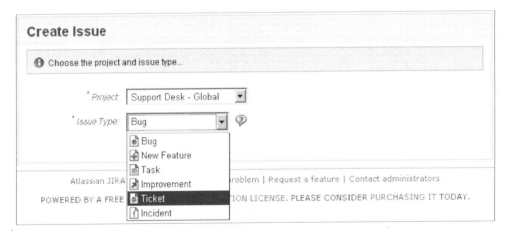

As we can see, our new **Ticket** and **Incident** issue types are now available in the selection. However, we are also getting the default issue types such as **Bug** and **New Feature**, which is not applicable for a support desk. By leaving them there, we are running the risk of confusing the users and allowing mistakes to be made. What we really want is to limit the issue types to only **Ticket** and **Incident** for the Support Desk–Global project.

If you remember from previous discussions, we can address this problem with a new issue type scheme. Let's go ahead and create one.

Creating an issue type scheme

We want to limit the issue types to be only **Incident** and **Ticket** for our **Support Desk–Global** project, but we do not want to affect other projects that still need to have **Bug** and other default issue types. We need to create a new issue type scheme specifically for support projects which can be used by us and other teams.

1. Browse to the **Manage Issue Types** page.

2. Click on the **Issue Type Scheme** tab to bring up the **Issue Type Scheme Configuration** page.

3. Type a meaningful name for our new scheme such as **Support Desk Issue Type Scheme**.

4. Give a short description of the scheme that is informative, allowing other administrators to easily know when to use this scheme.

5. Click on **Add** to create the new scheme.

6. Drag **Incident** and **Ticket** issue types from the **Available Issue Types** panel to the **Issue Types for Current Scheme** panel.

7. Select **Incident** as the **Default Issue Type**.

8. Click on the **Save** button.

9. Click on the **Associate** link for **Support Desk Issue Type Scheme**.

10. Select our **Support Desk – Global** project.

11. Click on the **Associate** button to apply this issue type scheme to the project.

12. Go back to the **Create Issue** page and we should check the **Issue Type** drop-down list.

You should now see that only **Incident** and **Ticket** are the only issue types that you can select when creating a new issue for **Support Desk–Global** project.

Creating new components

As discussed in earlier sections, components are sub-sections of a project. This makes logical sense for a software development project where each component will represent a deliverable software module. For other types of project, components may first appear useless or inappropriate.

It is true that components are not for every type of project out there, and this is the reason why you are not required to have them by default. Just like everything else in JIRA, all the features come from how you can best map them to your business needs.

The power of a component is more than just a flag field for an issue. For our example, let's imagine the company we are working for has a range of systems that need to be supported. These may range from phone systems and desktop computers, and other business applications. Let's also assume that our support team needs to support all of the systems. To help manage to delegate, we will create a component for each of the systems which the support desk team supports. We will also assign a lead for each of the components. This setup allows us to establish a structure where the Help Desk project is led by the support team lead, and each component is led by their respective system expert (who may or may not be the same as the team lead). As we will see in later chapters, this allows for a very flexible management process when we start wiring in other JIRA features such as notification schemes.

1. Browse to the **project administration** page for the **Support Desk–Global** project.
2. Click **Add a new component** from the Components panel.
3. Type **Internal Phone System** for the new component's name.
4. Provide a short description for the new component.
5. Select a user to be the lead of the component. Since we only have one user in our system at the moment, we will put **admin** as the component lead.
6. Click on **Add** to create the new component.

Creating new versions

As we have discussed earlier in this chapter, while versions are most applicable for projects with deliverables, they can still be helpful for tracking and reporting purposes. For our Support Desk project, we can use versions to represent different calendar months, and each ticket or incident raised by users will have a version number attached. This way it will be very easy for management to pull up a report to see how many issues are being raised for any given month.

1. Browse to the project administration page for the **Support Desk–Global** project.

2. Click on **Manage versions** from the Versions panel.

3. Type **August** for **Version Name**.

4. Provide a short description for the new version.

5. Click on the calendar icon and select the last day for the **Release Date**.

6. Click on **Add** to create the new version.

See it in action

Now that we have fully prepared our project, let's see how everything comes together by logging a ticket.

1. Click on the drop-down arrow of **Issues** from the top navigation bar.

2. Click **Create Issue** from the drop-down list.

3. Select **Support Desk–Global** as the Project.

4. Select **Incident** as the **Issue Type**.

5. Click on the **Next** button.

6. On the **Create Issue Detail** screen, you should see the components, versions, and priorities we have created.

7. Fill in the fields as shown in the following screenshot.

8. Click on the **Create** button to log the incident.

We will be exploring issues in more detail in the next chapter.

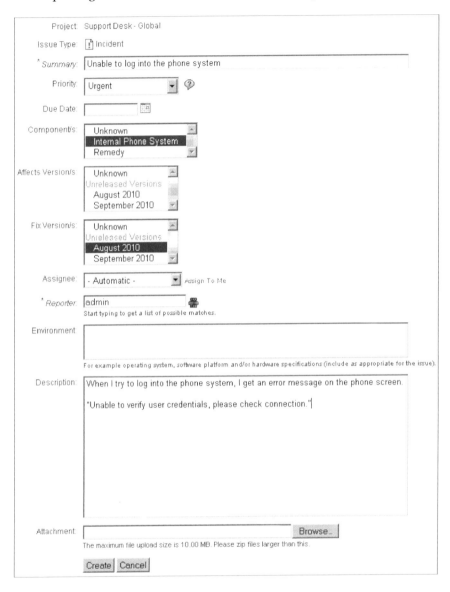

Summary

In this chapter, we looked at one of the most important concepts in JIRA, projects, and how to create and manage them. We also looked at various components that exist within a project and configuration options that can be set for a project. We concluded this chapter by starting on our exercise to implement a support desk system. In the next chapter, we will look further into an important concept in JIRA, issues.

3
Issue Management

As we already saw in the previous chapter, JIRA is a very flexible and versatile tool that can be used in different organizations for different purposes. A software development organization will use JIRA to manage its software development lifecycle and bug tracking while a customer service organization may choose to use JIRA for tracking and logging customer complaints and suggestions. For this reason, issues in JIRA can represent anything that is applicable to the real world scenario. Generally speaking, an issue in JIRA often represents a unit of work that can be acted upon by one or more people.

In this chapter, we will explore the basic and advanced features in JIRA for issue management. By the end of the chapter, you will have learned:

- Issues and what they are in JIRA
- Creating, editing, and deleting issues
- Moving issues between projects
- Expressing your interest on issues through voting and watching
- Advanced Issue operations including uploading attachments and linking issues

What an issue looks like

As we have discussed, an issue in JIRA can be anything in the real world to represent a problem domain. It can be a software bug, a help desk ticket, or a customer request, but what does an issue look like in JIRA? How does JIRA achieve this level of flexibility and still present it in a consistent manner?

Let's first take a look at an issue in JIRA. The following screenshot shows a typical example of an issue and breaks it down into more digestible sections, followed by an explanation on each of the highlighted sections. This view is often called the **Issue Summary** or the **View Issue** page.

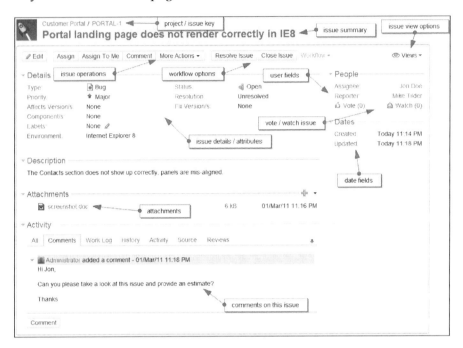

Section	Description
Project / Issue Key	The project that the issue belongs to. The issue key is the unique identifier of the current issue. This section acts as a breadcrumb for easy navigation.
Issue Summary	Gives a brief summary of the issue.
Issue Views	This shows the various view options for the issue. Options include XML, Excel, and Word.
Issue Operations	Operations which users can perform on the issue, such as edit, assign, and comment. These are covered in later sections of this chapter.
Workflow Options	Workflow transitions available. Workflow will be covered in *Chapter 6*.
Issue Details / Attributes	Lists fields such as **issue type** and **priority**. Custom fields are also displayed in this section. Fields will be covered in *Chapter 4*.
User Fields	Section-specific for user type fields such as assignee and reporter. Fields will be covered in *Chapter 4*.

Section	Description
Date Fields	Section-specific for date type fields such as **Create** and **Due** dates. Fields will be covered in *Chapter 4*.
Vote / Watch Issue	Options to allow users to vote on and watch an issue.
Attachments	Lists all attachments on this issue.
Comments	Lists all comments that are visible to the current user.

Creating an issue

JIRA is an issue-tracking system for users to log and track various types of issues they have. By default, all logged-in users will be able to log issues in JIRA. However, this can be controlled through permissions, which we will cover in *Chapter 9*.

When creating a new issue, you will need to fill in a number of fields. Some fields are mandatory, such as **summary** and **type**, while others are optional, such as **description**.

There are two ways in which you can create a new issue in JIRA. You can either:

1. Click on the **Create Issue** link at the top of the screen. This will bring up the **Create Issue Step 1** panel, where you can choose which project to create the issue in and the type of the issue.

2. Click on the **Create Issue** link from the issue drop down menu from the top bar. This will bring up the **Create Issue Step 1** page, which will be identical to the first option.

3. Select the **Project**, **Issue Type**, and click on the **Next** button. This will bring up the **Create Issue Step 2** page. The page contains a form of fields that you can fill to provide additional information for the issue. The fields with a red star (*) next to them are mandatory.

4. Fill in the fields and click on the **Create** button.

Once the issue has been created, JIRA will automatically take you to the issue summary page, which we have seen earlier.

If you do not fill in a mandatory field, JIRA will display an error message for the fields that are missing values, as shown in the following screenshot:

Editing an issue

After an issue has been created in JIRA, you can continue to modify and update its contents and provide additional information as it becomes available. When editing an issue, there are a few fields you cannot change.

- **Key**: This is a system-generated value and you will not be able to change or set it at any time.

- **Project**: You cannot change the issue's project association by editing the issue. You can change this, however, by moving the current issue to a different project. See the section *Moving an issue between projects* for more details.

- **Original Estimate**: You cannot change this value once someone has logged work against the issue. See the section *Time tracking* for more details.

To edit an issue, carry out the following steps:

1. Browse to the issue you wish to edit.
2. Click the **edit** option on the issue menu. You will be presented with a page similar to the **Create Issue Step 2** page.
3. Edit the fields values and click on **Update**.

After JIRA saves your update, you will be taken back to the issue summary page.

Deleting an issue

You may need to delete issues that have been created by mistake, or if the issue is redundant, although normally, it is better to close and mark the redundant issue. We will discuss closing an issue in *Chapter 6, Workflow and Business Process*.

Please note that issue deletion is permanent in JIRA. Unlike some other applications that may put deleted records in a trash bin, which you can retrieve later, JIRA completely deletes the issue from the system. The only way to retrieve the deleted issue is by restoring JIRA with a previous backup.

To delete an issue, carry out the following steps:

1. Browse to the issue you wish to delete.
2. Click on the **Delete** option from the **More Actions** menu. This will bring up the **Delete Issue** dialog.
3. Click on the **Delete** button to remove the issue permanently from JIRA.

Deleting an issue permanently removes it from JIRA, along with all of its data including attachments and comments.

Moving an issue between projects

Once an issue has been created, the issue is associated with a project. You can, however, move the issue around from one project to another project. This may sound like a very simple process, but there are a lot of steps involved and several considerations to make.

First, if the current issue type does not exist in the new project, you must decide on a new issue type. Second, you will need to map the status of the issue. Third, you will need to decide on the values for fields that exist in the new project but do not exist in the current project, if the new fields are mandatory. Sounds like a lot, but luckily, JIRA comes with a wizard that is designed to help you address all those items.

To start moving an issue, carry out the following steps:

1. Browse to the issue you wish to move.
2. Click on the **Move** option from the **More Actions** menu bar. This will bring up the **Move Issue** wizard.

There are essentially four steps in the move issue wizard.

The first step is to select which project you wish to move the issue to. You will also need to select the new issue type. If the same issue type exists in the new project, it is recommended that you continue to use the same issue type.

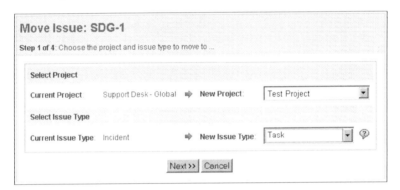

The second step allows you to map the current issue to the new project's workflow.

The third step shows all the fields that exist in the new project but not the current project which require a value.

The forth and last step shows you the summary of the changes that will be applied by moving the issue from project A to project B. This is your last chance to make sure that all the information is correct. If there are any mistakes, you can go back to step one and start over again. If you are happy with the change, confirm the move by clicking on **Move**.

Casting vote on an issue

The most straightforward way to express your interest in a JIRA issue is to vote for it. For organizations or teams that manage their priorities based on popularity, voting is a great mechanism to collect this information.

For example, a product company will have a public-facing JIRA application to track customer feature requests, and at the same time to allow customers to vote on these features based on their needs. This allows the product management and marketing team to have an insight on the market's needs and how to best evolve their offerings.

One thing to keep in mind is when voting, you can only vote once per issue. You can vote many times for many different issues, but for any given issue, you have only one vote. This helps prevent a single user from continuously voting on the same issue, which may blow the final statistics out of proportion. You can however, un-vote a vote that you have already cast on an issue, and vote on it again later if you choose to: it will still only count as one vote.

To vote on an issue, simply click on the tick icon next to **Votes**. Once you have voted for an issue, the icon will appear in color. If you have not yet voted for an issue, the icon will appear gray.

Receiving notifications about issues

JIRA is able to send out automated e-mail notifications about updates on issues to users. Normally, notification e-mails will only be sent out to the issue's reporter, assignee, and people who have registered interest in the issue. This behavior can be changed through **Notification Schemes**, which we will discuss in *Chapter 7, E-mail and Notification*.

You can register your interest in the issue by choosing to watch the issue. By watching an issue, you become a watcher of an issue and receive e-mail notifications on activity updates. Users watching the issue can also choose to stop watching, thus cancelling e-mail updates from JIRA.

To watch an issue, simply click on the mail icon next to **Watchers**. When you are watching an issue, the icon will appear in color. When you are not watching an issue, the icon will appear grayed out.

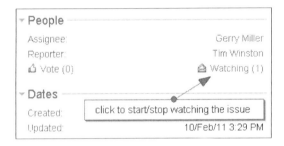

JIRA also shows how many people are actively watching the issue by displaying the total watchers next to the watch icon. You can click on the **Watchers** link to bring up the **Watchers** page, which will show a list of users that are currently watching the issue.

If you are the project administrator, by default, you can invite others to watch the issue by adding them as watchings yourself from the same page. This can be changed through modifying permissions, which we will cover in *Chapter 9*.

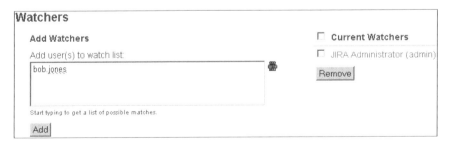

Re-assigning issues to others

Once an issue has been created, the user assigned to the issue will normally start working on it. However, this does not mean the issue will stay with the same person forever.

There are many instances where an issue needs to be re-assigned to a different user. For example, the current assignee may be unavailable, or if issues are created with no specific assignees. Another example is when issues are assigned to different people at different stages of the workflow. For this reason, JIRA allows users to re-assign issues once they have been created.

To re-assign an issue, carry out the following steps:

1. Browse to the issue you wish to assign.
2. Click on the **Assign** option from the issue menu bar. This will bring up the **Assign Issue** page.
3. Select the new assignee for the issue, and optionally put in a comment to provide some information to the new assignee.
4. Click on the **Assign** button.

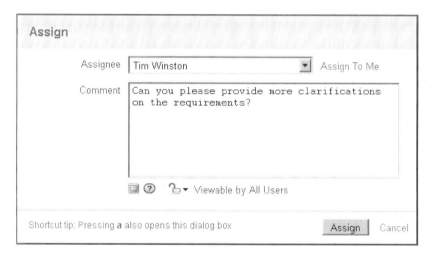

Once this issue has been re-assigned, its assignee value will be updated to the new assignee. The new assignee will also receive a notification e-mail alerting him/her that a new issue has been assigned and waiting to be worked on. It is possible to set up JIRA to allow issues to be unassigned. Unassigned issues do not have an assignee and will not show up on anyone's list of active issues.

Issues and comments

JIRA lets users to create comments on issues. As we have already seen, you will be able to create comments when you assign an issue to a different user. This is a very useful feature that allows multiple users to collaborate on the same issue and share information. For example, the support staff (issue assignee) may request more clarification from the business user (issue reporter) by adding a comment to the issue. When combined with JIRA's built-in notification system, automatic e-mail notifications will be sent out to the issue's reporter, assignee, and any other user watching the issue. Notifications are covered in *Chapter 7*.

Adding comments

By default, all logged-in users will be able to add comments to issues they can access. To add a comment to an issue,

1. Browse to the issue you wish to add a comment for.

2. Click on the **Comment** option from the issue menu bar. This will bring up the **Comment** input section.

3. Type the comment into the text box. The text box will adjust its size as you type.

4. Click on the **Add** button to add the comment.

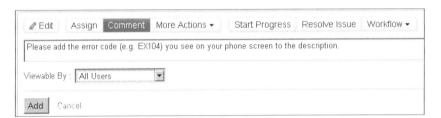

Once a comment has been added, the comment will be visible in the **Comments** tab in the **Issue Activity** section.

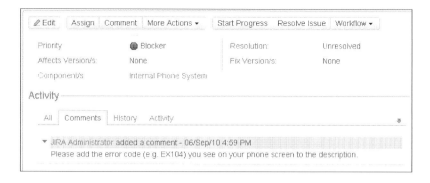

Managing your comments

After you have added your comment to an issue, you can edit its contents, security setting, or delete it altogether. To edit or delete a comment, simply hover over the comment and the comment management options will appear on the right-hand side.

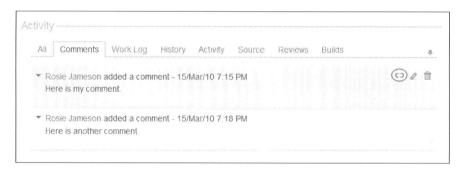

Creating a Permalink

From time to time, you will often want to refer other people to a comment you have previously made. While you could tell them the name of the issue and let them scroll down to the bottom until they find your comment amongst hundreds of others, JIRA allows you to create a quick Permalink to your comment that will take you directly to the comment of interest.

To create a permalink for a comment, carry out the following steps:

1. Browse to the comment you wish to permalink.
2. Hover over the comment to bring up the comment management options.
3. Click on the permalink icon. This will highlight the comment in pale blue.

You will now notice that your browser's URL bar will look something like

`http://localhost:8080/jira/browse/HD-13?focusedCommentId=94796#acti on_94796` (notice the `focusedCommendId` section after the issue key). Cut and paste that URL and give it to your colleagues. Once they click on that link, they will be taken directly to your comment, which will be highlighted.

Attachments

As we have seen, JIRA uses fields such as **summary** and **description** to capture data. This works for most cases, but when you have complex data such as application log files or screenshots, fields become insufficient. This is where attachments come into play. JIRA allows you to attach files to an issue as support documents.

Enabling attachments in JIRA

Attachments are saved as files on the JIRA file server, not in the database, so you need to ensure there is sufficient disk space to accommodate the volume of attachments for now and in the future. As attachments are not stored in the database, JIRA will not backup the files as part of its backup process, and need to be backed up separately.

Attachments are enabled by default in JIRA so users will be able to attach files to issues as soon as JIRA is installed. However, if it is disabled for some reason, you can re-enable it. To enable attachments for JIRA, carry out the following steps:

1. Login JIRA as a JIRA Administrator.
2. Browse to the administration console by clicking on the **Administration** link on the top navigation panel.
3. Click on **Attachments** under **Global Setting** from the left navigation panel. This will take you to the **Attachment Settings** page.
4. Click on the **Edit Configuration** link. This will bring up the **Edit Attachment Settings** page.
5. Select **Use Default Directory** for **Attachment Path**.
6. Click on the **Update** button to enable attachments in JIRA.

On the **Attachment Settings** page, there are a few options you need to configure when you enable attachments in JIRA. The following table summarizes the configuration options.

Options	Description
Attachment Path	Where attachments will be stored on the file system. The only options are the default directory, which is inside your JIRA_HOME directory, or to disable attachments in JIRA.
Attachment Size	The maximum size of the attachment users can upload, in bytes
Enable Thumbnails	Whether or not to enable thumbnail generation when the attachment is an image.
Enable ZIP support	Whether or not to enable ZIP support, which allows users to download multiple attachments as a single ZIP file, and also view contents of ZIP attachment files.

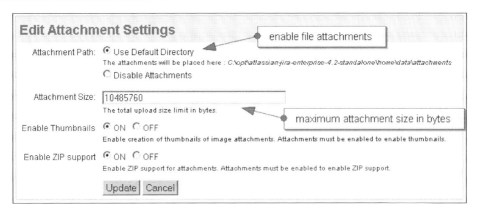

Attachments are enabled and disabled globally across JIRA. You cannot selectively enable or disable attachment function on a per project basis. You can however, achieve a similar result by controlling the permission around who can attach files. Permissions are discussed in *Chapter 8, Securing your JIRA*.

Attaching files

JIRA allows you to attach any arbitrary file to an issue. These can be images, Microsoft Office documents, and other binary files. To attach a file to an issue, carry out the following steps:

1. Browse to the issue you wish to attach a file to.

2. Select **Attach File** from the **More Actions** menu. This will bring up the **Attach Files** page.

3. Click on the **Browse** button to select the file you wish to attach.

4. Optionally, provide a comment for the attached file. The comment will be added as a normal comment to the issue.

5. Optionally, select the security level for who can see the comment.

6. Click on the **Attach** button.

When attaching files to JIRA, you need to remember the file name cannot contain the following characters – '\', '/','\', '%', ':', '$', '?', '*'.

Attaching screenshots

Apart from letting you attach any file to an issue, JIRA also allows you to directly attach a screenshot from your system clipboard to issues. This saves you from having to take a screenshot, save it as a physical file on the disk, and finally attach it in JIRA.

To attach a screenshot, carry out the following steps:

1. Browse to the issue you wish to attach a screenshot to.

2. Select **Attach Screenshot** from the **More Actions** menu. This will bring up the **Attach Screenshot** page.

3. Click on **Yes** when prompted whether you want to trust the applet.

4. Click on the **Paste** button and the screenshot will be pasted into the panel.

5. Enter a file name for the screenshot or accept the default name.

6. Optionally, provide a comment for the attached file. The comment will be added as a normal comment to the issue.

7. Optionally, select the security level for who can see the comment.

8. Click on the **Attach** button.

Just like attaching a file to JIRA, the same file name restriction applies to attaching a screenshot.

Sub-tasks

JIRA allows only one person (assignee) to work on one issue at a time. This design ensures that an issue is a single unit of work that can be tracked against one person. However, in the real world, we often find ourselves in situations where we need to have multiple people working on the same issue. This may be caused by a poor breakdown of tasks or simply because of the nature of task at hand. Whatever the reason, JIRA provides a mechanism to address this problem through **sub-tasks**.

Sub-tasks are similar to issues in many ways, and as a matter of fact, sub-tasks are a special kind of issue. They must have a parent issue, and their issue types are flagged as sub-task issue types. You can say that all sub-tasks are issues, but not all issues are sub-tasks.

For every issue, you can have one or more sub-tasks that can be assigned and tracked separately from one another. Sub-tasks cannot have other sub-tasks. JIRA allows only one level of sub-task.

Enabling sub-tasks

Sub-tasks are enabled by default. If you have sub-tasks disabled for some reason (for example, upgrading from a version prior to 4.2), you will need to enable this feature.

To enable sub-tasks in JIRA, carry out the following steps:

1. Log in as a JIRA Administrator user.
2. Browse to the administration console by clicking on the **Administration** link on the top navigation panel.
3. Click on **Sub-Tasks** under **Global Setting** from the left navigation panel. This will take you to the **Sub-Tasks Administration** page.
4. Click on **Enable** to enable sub-tasks in JIRA.

Creating sub-tasks

Since sub-tasks belong to an issue, you need to first browse to the issue before you can create a new sub-task.

1. Browse to the issue you wish to create a sub-task for.

2. Select **Create Sub-Task** from the **More Actions** menu. This will take you to the familiar **Issue Creation Step 1** page.

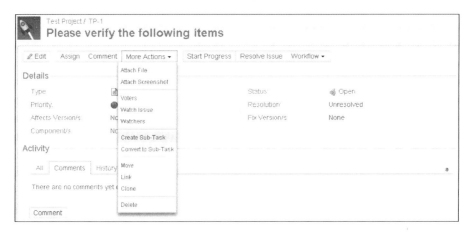

Unlike the normal **Issue Creation** page, you do not select the project. This is because JIRA can determine the project value based on the parent issue. The issue type selection also only contains issue types of sub-tasks.

3. Select the sub-task **issue type** and click **next**, this will take you to the **Issue Creation Step 2** page.

4. Fill in the fields and click the **Create** button.

Once the sub-task has been created, you will be taken directly to the **sub-task summary** page. From here, you will be able perform normal issue actions on the sub-task and navigate back to the parent issue.

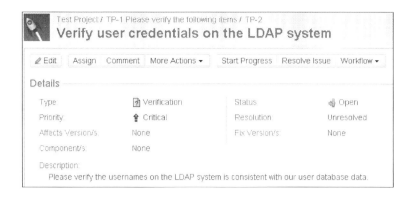

Issue linking

Issues can have relationships between themselves. Sometimes, two issues might be related to each other, and in other cases, one issue might be a duplicate of another issue. Instead of capturing all these associations in the issue description or comments, JIRA provides the facility to create links between issues.

Enabling issue linking

Issue linking is enabled by default when you first install JIRA. If for some reason it is disabled, you will need to re-enable it. Issue linking is configured globally, so once it is enabled, issue linking will become available for all projects in JIRA.

You need to be a JIRA Administrator to enable issue linking. To do so, follow the steps below:

1. Log in as a JIRA Administrator user.
2. Browse to the administration console by clicking on the **Administration** link on the top navigation panel.
3. Click on **Issue Linking** under **Global Setting** from the left navigation panel. This will take you to the **Issue Link Administration** page.

4. Click on **Activate** to enable issue linking in JIRA.

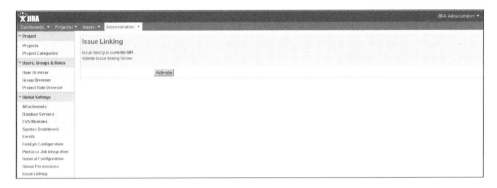

From this page, you will be able to see a list of **Link Types** available. A link type defines the nature of the link between issues. For example, the default **Blocks link** type defines that issue A blocks issue B, thus issue B cannot be completed until issue A is resolved. It is important to note that issue linking does not place any restrictions on issues. This means, although the link states that issue B cannot be completed until issue A is resolved, this is not enforced and users can close issue A while issue B remains open.

Creating link types

JIRA comes with four link types by default: **Blocks**, **Cloners**, **Duplicate**, and **Relates**. As we discussed earlier, a link type is simply a type of association that describes the relationship between two issues, and so you can define your own link types in JIRA. For example, one issue can support another issue, and we can create a link type called **Supports**.

To create a new link type, follow the following steps:

1. Browse to the **Issue Linking Administration** page.
2. Make sure issue linking is enabled.
3. Fill in the **Add New Link Type** form. For a duplicate link type:
   ◦ Enter **Supports** for the **Name** field.
   ◦ Enter **Supports** for the **Outward Link Description** field.
   ◦ Enter **is supported by** in the **Inward Link Description** field.
4. Click on the **Add** button.

Outward and inward link descriptions define what are shown when users select the type of link to use when linking two issues together. We will see an example of this later in the section.

Once a new link type is added, it will be displayed in the table on the **Issue Linking Administration** page.

Linking issues

When linking issues, it is important to select the correct link. As we have seen, for each link type defined, there is an outward and inward link description. Outward links are links going out of the current issue. You can think of outward links as "active links". Inward links are links coming into the current issue. You can think of inward links as "passive links".

For example, we have a bug issue which states that a page is not displaying correctly. We also have a new feature issue that requires us to add some new items onto the same page. For us to implement the new change, we must first fix the bug. In other words, the bug (Issue A) blocks (outward) the feature (Issue B), or the feature is blocked by (inward) the bug. In JIRA, outward links are displayed on the left side of the **Issue Links** section.

Inward links are displayed on the right side of the Issue Links section.

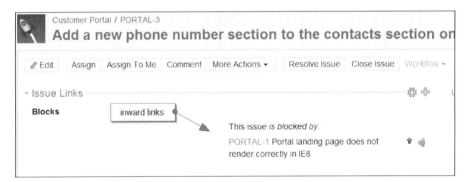

Now that we have explained outward and inward links, let's look at how to create a link between issues.

1. Browse to the issue you wish to create a link for.

2. Select **Link** from the **More Actions** menu. This will bring up the **Link Issue** page.

3. Select the type of issue linking.

4. Select the issue(s) to link to.

5. Optionally, add a comment for adding the issue link.

6. Optionally, select the security level for who can see the comment.

7. Click on the **Link** button.

Issue cloning

When you need to create a new issue and you already have a similar issue, JIRA allows you to quickly create the new issue with data based on your existing issues, by cloning the original issue. Cloning an issue allows you to quickly create a new issue with most of its fields populated.

A cloned issue has the same values for its fields such as **description**, **issue type**, and **priority** as the original issue, but it is a separate entity nonetheless. Further actions performed on either of the two issues will not affect the other.

When an issue is being cloned, a **Clone link** is automatically created between the two issues, establishing the relationship.

Cloning an existing issue

Cloning an issue in JIRA is simple and straightforward, all you have to do is specify a new summary for the cloned issue. To clone an issue, follow these steps:

1. Browse to the issue you wish to clone.
2. Select **Clone** from the **More Actions** menu. This will bring up the **Clone Issue** page.
3. Type in a new summary for the new cloned issue.
4. Click on the **Create** button.

Once the issue is successfully cloned, you will be taken to the issue summary page for the newly cloned issue.

Time tracking

Since issues often represent a single unit of work that can be worked on, it is logical for users to log time they have spent on working on the issue. You can specify an estimated effort required to complete an issue and JIRA will be able to help you track the progress. JIRA displays the time tracking information of an issue in the **Time Tracking** panel at the right-hand side.

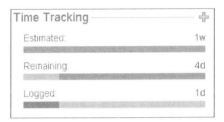

1. **Estimated**: Represents the original estimated effort required to complete the issue.

2. **Remaining**: The remaining time for the issue to be completed. This is calculated automatically by JIRA based on the original estimate and total time logged by users.

3. **Logged**: Total time logged by all users on this issue.

Enabling time tracking

Time tracking is enabled by default when you install JIRA. If for some reason it is disabled, such as when you upgrade from an older version of JIRA, you must first re-enable it. To enable time tracking, follow these steps:

1. Log in as a JIRA Administrator user.

2. Browse to the administration console by clicking on the **Administration** link on the top navigation panel.

3. Click on **Time Tracking** under **Global Setting** from the left navigation panel. This will take you to the **Time Tracking** page.

4. Click on **Activate** to enable issue linking in JIRA.

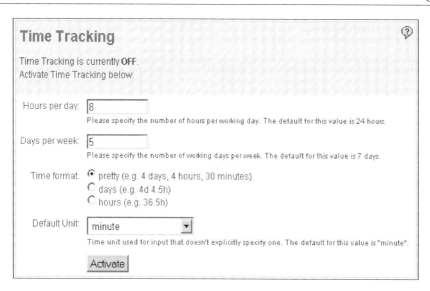

On the **Time Tracking** page, you can set several parameters. As we will see in later sections, these parameters will determine the time tracking behavior for JIRA.

Parameter	Description
Hours per day	Number of hours that JIRA will consider a working day. For example, if this is set to 8 hours per day, when the user puts in 16 hours, JIRA will automatically convert it to 2 days.
Days per week	Number of working days per week in JIRA. For example, if this is set to 5 days per week, when the user puts in 10 days, JIRA will automatically convert it to 2 weeks.
Time format	How JIRA will display time in the **Time Spent** field.
Default unit	The default time tracking unit if the user does not supply one.

Specifying original estimates

Original estimate represents the anticipated time required to complete the work represented by the issue. It is shown as the blue bar under the **Time Tracking** section.

In order for you to specify an original estimate value, you need to make sure that time tracking is enabled and the **Time Tracking** field is added to the issue's create and/or edit screen. We will discuss fields and screens in *Chapter 4* and *Chapter 5*, respectively.

To specify an original estimate value, **On** the create issue and/or edit issue screen. Provide a value for the **Original Estimate** field.

Logging work

Logging work in JIRA allows you to specify the amount of time (work) you have spent working on an issue. You can log work against any issues, provided time tracking is enabled and you have permission to do so. We will cover permissions in *Chapter 8, Securing your JIRA*.

To log work against an issue, follow the steps below:

1. Browse to the issue you wish to log work against.

2. Select **Log Work** from the **More Actions** menu. This will bring up the **Log Work** page.

3. Enter the amount of time you wish to log. Use "w", "d", "h", "m" to specify week, day, hour, and minute, respectively.

4. Select the date you wish the log your work against.

5. Optionally, select how the remaining estimate should be adjusted.

6. Optionally, add a description to the work you have done.

7. Optionally, select the security on who can view the work log entry.

8. Click on the **Log** button.

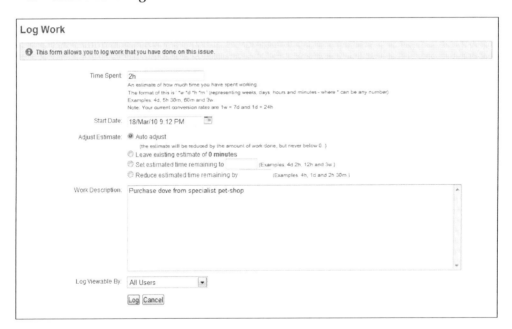

Help Desk Project

In this exercise, we will follow up from the previous chapter where we created a project for our Global Help Desk team.

Configuring sub-tasks

Since we are building a system for our support team, we will allow business users to directly log issues into the system. This means there is the potential possibility of users logging issues that are broad in scope and require several tasks to be undertaken in order to resolve the problem. We will need to enable sub-tasks to help our support staff to better break down the issue.

The first step is to enable sub-tasks in JIRA.

1. Log in as a JIRA Administrator user.
2. Browse to **Sub-Tasks administration** page.
3. Click **Enable** to enable sub-tasks in JIRA.

Now that we have enabled sub-tasks, the next step is to create some new types of sub-tasks. JIRA comes with a generic sub-task type called **Sub-task**, but we will need some more specific ones applicable to our problem domain.

1. Browse to **Sub-Tasks administration** page.
2. Set **Name** to **Verification**.
3. Set **Description** to **A verification task for this issue**.
4. Set **Icon URL** to /images/icons/undefined.gif.
5. Click on **Add** to add the new sub-task type.

We have now added a new sub-task type to JIRA. When we create new sub-tasks, we will have the option to choose either creating a generic sub-task or our verification sub-task.

Configuring time tracking

For our support desk team, we would like to allow our team members to log the amount of time they have spent working on support requests submitted by business users. For the purpose of our team, we will be providing support during normal business hours, this means 8 hours per day, and 5 days per week.

Armed with the knowledge we have gathered throughout this chapter, let's go ahead and enable time tracking for our system.

1. Log in as a JIRA Administrator user.

2. Browse to the **Time Tracking** Administration page.

3. Set **Hours per day** to **8**.

4. Set **Days per week** to **5**.

5. Set **Time format** to **pretty**.

6. Set **Default unit** to **minute**.

7. Click on **Activate** to enable Time Tracking.

Now we have globally enabled time tracking. We will be looking at how to provide finer control over time tracking in later chapters. With this configuration, we have set JIRA to perform the following automatic conversions.

1. When the user inputs **8h** (8 hours), it will be interpreted as 1d (1 day).

2. When the user inputs **5d** (5 days), it will be interpreted as 1w (1 week).

3. When the user does not specify the unit, JIRA will interpret it as in minutes by default. For example, if the user inputs **60**, it will be interpreted as 60 minutes and converted to 1h (1 hour).

Enabling issue linking

As our support team supports a wide range of IT systems in the organization, if one system fails, many users will be affected. As a result, a single failure may result in multiple support request or error reports being logged. Instead of working on each of the issues individually as separate cases, it will be a lot more efficient to link related issues through issue linking.

The first step is to enable issue linking in JIRA.

1. Log in as a JIRA Administrator.

2. Browse to the **Issue Linking Administration** page.

3. Click on **Activate** to enable issue linking in JIRA.

Now that we have enabled issue linking, we need to create a few issue link types to support our needs. For our support team, we will need two issue link types. A **relate link** that ties together issues that are related to each other and a **duplicate link** that specifies that one issue is a duplicate of another.

1. Browse to the **Issue Linking Administration** page.
2. Fill in the **Add New Link Type** form. For a duplicate link type
   - ○ Enter **Relate** for the **Name** field.
   - ○ Enter **relates to** for the **Outward Link Description** field.
   - ○ Enter **is related to** in the **Inward Link Description** field.
3. Click on the **Add** button.

Use the same steps to create an issue link called **Duplicate**, adjusting the values as needed.

Putting it together

Now that we have configured JIRA to support the additional features for issue management, let's start some tests.

First, start by logging an incident about our internal phone system.

1. Click on **Create Issue** from the **Issues** drop-down menu.
2. Select our **Support Desk – Global** project.
3. Select **Incident** as our **Issue Type**.
4. Click on the **Next** button to move onto the second stage of issue creation.

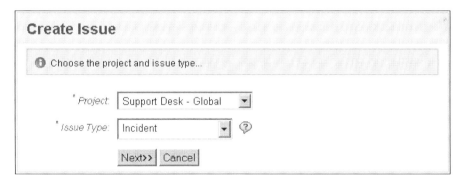

On the next screen, fill in the form to provide more information about the incident. Provide a summary of the incident in one line, and select **Internal Phone System** for the component. For **Affects Versions**, select **September** as this is the month when the incident occurred. You should not fill in the **Fix Version** field as this should be filled in by the support team once the issue is resolved. We will be looking at how to customize the fields on the form in *Chapter 5, Screen Management*. Click on the **Create** button to create and submit the issue.

Now let's log another issue with similar data to simulate another user that has logged a duplicate incident due to the same system failure. As a shortcut, let's clone the original issue to save some typing.

From the **Issue Summary** screen, select the **Clone** option from the **More Actions** menu item. On the **Clone Issue** screen, change the summary and click on **Clone**. You may choose to edit the cloned issue with different details.

As a support staff, you would see that there are two issues waiting for you to resolve. Upon initial investigation, you will realize that both issues are caused by the same problem. Instead of wasting time checking the same problem twice, let's create a link for the two issues and mark them as **related**.

From either of the two issues, click on the **Link** option from the **More Actions** menu. On the **Link Issue** screen, select **relates to** and **type** in the issue key of the other issue. Click on **Link** to establish the link between the two issues.

Since a failure of the phone system may be caused due to many different reasons, you decide to break the problem down further to find out the root cause of the issue. Let's create some sub-tasks. Bring down the **More Actions** menu item and you will find that the option to create sub-tasks is not there. What could be wrong?

Recall from the previous chapter when we set up our project, we strictly limited the issue types that we can create in our Help Desk project so we do not confuse users with irrelevant issue types such as **bugs** and **improvements**, by creating a separate issue type scheme. When we create a new issue type and/or sub-task type, it is automatically added to the default issue type scheme. What we need to do now is manually add our new sub-task types to our issue type scheme.

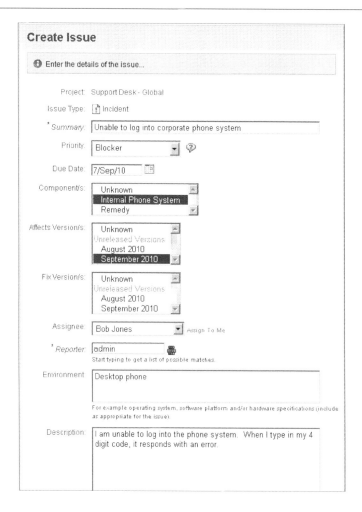

To add our new sub-task type:

1. Log in as a JIRA Administrator user.
2. Browse to the **Manage Issue Types** page.
3. Click on the **Issue Type Scheme** tab.
4. Click on **Edit for Help Desk Issue Type Scheme**.
5. Drag-and-drop **Verification issue type** from **Available Issue Types** to **Issue Types for Current Scheme**.

6. Click on **Save** to update the changes.

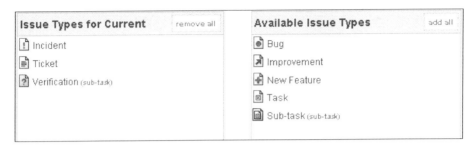

Now that we have associated our new issue type with our project, let's go back to our issue and bring down the **More Actions** menu. This time, you should see the **Create Sub-Task** option available in the menu. Click on **Create Sub-Task** and fill in the form. Click on **Create** to create the sub-task.

If we now browse back to the original issue, we will see that it has a link indication that it is related to another issue, and one sub-task underneath the issue.

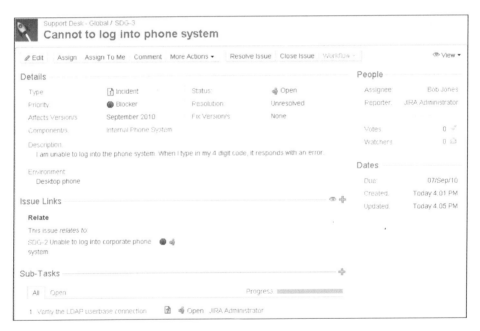

Summary

In this chapter, we looked at what issues in JIRA and explored the basic operations of creating, editing, and deleting issues. We also looked at advanced operations that are offered in JIRA to enhance and manipulate issues, such as adding attachments, creating sub-tasks, linking multiple issues, and more. In the next chapter, we will look at fields and what we can do with them.

4

Field Management

Projects are collections of issues, and issues are collections of fields. As we have seen in earlier chapters, fields are what captures and displays data to users. There are many different types of fields in JIRA, ranging from simple text fields to more complicated picker-style fields with auto-completion. An information system is only as useful as the data that it stores. By understanding how to effectively use fields, you can turn JIRA into a powerful information system for data collection, processing, and reporting.

In this chapter, we will explore fields in detail and how they relate to other aspects of JIRA. By the end of the chapter, you will have learned:

- What are built-in fields and custom fields
- How to extend JIRA through custom fields
- Adding behaviors to fields with field configurations
- Field configuration schemes and how to apply them to projects

Built-in fields

JIRA comes with a number of built-in fields. You have already seen a few of them in previous chapters, such as **summary**, **priority**, and **assignee**. These fields make up the backbone of an issue and you cannot remove them from the system. For this reason, they are referred to as **system fields**. The following table lists the most important system fields in JIRA.

System field	Description
Assignee	The user who is currently assigned to work on the issue.
Summary	A one-line summary of the issue.
Description	A detailed description of the issue.
Reporter	The user who reported this issue (although most of the time also the person who has created the issue, but not always).
Component/s	Project component(s) that the issue belongs to.
Affects Version/s	The version/s that the issue affects.
Fix Version/s	The version/s that the issue fixes.
Due Date	The date when this issue is due.
Issue Type	The type of the issue (for example, Bug or New Feature).
Priority	How important is the issue compared to other issues.
Resolution	The current resolution value of the issue (for example, Unresolved or Fixed).
Time Tracking	Lets users specify estimates of how long the issue will take to complete.

Custom fields

While JIRA's built-in system fields are quite comprehensive for basic general uses, most organizations will soon find that they have special requirements that cannot be addressed simply with the system fields available. To help you tailor JIRA to your organization's needs, JIRA lets you create and add your own fields to the system, called **custom fields**.

Custom field types

Every custom field belongs to a custom field type, which dictates its behavior, appearance, and functionality. When you are adding a custom field to JIRA, you are really adding another instance of a custom field type.

JIRA comes with over 20 custom field types that you can use straight out of the box. Many of the custom field types are identical to the built-in fields but provide you with more control and flexibility that is not available with their built-in counterparts. The following tables break down and list all the JIRA standard custom field types and their characteristics.

Simple fields

These fields are the most basic field types in JIRA. They are usually simple and straightforward to use, such as a text field, which allow users to input any text.

Custom field type	Description
Free Text Field (unlimited text)	Multiple line text-area enabling entry for large text contents.
Number Field	Input field storing and validating numeric values.
Radio Buttons	Radio buttons ensuring only one value can be selected.
Select List	Single select list with a configurable list of options.
Text Field	Basic single link input field to allow simple text input of less than 255 characters.
URL Field	Input field that validates a URL.

JIRA specialized fields

These fields provide specialized functions. For example, the **Date Picker** field provides you with a calendar to let you pick a date from, and the **User Picker** has an auto-complete feature to help you find the user you want to select.

Custom field type	Description
Cascading Select	Multiple select lists where the options for the second select list are dynamically updated based on the value of the first.
Date Picker	Input field allowing input with a date picker and enforces valid dates.
Date Time	Input field allowing input with a date and time picker and enforces valid dates timestamp.
Group Picker	Choose a user group using a pop up picker window.
Labels	Input field allowing labels to be added to an issue.
Project Picker	Select list displaying the projects viewable by the user in the system.
Read-only Text Field	A read-only text field that does not allow users to set its data but to only possible to programmatically set its data.
Single Version Picker	Choose a single version from available versions in the project.
User Picker	Choose a user from the JIRA user base via either a pop up user picker window, or through auto completion.
Version Picker	Choose one or more versions from available versions in the current project.

Multi fields

These fields are like their singular versions and allow you to select multiple values rather than only one. For example, the **Multi Select** field lets you select one or more values, while its singular equivalent, the **Select List** field only lets you choose one. The only exception is the **Multi Checkboxes** field, which does not come with a singular variety.

Custom field type	Description
Multi Checkboxes	Checkboxes allowing multiple values to be selected.
Multi Group Picker	Choose one or more user groups using a pop up picker window.
Multi Select	Select list allowing multiple values to be selected.
Multi User Picker	Choose one or more users from the user base via a pop up picker window.

As you can see, JIRA provides you with a comprehensive list of custom field types. In addition, there are third-party custom field types (called **plugins**) that you can add to your JIRA to enhance its functionality. We will look at plugins in *Chapter 10, General Administration*.

Searchers

For any information system, capturing data is only half of the equation. Users will need to be able to retrieve the data at a later stage, usually through searching, and JIRA is no different. While fields in JIRA are responsible for capturing and displaying data, it is their corresponding searchers that provide the search functionality.

In JIRA, all of the built-in fields have their associated searchers by default, so you will be able to search issues by their summary or assignee without any further configuration. For custom fields however, you will need to specify a searcher for each custom field you add. If you do not specify a searcher, you will not be able to search data based on that field. For each of the default custom field types, JIRA also provides you with one or more searchers. You can select a searcher when you create a new custom field and later change the searcher, as we will see later when we cover how to manage custom fields.

Custom field context

Unlike built-in fields, custom fields can also have contexts. A custom field context is made up of a combination of issue types and projects. This means that a custom field can behave differently depending on the issue type and project (its context). An example is a select list custom field. You will be able to set a different set of selection values based on different issue types and project combinations.

When a custom field is initially created, it will have a default context. You can add more custom field contexts for the custom field once it has been created.

Managing custom fields

Just like built-in fields, custom fields are used globally across JIRA, so you will need to have JIRA Administrator global permissions to carry out management operations such as creation and configuration.

JIRA maintains all the custom fields in a centralized location for easy management. To access the custom field management page:

1. Log into JIRA as a JIRA Administrator.

2. Click on **Administration** from the top menu bar.

3. Select **Custom Fields** from the left panel to bring up the **View Custom Fields** page.

Adding a custom field

Creating a new custom field is a multi-step process. You first need to determine the type of custom field, and then its searcher and context. We will be walking through the process below:

1. Browse to the **View Custom Fields** page.

2. Click on the **Add Custom Field** link. This will bring you to step 1 of the process where you can select the custom field type.

3. Select the custom field type you wish to add and click on **Next**. This will bring you to step 2 of the process where you can specify other aspects of the new custom field.

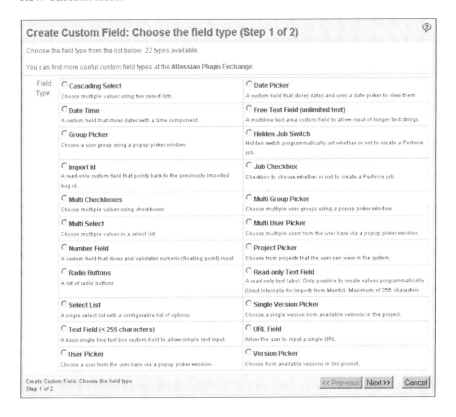

4. Fill in the **Field Name** and **Field Description**. You can have multiple custom fields with the same name; however, doing so will make it harder for maintenance.

5. Select a search template, if available. All custom field types that are shipped with JIRA will have one or more search templates.

6. Select which issue types the custom field will be available for. If you select the **All issue type** option, the custom field will be available to all issue types (assuming it is also available for the project, see the following screenshot).

7. Select the projects the custom field will be available for. **Global context** means all projects in JIRA. If you select specific projects, then the custom field will only be available for issues within those projects (if it is available for the issue type, see the preceding screenshot).

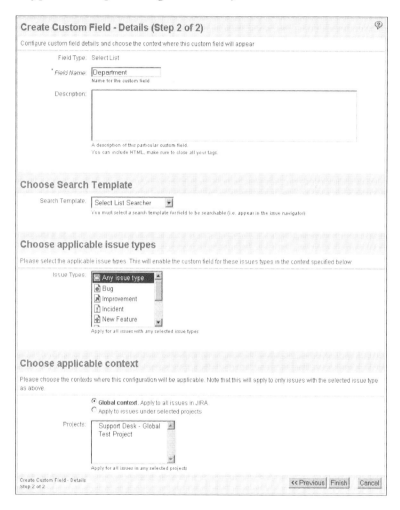

8. Click on **Finish**. This will bring you to the last step of the process where you can specify the screen on which you would like to add the field. You do not have to add the field to a screen. We will be discussing fields and screens in *Chapter 5, Screen Management*.

9. Select the screens and click on **Update**.

Once a custom field has been created, you will be able to manage its configurations and settings.

Editing/Deleting a custom field

Once a custom field has been created, you can edit its details at any time. You might have already noticed that there is a **configure** option and an **edit** option for each custom field. At first, the difference between the two may not be clear. One way to distinguish the two is that **configure** specifies options related to custom field context, which we will discuss in the following sections. **Edit** specifies options that are global across JIRA for the custom field, these include its name, description, and search template.

1. Browse to the **View Custom Fields** page.
2. Click on the **Edit** link for the custom field you wish to edit from the list of custom fields. This will bring you to the **Edit Custom Field Details** page.
3. Change the custom field details.
4. Click on the **Update** button to apply the changes.

When making changes to the search templates for your custom fields, it is critical to note that while the change will take effect immediately, you need to perform a full system re-index in order for JIRA to return correct search results. This is because for each search template, the underlying search data structure might be different, and JIRA will need to update its search index for the newly applied search template. We will be discussing searching and indexing in more detail in *Chapter 9, Saerching, Reporting, and Analysis*.

Edit Custom Field Details

If the search template is changed, manual reindexing must follow

Field Name: Department

Description:

A description of this particular custom field.
You can include HTML, make sure to close all your tags.

Search Template: Select List Searcher

Note that changing a custom field searcher may require a re-index.

(Update) (Cancel)

You can also delete existing custom fields by carrying out the following steps:

1. Browse to the **View Custom Fields** page.
2. Click on the **Delete** link for the custom field you wish to delete. This will bring you to the **Delete Custom Field** page.
3. Click on the **Delete** button to delete the custom field.

Once deleted, you cannot get the custom field back and you will not be able to retrieve and search the data held by those fields. If you try to create another custom field of the same type and name, it will not inherit the data from the previous custom field as JIRA assigns unique identifiers to each custom field. It is highly recommended that you backup JIRA before you delete the field. We will discuss backup strategies in *Chapter 10*.

Configuring a custom field

Now that we have seen how to create and manage custom fields, we can start looking at the more advanced configuration options. Different custom field types will have different configuration options available to them. For example, while all custom fields will have the option to specify one or more contexts, select list-based custom fields will also allow you to specify the list of options users can choose from. We will look at each of the configuration options in the following sections.

To configure a custom field, you need to access the **Configure Custom Field** page:

1. Browse to the **View Custom Fields** page.
2. Click on the **Configure** link for the custom field you wish to configure from the list of custom fields. This will bring you to the **Configure Custom Field** page.

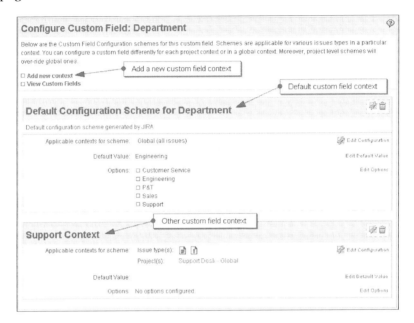

Adding custom field contexts

From time to time, you may need your custom fields to have different behaviors depending on the issue's project or issue type. For example, if we have a select list custom field called **Department**, we may want it to have a different set of options based on which project the issue is being created, or even a different default value.

To achieve this level of customization, JIRA allows you to create multiple custom field contexts for a custom field. As we have seen already, a custom field context is a combination of issue types and projects. In our example, we can create a context for issue type of **Bug** and project of **Support**, and set the default department to **Engineering**. The key message here is, JIRA allows you to configure custom fields based on issue types and projects through contexts.

Creating a new custom field context is simple. All you need to do is decide the issue type and project combination that will define the context.

1. Browse to the **Configure Custom Field** page for the custom field you wish to create a new context for.

2. Click on the **Add new context** link. This will take you to the **Add configuration scheme context** page.

3. Give a name to the new custom field context in the **Configuration scheme label** field.

4. Select the applicable issue types.

5. Select the applicable projects.

6. Click on the **Add** button to create the new custom field context.

Each project can only belong to one custom field context (Global context is not counted for this). Once you have selected a project for a context, it will not be available the next time you create a new context. For example, if you have created a new context for Project A, it will not be listed as an option when you create another context for the same custom field. This is to prevent you from accidentally creating two contexts for the same project.

After a new custom field context has been created, it will not "inherit" any configuration values, such as **Default Value** and **Select Options** from other contexts, such as the default context. You will need to re-populate and maintain the configuration options for each newly created context.

Configuring select options

For custom field of types select list, checkboxes, radio buttons and their multi versions, you need to configure their select options before they can become useful to the users. The select options are configured and set on a per custom field context basis. This provides the custom field with the flexibility to have a different set of options for a different context.

To configure the select options, you need to first select the custom field and then the context that the options will be applied to.

1. Browse to the **View Custom Fields** page.

2. Click on the **Configure** link for the custom field you wish to configure select options for.

3. Click on the **Edit Options** link for the custom field context to apply the options for.

4. Fill in the option values in the **Add New Custom Field Option** section and click on the **Add** button to add the value. The options will be added in the order in which they are entered into the system. You can manually move the option values up and down or click on **Sort options alphabetically** to let JIRA perform the sorting for you.

5. Click on the **Done** button once you have finished configuring the select options.

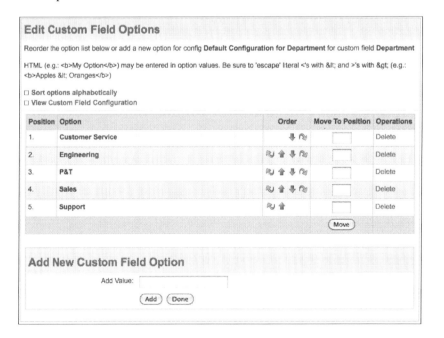

Once you have added an option, you cannot change its name. You will have to delete it and create a new option with the new name.

Setting default values

For most custom fields, you can set a default value so that your users will not need to fill them in unless they have special needs. For text-based custom fields, the default values will be text displayed by default when the users create or edit an issue. For selection-based custom fields, the default values will be options preselected for the users.

Just like setting selection options, default options are also set on a per custom field context-basis.

1. Browse to the **View Custom Fields** page.
2. Click on the **Configure** link for the custom field you wish to configure select options for.
3. Click the **Edit Default Value** link for the custom field context you wish to set a default value for.
4. Set the default value for the custom field.
5. Click on the **Set Default** button to set the default value.

The way to set default values will be different for different custom field types. For text-based custom fields, you will be able to type any text string. For select-based custom fields, you will be able to select from the options you have added (if you have not set any options for the custom field, the only option available as a default value will be **None**). For picker-based custom fields such as user picker, you will be able to select a user directly from the user base.

Field configuration

As we have seen already, fields are used to capture and display data in JIRA. Fields can also have behaviors, which are defined by field configuration. For each field in JIRA, one or more behaviors from the list below can be specified.

- **Field description**: The description text that appears under the field when an issue is edited.

- **Visibility**: Determines if a field will be visible or hidden.

- **Required**: Specifies if a field will be optional or required to have a value when an issue is being created / updated. When applied to a select, checkbox, or radio button custom fields, this will remove the **None** option from the list.

- **Rendering**: For text-based fields, how the content is to be rendered (for example, rich text).

A field configuration provides you with control over each individual field in your JIRA, including both built-in fields and custom fields. Since it is usually good practice to reuse the same set of fields instead of creating new ones for every project's needs, JIRA allows us to create multiple field configurations, in which we can specify different behaviors on the same set of fields and apply them to different projects.

We will be looking at how to manage and apply multiple field configurations in later sections in this chapter, but first, let's take a close look at how to create new field configurations and what we can do with the configurations.

You can access the field configuration management page through the JIRA Administration console.

1. Log into JIRA as a JIRA Administrator.
2. Click on **Administration** from the top menu bar.
3. Select **Field Configurations** from the left-hand side panel. This will bring you to the **View Field Configurations** page.

Adding a field configuration

Creating new field configurations is simple. All you need to do is specify the name and a short description for the new configuration.

1. Browse to the **View Field Configurations** page.

2. Specify the name for the new field configuration in the **Add Field Configuration** section.

3. Provide a short description for the field configuration.

4. Click on the **Add** button to create.

As we will see later in the *Field configuration scheme* section, field configurations are linked to issue types, so it is recommended to name your field configurations based on the issue type it will be applied to and with a version number at the end, for example, Bugs Field Configuration 1.0. This way, when you need make changes to the field configuration, you can increment the version number, leaving you a history of changes that you can revert back to.

After a field configuration is created, it is put into what we call the inactive state. This means the configuration is not being used anywhere in JIRA and you are free to edit and delete it. In order to activate the field configuration, we need to associate it with a field configuration scheme. We will look at how to do this in later sections.

Add Field Configuration

To create a new Field Configuration please specify a name and optionally the description and press **Add**.

* *Name:*

Description:

Add

Editing/Deleting a field configuration

You can update the existing field configuration details or delete it altogether. The details you can edit are the configuration's **name** and **description**.

1. Browse to the **View Field Configurations** page.

2. Click the **Edit** link for the field configuration you wish to edit. This will take you to the **Edit Field Configuration** page.

3. Update the **Name** and **Description** fields with new values.

4. Click on the **Update** button to apply the changes.

You will be able to edit field configuration details at anytime. However, for deletion, you can only delete the configuration when it is inactive. Once you have associated the configuration with a scheme, which will put the configuration into the active state, you cannot delete it until it is back in the inactive state. For you to put the field configuration back into the inactive state, you need to unassociate it from the field configuration scheme.

1. Browse to the **View Field Configurations** page.
2. Click on the **Delete** link for the field configuration you wish to delete. This will take you to the **Delete Field Configuration** page for confirmation.
3. Click on the **Delete** button to delete the field configuration.

Copying a field configuration

A field configuration contains configuration details for all fields in JIRA. For a moderately complicated instance, you are likely to have over twenty fields. It will be very unproductive if have to reconfigure every single field whenever you need to create a new set of field configurations, usually with only minor differences for a few fields.

To simplify your task, JIRA allows you to copy an existing field configuration and use that as a base for you to make only the necessary changes. This greatly reduces the amount of effort required as you will not be required to reconfigure all the fields that are common across all the use cases.

1. Browse to the **View Field Configurations** page.
2. Click on the **Copy** link for the field configuration you wish to copy. This will take you to the **Copy Field Configuration** page.
3. Specify a new name for the field configuration.
4. Specify a description.
5. Click on the **Copy** button to copy the field configuration.

Managing field configurations

Now that we have seen how to create, edit, delete, and copy field configurations, it is time for us to take a closer look at the different configuration options. Just a quick recap, each field configuration includes all fields available in JIRA, and their behaviors are defined specifically to each field configuration. We will then set a context for the field configuration through the use of a field configuration scheme, which will determine when a field configuration will become active for a given issue.

To access the field configuration options,

1. Browse to the **View Field Configurations** page.

2. Click on the **Configure** link for the field configuration you wish to configure. This will take you to the **View Field Configuration** page.

On this page, all the fields and their current configuration options that are currently set for the selected field configuration are listed.

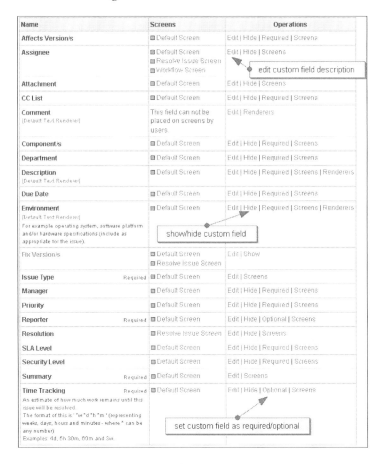

As you can see, there are several options you can configure for each field, and depending on the field type, the options may vary. While we will be looking at each of the options, it is important to note that some of the options will override each other. This is JIRA trying to protect you from accidentally creating a configuration combination that will break your JIRA. For example, if a field is set to both **hidden** and **required**, your users will not be able to enter a value in the field, and thus be unable to create or edit issues, and so JIRA will not allow you to set a field to required if you have already set it to hidden.

Field description

While having a meaningful name for your fields will help your users to understand what the fields are for, providing a short description will provide more context and meaning. Field descriptions are displayed under the fields when you are creating or editing an issue.

To add a description for a field:

1. Browse to the **View Field Configuration** page for the field configuration you wish to use.
2. Click on the **Edit** link for the field you wish to set a description for.
3. Add the description for the field, and click on **Update**.

Field requirement

You can set certain fields to be required, or compulsory for issues. This is a very useful feature as this ensures that critical information will be captured when users create issues. For example, for our support system, it makes sense to have our users fill in the system that is misbehaving and make that field compulsory to help our support engineers.

You have already seen required fields in action. System fields such as **Summary** and **Issue Type** are compulsory in JIRA (and you cannot change that). When you do not specify a value for a required field, JIRA will highlight the field in red with an error message telling you that the field is required.

When you add a new field into JIRA, such as a custom field, they are optional by default, meaning users do not need to specify a value. You can change the setting to make those fields required.

1. Browse to the **View Field Configuration** page for the field configuration you change to adjust.
2. Click the **Required/Optional** link for the field you wish set as its mandatory requirement.

You will notice that once a field is set to required, there will be a small text label, **Required,** in red next to the field name, and when you create or edit an issue, the field will have a red * character next to its name. This is JIRA's way to indicate that a field is required.

Field visibility

Most fields in JIRA can be hidden from users. When a field is set to hidden, users will not see the fields on any screens including issue create, update, and view.

To show or hide a field:

1. Browse to the **View Field Configuration** page for the field configuration you wish to adjust.
2. Click the **Show/Hide** link for the field you wish to show or hide, respectively.

You will notice that when a field is set to be hidden, the field name becomes grayed out. Once a field has been set to hidden, it will not appear onscreen and you will not be able to search with it.

Not all fields can be hidden; required fields such as **Summary** and **Issue Type** cannot be hidden. When you set a field to **hidden**, you will notice that you are no longer able to set the same field to **required**. As stated earlier, setting a field to **required** will make JIRA enforce a value to be entered into the field when you create or edit an issue. If the field is hidden, there will be no way for you to set a value and you will be stuck. This is why JIRA will automatically disable the required option if you have already hidden a field. On the other hand, if you have made a field required, when you hide the same field, you will notice that the field is no longer required. The rule of thumb is that field visibility will override field requirement.

Field rendering

By default, all fields in JIRA are displayed in plain text without an additional mark up. There are some fields that can be configured to allow different markups to enhance their visual presentation, through the use of renderers.

JIRA ships with 4 different renderers:

- **Default Text Renderer**: The default renderer is for text-based fields. Contents are rendered as plain text. If the text resolves to a JIRA issue key, the renderer will automatically turn that into an HTML link.
- **Wiki Style Renderer**: Wiki style renderer is an enhanced renderer for text-based fields. Allows you to use wiki markup to decorate your text content.

- **Select List Renderer**: The default renderer for selection-based fields. It is rendered as standard HTML select list.

- **Autocomplete Renderer**: An enhanced renderer for selection-based fields. Provides an autocomplete feature to assist users as they start typing into the fields.

The following table lists all the fields that can have special renders configured and their available options.

Field	Available renderers
Description	Wiki Style Renderer, Default Text Renderer
Comment	Wiki Style Renderer, Default Text Renderer
Environment	Wiki Style Renderer, Default Text Renderer
Component	Autocomplete Renderer, Select List Renderer
Affects Version	Autocomplete Renderer, Select List Renderer
Fix Versions	Autocomplete Renderer, Select List Renderer
Custom field of type "Free Text Field (unlimited text)"	Wiki Style Renderer, Default Text Renderer
Custom field of type "Text Field"	Wiki Style Renderer, Default Text Renderer
Custom field of type "Multi Select"	Autocomplete Renderer, Select List Renderer
Custom Field of type "Version Picker"	Autocomplete Renderer, Select List Renderer

To set the renderer for a field:

1. Browse to the **View Field Configuration** page for the field configuration you wish to use.

2. Click on the **Renderer** link for the field you wish to set a renderer for (if it is available). You will be taken to the **Edit Field Renderer** page.

3. Select the renderer from the available drop down list.

4. Click on the **Update** button to set the renderer.

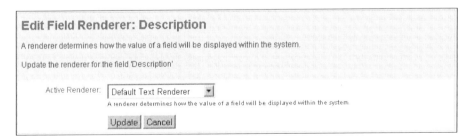

Screens

In order for a field to appear, it needs to be placed onto a screen. You have already seen this when creating new custom fields. One of the steps in the creation process is to select what screens to add the custom field to. Screens will be discussed further in *Chapter 5, Screen Management,* so we will not be spend much time right now. What you need to know for now is that after a field has been added to a screen, you can add it to additional screens or take it off completely. If you are working with just one field, you can configure it here from field configurations. If you have multiple fields to update, a better approach will be to work directly with screens, as we will see in *Chapter 5.*

Field configuration scheme

With multiple field configurations, JIRA determines when to apply each of the configurations through **Field Configuration Scheme**. A field configuration scheme maps field configurations to issue types. The field configuration scheme can then be associated with one or more projects.

This allows you to group multiple field configurations mapped to issue types, and apply them to a project in one go. The project will then be able to determine which field configuration to apply based on the issue type of the issue. For example, for a given project, you can have different field configurations for **Bugs** and **Tasks**.

This grouping of configurations into schemes also provides you with the option to reuse existing configurations without duplicating work as each scheme can be reused and associated to multiple projects.

Managing field configuration schemes

You can manage all your field configuration schemes from the **View Field Configuration Schemes** page. From there, you will be able to add, configure, edit, delete, and copy schemes.

1. Log into JIRA as a JIRA Administrator.
2. Click on **Administration** from the top menu bar.
3. Select **Field Configuration Schemes** from the left hand side panel. This will bring you to the **View Field Configuration Schemes** page.

Adding a field configuration scheme

The first step to group your field configurations is to create a new field configuration scheme. JIRA comes with a System Default Field Configuration, which is used by all projects that do not have a specific scheme selected. The new field configuration scheme will hold all the mappings between our field configurations and issue types.

To create a new field configuration scheme, all you need to do is specify the name and an optional description for the scheme.

1. Browse to the **View Field Configuration Schemes** page.

2. Fill in a name for the new field configuration scheme in the **Add Field Configuration Scheme** section.

3. Optionally, provide a short description for the scheme.

4. Click on the **Add** button to create the scheme.

Since field configuration schemes are applied to projects, it is good practice to name your field configuration schemes according to the projects. For example, the scheme for a Sales Project can be named Sales Field Configuration Scheme. You can add a version number after the name to help you maintain changes.

Once the new field configuration scheme is created, it will be displayed in the table listing all existing schemes. At this time, the scheme is in the inactive state, as it does not contain any configuration mappings and thus is not yet active in JIRA.

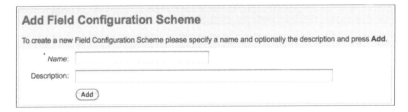

Editing/Deleting a field configuration scheme

You can update existing field configuration scheme details or delete it altogether. The details you can edit are the scheme's name and description. You can also update its field configurations mapping, which will be covered in later sections.

1. Browse to the **View Field Configuration Schemes** page.

2. Click on the **Edit** link for the field configuration scheme you wish to edit. This will take you to the **Edit Field Configuration Scheme** page.

3. Update the **Name** and **Description** fields with new values.

4. Click on the **Update** button to apply the changes.

Just like field configurations, you can only delete a field configuration scheme if it is in the inactive state. Once you have associated the scheme with a project, which will put the scheme into the active state, you cannot delete it until it is back in the inactive state. To deactivate a field configuration scheme, you will have to unassociate the scheme from all projects you have applied it to.

1. Browse to the **View Field Configuration Schemes** page.
2. Click on the **Delete** link for the field configuration scheme you wish to delete. This will take you to the **Delete Field Configuration Scheme** page for confirmation.
3. Click on the **Delete** button to delete the scheme.

Copying a field configuration scheme

There will be times when you need a new field configuration scheme and the requirements are very similar to those of a scheme that you already have. Instead of creating a new scheme from scratch, you can choose to copy the existing scheme as a base, and simply make some quick modifications. JIRA allows you to achieve exactly this by letting you copy existing schemes.

1. Browse to the **View Field Configuration Schemes** page.
2. Click on the **Copy** link for the field configuration scheme you wish to copy. This will take you to the **Copy Field Layout Configuration** page.
3. Specify the name and description of the new scheme.
4. Click on the **Copy** button to create the copy.

Once the newly-copied scheme is created, you will be able to modify its field configuration and issue type mappings as per your requirements, which we will look at in the next section.

Configuring a field configuration scheme

Once we have a new field configuration scheme setup, we will be able to add mapping between field configurations and issue types. For each field configuration scheme, one issue type can be mapped to only one field configuration, while each field configuration can be mapped to multiple issue types. The following screenshot shows the **General Task Field Configuration** being applied to both **Task** and **Improvement** issue types, but each issue type can only have one field configuration.

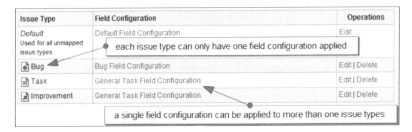

When a field configuration scheme is first created, JIRA creates a default mapping which maps all unmapped issue types to the default field configuration. You cannot delete this default mapping as it acts as a "catch all" condition for mappings that you do not specify in your scheme. What you need to do is to add more specific mappings that will take precedence over this default mapping.

1. Browse to the **View Field Configuration Schemes** page.
2. Click on the **Configure** link for the field configuration scheme you wish to configure. This will take you to the **Configure Field Configuration Scheme** page.
3. Select the issue type and field configuration from the **Add Issue Type To Field Configuration Association** section to establish the mapping.
4. Click on the **Add** button to add the mapping.

You will notice that once you have added a mapping, the mapped issue type will disappear from the list of selectable issue types. This is JIRA's way of preventing you from double-mapping an issue type by accident. Once you have mapped all available issue types, you will not be able to add any more mappings.

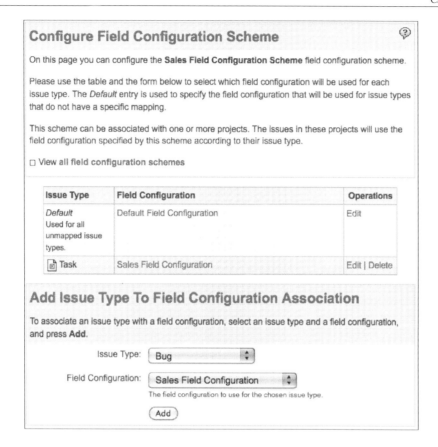

Associating a field configuration scheme with a project

After we have created a new field configuration scheme and established the mappings, the configurations will not take effect immediately. The scheme is still in the inactive state. In order to activate the scheme, we need to associate the scheme with a project for the configurations to take effect.

It is important to note that once you have associated the field configuration scheme with a project, you cannot delete the scheme until you have removed all the associations, so the scheme becomes inactive again.

To activate a field configuration scheme, you need to establish the association on a per project level. This means you need to go to each individual project and set the field configuration scheme option for them.

1. Log in JIRA as a JIRA Administrator.

2. Click on **Administration** from the top menu bar.

3. Select the project you wish to associate the field configuration scheme with. This will bring up the **Project Administration** page.

4. Click on the **Select** link for **Field Configuration Scheme**. This will bring up the **Field Layout Configuration Association** page.

5. Select the field configuration scheme from the **Scheme** select list.

6. Click on the **Associate** button.

You can repeat step 3 to 6 to associate the field configuration scheme with more projects.

Help Desk Project

Now that we have seen how to manage fields in JIRA, it is time to expand on our Help Desk project to include some customized fields and configurations to help our support staff.

What we will do this time is add a few new custom fields to help capture some additional useful data from the business users when they log an incident. We will also create a customized field configuration specially designed for our support team. Lastly, we will tie everything together by associating our fields, configurations, and projects through field configuration schemes.

Setting up custom fields

Since we are implementing a support system, one common feature is to be able to escalate the incident, and for every escalation, a group of users will be notified automatically. The automatic escalation and notification aspects of this feature will be covered and implemented in later chapters, but what we do need right now is a way to answer questions such as:

- Does the issue require escalation?
- What is the current escalation level?
- Who should be notified when the issue is escalated?

To address these requirements, we will be adding 3 custom fields, one per question.

The first custom field we are going to add is the **Is Escalation Required** field. We want to have the option so that not all tickets raised will require escalation. Some tickets may not be urgent or they are simply for investigative purposes. We will also make this field required so the users will need to indicate if they would require escalation. To help our users, we will provide a default value of **Yes** so that tickets will require escalation by default. Since this is a single selection field, we will be using radio buttons.

1. Browse to the **View Custom Fields** page.
2. Click on the **Add Custom Field** link.
3. Select the **Radio Buttons** custom field type.
4. Give the custom field the name of **Is Escalation Required**.
5. Accept the default options and click on **Finish**.
6. Check **Default Screen** and click on **Update**.

The second custom field is a simple text-based field that will indicate what level of escalation the ticket is currently at. We do not want users (support or business) to be able to change the values as this should be determined by the system automatically, so we will be using a **read-only text** field.

1. Browse to the **View Custom Fields** page.

2. Click on the **Add Custom Field** link.

3. Select **Read-only Text Field** custom field type.

4. Give the custom field the name of **Escalation Level**.

5. Accept the default options and click on **Finish**.

6. Check **Default Screen** and click on **Update**.

Finally, the third custom field will contain a list of users from JIRA's user base who will receive notifications when the ticket is being escalated.

1. Browse to the **View Custom Fields** page.

2. Click on the **Add Custom Field** link.

3. Select **Multi User Picker** custom field type.

4. Give the custom field the name of **Escalation List**.

5. Accept the default options and click on **Finish**.

6. Check **Default Screen** and click on **Update**.

Now that we have created the necessary custom fields, the next step is to configure them. Remember our **Is Escalation Required** custom field will allow users to specify if the tickets they raised need escalation, so we need to add the options **Yes** and **No** to the field. We also need to set the default all tickets to require escalation.

1. Browse to the **View Custom Fields** page.

2. Click the **Configure** link for **Is Escalation Required** custom field.

3. Click on **Edit Options**.

4. Add the options of **Yes** and **No**, and click on the **Done** button when finished.

5. Click on the **Edit Default Value** link.

6. Select the **Yes** option for the default value.

Setting up field configuration

Now that we have our custom fields, the next step is to create a new field configuration so we can specify the behaviors of our custom fields. Previously, we had decided to make the **Is Escalation Required** field "required" so there will be no ambiguity when it comes to determining if a ticket needs to be escalated. Let's start by creating a new field configuration first.

1. Browse to the **View Field Configurations** page.

2. Name the new field configuration **Help Desk Field Configuration**.

3. Provide a helpful description **Field configuration** for the help desk team.

4. Click on the **Add** button to create.

Now that we have our new field configuration, we can start add configurations to our new custom fields.

1. Click on the **Configure** link for **Help Desk Field Configuration**.

2. Click on the **Required** link for the **Is Escalation Required** custom field. (If you do not see the **Is Escalation Required** field in the list of fields, please go back to the **View Custom Fields** page to verify that the field has been created successfully.)

Setting up a field configuration scheme

We have our custom fields, we have configured the relevant options, created a new field configuration, and set the behaviors for our fields, now it is time to add them to a scheme.

1. Browse to the **View Field Configuration Schemes** page.

2. Name the new field configuration scheme **Help Desk Field Configuration Scheme**, as we will be applying this to our Help Desk project.

3. Provide a helpful description **Field configuration scheme** for the help desk team.

4. Click on the **Add** button to create.

With the field configuration scheme in place, we can now activate our configurations. Since this is designed for our help desk team, we would want to apply the field configurations to the issue types that are applicable to the Help Desk project, that is **Ticket** and **Incident**.

1. Click on the **Configure** link for the **Help Desk Field Configuration** Scheme.

2. Select the issue type **Ticket** and field configuration **Help Desk Field Configuration**.

3. Click on the **Add** button to add the association.

4. Repeat steps 2 and 3 for the **Incident** issue type.

Putting it all together

OK, we have done all the hard work. We have created new custom fields, a new field configuration, and a new field configuration scheme. The last step is to put everything together and see it in action!

1. Browse to the **Project Administration** page for our **Help Desk** project.

2. Click on the **Select** link for **Field Configuration Scheme**.

3. Select **Help Desk Field Configuration Scheme** and click on the **Associate** button.

All right, we are all done! You can pat yourself on the back, sit back, and take a look at our hard work in action.

Create a new **Incident** under **Help Desk** project and you will see our new custom fields at the bottom of the page (you will not see **Escalation Level**, as it is a read-only and will not appear on the create/edit screens).

Go ahead and create the incident by filling the fields. On the view issue page, you will see our new custom fields displayed along with the values you have provided.

Summary

In this chapter, we looked in-depth at fields in JIRA. We saw how JIRA is able to extend its ability to capture user data through custom fields. We have also explored how we can specify different behaviors for fields under different contexts through the use of field configurations and schemes. In the next chapter, we will expand on what have learned about fields by formally introducing you to **screens** and showing you how to combine fields and screens together to provide your users with the most natural and logical forms to assist them in creating and logging issues.

5
Screen Management

Fields collect data from users and we have seen how to create our own custom fields from a wide range of field types to address our different requirements. Indeed data collection is at the center of any information system, but that is only half of the story. How the data is captured is just as critical. Data input forms need to be organized so users do not feel overwhelmed, and the general flow of fields needs to be logically structured and grouped into sections; this is where screens come into play.

In this chapter, we will pick up where we left off from the last chapter and explore the relationship between fields and screens. We will further discuss how you can use screens to customize your JIRA to provide your users with a better user experience. By the end of the chapter, you will have learned:

- What screens are and how to create your own
- How to add fields onto screens
- How to logically breakdown your screen into logical sections with tabs
- About the relationship between screens and issue operations
- How to link screens with projects and issue types

Screens

In comparison to a normal paper-based form, fields in JIRA are the check boxes and spaces you have to fill in, while the screens are the form documents themselves. When fields are created in JIRA, they need to be added onto screens in order to be presented to users. You can say that screens are like groupings or "containers" for fields.

While many other software systems provide users with limited control over the presentation of screens, JIRA is very flexible when it comes to screen customization. You can create you own screens and decide what fields are to be placed on them and in what order. You can also decide which screens are to be displayed for major issue operations. In JIRA, you can create and design customized screens for the following operations:

- **Create issue**: The **create issue details** screen (or step 2) of the issue creation process.
- **Edit issue**: When an issue is being updated.
- **View issue**: After an issue is created and being viewed by users.
- **Workflows**: During workflow transitions (workflows will be covered in *Chapter 6, Workflow and Business Process*).

Screens are maintained centrally from the administrator console, which means you need to be a JIRA administrator to create and configure screens.

1. Log into JIRA as a JIRA Administrator.
2. Click on **Administration** from the top menu bar.
3. Select **Screens** from the left panel to bring up the **View Screens** page.

From this screen, you can see a list of existing screens and also create new ones. You can also manage each individual screen by updating its details, copying or deleting it, and most important of all, configuring its settings. Configuring a screen includes deciding what fields will go in them and how you can divide a screen into various tabs. We will be looking at each of these in the following sections.

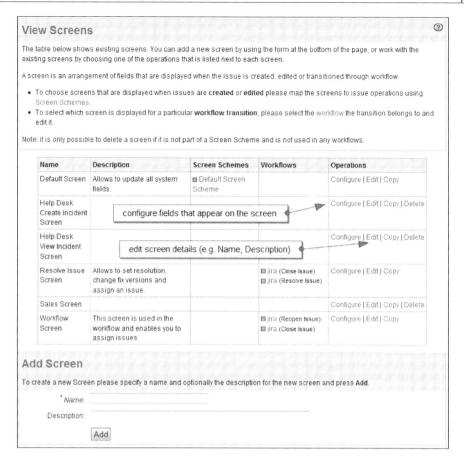

Adding a screen

JIRA comes with three screens by default. You have already seen them when adding a new custom field, resolving an issue, and transitioning an issue through a workflow. As a matter of fact, if you have not made any customizations to the screens, every issue screen you see will be one of the three following screens:

- **Default Screen**: The screen used for creating, editing, and viewing issues.

- **Resolve Issue Screen**: The screen used when resolving and closing issues.

- **Workflow Screen**: The screen used when transitioning issues through workflow (if configured to have a screen, such as **Reopen Issue**).

While these screens are able to cover most basic requirements, you will soon find adjustments need to be made. For example, an engineering bug issue will have a that different field layout a sales inquiry issue. To add a new screen in JIRA:

1. Browse to the **View Screens** page.

2. Provide a meaningful name for the new screen in the **Add Screen** section. It is a good idea to name your screen after its purpose, for example, **Bug Create Screen**.

3. Provide an optional short description for the screen.

4. Click on the **Add** button to create the screen.

After a new screen has been created, it is put into the inactive state. The screen is not used by JIRA until it has been associated with a screen scheme or workflow transition. Workflows will be discussed in *Chapter 6, Workflow and Business Process*.

Editing/Deleting a screen

You can edit existing screens to update their details to help keep your configurations up to date and consistent. To edit a screen:

1. Browse to the **View Screens** page.

2. Click on the **Edit** link for the screen you wish to update. This will take you to the **Edit Screen** page.

3. Update the name and description of the screen.

4. Click on the **Update** button to apply your changes.

To delete an existing screen, the screen must not be used by any screen schemes. If the screen is associated with a screen scheme or workflow, you will not be able to delete the screen. You will need to undo the association first. To delete a screen:

1. Browse to the **View Screens** page.

2. Click on the **Delete** link for the screen you wish to remove. This will take you to the **Delete Screen** page.

3. Click on the **Delete** button to remove the screen.

By deleting a screen, you are not deleting the fields that are on the screen.

Copying a screen

Screens can be complicated with many fields, so creating a new screen from scratch may not be the most efficient method if there is already a similar screen available. Just like with many other entities in JIRA, you can make a copy of an existing screen, thus cutting down the time that would otherwise take you to re-add all the fields.

1. Browse to the **View Screens** page.
2. Click on the **Copy** link for the screen you wish to copy. This will take you to the **Copy Screen** page.
3. Provide a new name and description for the screen.
4. Click on the **Copy** button to copy the screen.

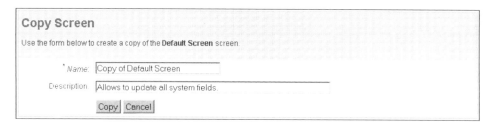

Just like newly created screens, cloned screens are inactive until they have been associated.

Configuring a screen

Creating a new screen is like getting a blank piece of paper, the fun part is to add and arrange the fields on the screen. Fields in JIRA are arranged and displayed from top to bottom in a single column, and you have full control of what fields to add and in what order they should be arranged. Furthermore, JIRA allows you to break your screens up into tabs, or "pages within a form", and you can do all of this within a single configuration page. It is this level of flexibility combined with its simplicity that makes JIRA a very powerful tool.

To configure a screen:

1. Browse to the **View Screens** page.

2. Click on the **Configure** link for the screen you wish to configure.

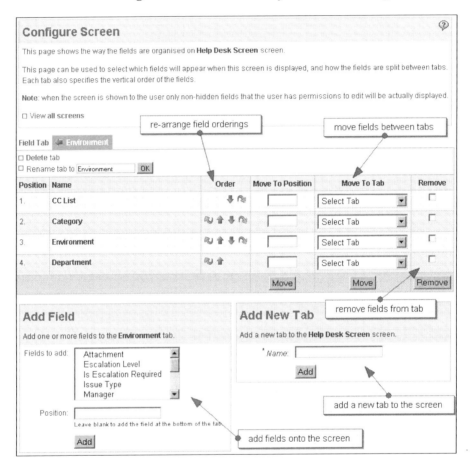

On this page, you can:

*   Add/remove fields on the screen
*   Change the order of the fields
*   Create/delete tabs on the screen
*   Move fields from one tab to another

Adding a field to a screen

When you first create a screen, it is of little use. In order for the screens to have items to present to the users, you must first add fields onto the screen.

1. Browse to the **Configure Screen** page for the screen you wish to configure.

2. Select the fields you would like to place onto the screen from the **Add Field** section. You can select multiple fields to be added at once by selecting multiple options while holding down the *Ctrl* key.

3. Optionally, specify the position of where you would like to add those fields.

4. Click on the **Add** button to add the fields onto the screen.

Deleting a field from screen

Fields can be taken off of a screen completely. When a field is taken off, it will not appear when the screen is presented to users. There is a subtle difference between deleting a field from a screen and hiding a field from a screen (discussed in the previous chapter). Although both actions will prevent the field from showing up, by removing the field, issues will not receive a value for that field when they are created. This becomes important when a field is configured to have a default value. When the field is removed, the issue will not have the default value for the field, while if the field is simply hidden, the default value will apply.

You will also need to pay close attention to not delete required fields, such as **summary**, from a screen. As we saw in *Chapter 4, Field Management*, JIRA will prevent you from hiding fields that are marked as required, but JIRA does not prevent you from removing required fields. It is possible for you to end up in a situation where JIRA requires a value for a field that does not exist on the screen. This can lead to very confusing error messages being delivered to the end users.

1. Browse to the **Configure Screen** page for the screen you wish to configure.

2. Change the checkbox for the fields you wish to delete from the screen under the **Remove** column.

3. Click on the **Remove** button to delete the selected fields from the screen.

Reordering fields on screen

By default, fields are displayed from top to bottom and new fields are added to the bottom. As your requirements for screen design continue to evolve, the order of fields will need to be re-arranged as fields are being added and deleted.

JIRA provides two methods for you to move fields around on a screen. You can move a field up and down one position at a time, or you can specify the position where you would like to place the field.

To move a field up or down one position at a time:

1. Browse to the **Configure Screen** page for the screen you wish to configure.
2. Click the up and down arrow icon for the field you wish to move.

You can also click the **Move to First** and **Move to Last** arrows to move the field instantly to the top bottom of the list, respectively.

When your list of fields are long, instead of clicking multiple times to move your field to the desired position, you can specify directly where you would like it to go.

1. Browse to the **Configure Screen** page for the screen you wish to configure.
2. Specify the desired position in the **Move To Position** field for the field you would like to move (first field has a value of 1).
3. Click on the **Move** button to move the field.

You can move multiple fields at once by using the **Move To Position** field on each field, but you cannot specify the same position for more than one field.

Screen tabs

For most cases, you will be adding fields sequentially onto a screen and users will fill them in from top to bottom. However, there will be cases where your screen becomes over-complicated and cluttered due to the sheer number of fields you need. In order to retain clarity on the screen, you may want to group several fields together to separate them from the rest. This is where tabs come in.

If you think of screens as the entire form a user must fill in, then tabs will be individual pages or sections that make up the whole document. Tabs go from left to right, so it is a good practice to design your tabs to flow logically from left to right. For example, the first tab can gather general information such as summary and description. Subsequent tabs will gather more domain-specific information.

Adding a tab

Every page in JIRA has a default tab. This is the tab where fields are initially added and displayed. You can add new tabs to a screen to break down and better manage your screen presentation. To create a new tab:

1. Browse to the **View Screens** page.
2. Click on the **Configure** link for the screen you wish to add a new tab for.
3. Provide a meaningful name for the new tab.
4. Click on the **Add** button to create the tab.

Once a tab is created, you will be able to add fields onto the tab.

Editing/Deleting a tab

Just like screens, you can maintain existing tabs by editing their names or removing them from the screen. To edit a tab's name:

1. Browse to the **View Screens** page.
2. Click on the **Configure** link for the screen that has the tab you wish to edit.
3. Select the tab.
4. Provide a new name for the tab.
5. Click on the **OK** button to apply the change.

When you are deleting a tab, the fields that are on the tab will be taken off the screen. You will need to re-add or move them to a different tab if you still want those fields to appear on the screen. Each screen must contain at least one tab; you cannot delete the last tab remaining.

1. Browse to the **View Screens** page.
2. Click on the **Configure** link for the screen that has the tab you wish to edit.
3. Select the tab.
4. Click on the **Delete** link. This will take you to the **Delete Screen Tab** page.
5. Click on the **Delete** button to remove the tab from the screen.

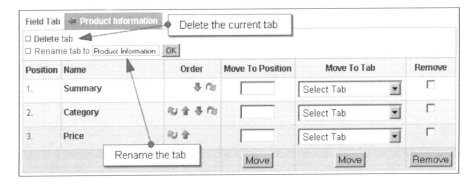

Reordering tabs

Tabs are organized horizontally from left to right. When you add a new tab to the screen, it is appended to the end of the list. There will be times when you need to rearrange them so your screen flow will make more sense to the users.

When you add new tabs, they are appended to the end of existing tabs. You can however, reshuffle the ordering. To reorder your tabs:

1. Browse to the **View Screens** page.

2. Click on the **Configure** link for the screen with tabs you wish to reorder.

3. Select the tab you would like to move.

4. Click on either the **Left** or **Right** arrow to move the tab.

When you move tabs around, their fields will move along with the tabs.

Screen schemes

We have seen how we can create and manage screens and how to configure what fields appear on the screens. The next step is letting JIRA know how to choose which screen to display for each operation.

Screens are displayed during issue operations and a screen scheme defines the mapping between screens and the operations. With a screen scheme, you can control the screen to display for each of the issue operations listed below.

- **Create Issue**: This screen is shown when you are creating a new issue.

- **Edit Issue**: This screen is show when you are editing an existing issue.

- **View Issue**: This screen is shown when you are viewing an issue.

By default, all three operations use the same screen, the **Default Screen**. This is a sensible default as it displays information to users consistently across all three operations. However, there will be times when you do not wish certain fields to be available for editing once the issue is created, such as **Issue Type**. You may want to have finer control over the type of issues raised for reporting and statistical measurement reasons, so it is not a good idea to let users freely change the issue type. Another example would be that certain fields are not required during creation time because the required information may be not available at the time, so instead of confusing and/or overwhelming your users, you leave those fields out during issue creation, and only ask them to be filled in at a later time when the information becomes available.

As you can see, dividing the screens up into multiple issue operations rather than having this one-screen-fits-all approach, JIRA provides you with a new level of flexibility to control and design your screens. As always, if there are no significant differences between the screens, for example **Create** and **Edit**, it is recommended that you create a base screen and use the **Copy Screen** feature to reduce your workload.

Screen schemes are maintained centrally by the JIRA Administrator.

1. Log into JIRA as a JIRA Administrator.

2. Click on **Administration** from the top menu bar.

3. Select **Screen Schemes** from the left panel to bring up the **View Screen Schemes** page.

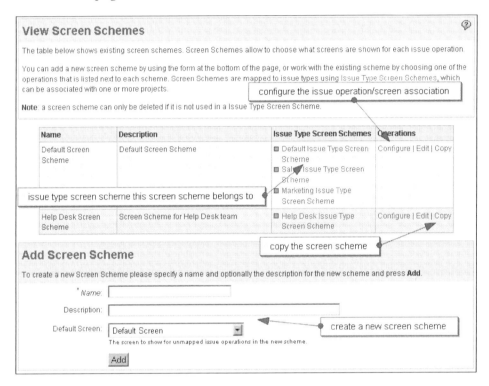

From the **View Screen Schemes** page, you will be able to see a list of all existing screen schemes, create and delete screen schemes, and manage each scheme's configurations such as issue operation and screen associations.

Adding a screen scheme

JIRA ships with a **Default Screen Scheme**, which uses the **Default Screen** for all of the issue operations. Whenever you add a new field, it will be placed onto that screen. When you create a new project, it will be assigned this default screen scheme. All issues will have those fields present.

As your JIRA application grows and different projects get created, it is a good practice to create separate, specialized screen schemes to better manage screen presentations. This way, you will have a finer control over the screens used by the different issue operations and issue types. To create a new screen scheme:

1. Browse to the **View Screen Schemes** page.
2. Provide a meaningful name for the new screen scheme in the **Add Screen Scheme** section.
3. Provide an optional short description for the screen scheme.
4. Select a default screen from the list of screens.
5. Click on the **Add** button to create the screen scheme.

At this stage, the new screen scheme is **not in use**. This means that is it not yet associated with any **Issue Type Screen Schemes** (Issue Type Screen Schemes are covered in later sections). You can tell whether a screen scheme is active by checking if the **Delete** option is available. You cannot delete active screen schemes.

After an issue screen scheme is created, it will apply the selected default screen to all issue operations. We will look at how to associate screens to issue operations in later sections.

Editing/Deleting a screen scheme

You can update the details of an existing screen scheme such as its name and description. In order for you to make changes to the default screen selection, you need to configure the screen scheme, which will be covered in later sections. To edit an existing screen scheme:

1. Browse to the **View Screen Schemes** page.
2. Click on the **Edit** link for the screen scheme you with to edit. This will take you to the **Edit Screen Scheme** page.
3. Update the name and description with new values.
4. Click on the **Update** button to apply the changes.

Inactive screen schemes can also be deleted. If the screen scheme is active (that is associated with an issue type screen scheme), then the delete option will not be present. To delete a screen scheme:

1. Browse to the **View Screen Schemes** page.

2. Click on the **Delete** link for the screen scheme you with to edit. This will take you to the **Delete Screen Scheme** page.

3. Click on the **Delete** button to confirm that you wish to delete the screen scheme.

Copying a screen scheme

While screen schemes are not as complicated as screens, there are still be times when you will want to copy an existing screen scheme rather than creating one from scratch. You might want to copy the scheme's screens/issue operations associations, which we will cover in the next section, or make a quick backup copy before making any changes to the scheme.

To copy an existing screen scheme:

1. Browse to the **View Screen Schemes** page.

2. Click the **Copy** link for the screen scheme you with to copy. This will take you to the **Copy Screen Scheme** page.

3. Provide a new name and description for the screen scheme.

4. Click the **Copy** button to copy the selected screen scheme.

Just like a new screen scheme, copied screen schemes are inactive by default.

Configuring a screen scheme

As mentioned earlier, when we create a new screen scheme, it will use the same screen selected as our default screen for all issue operations. Now, if you want to use the same screen for create, edit, and view, then you are set. There is no need to perform any further configuration to your screen scheme. However, if you need to have different screens displayed for different issue operations, then you will need to establish this association.

When an issue operation does not have an association with a screen, the default screen will be applied. If the issue operation is later given a screen association, then the specific association will take precedence over the general fall back default screen.

The associations between screens and issue operations are managed on a per screen scheme level. To configure a screen scheme:

1. Browse to the **View Screen Schemes** page.
2. Click on the **Configure** link for the screen scheme you wish to configure. This will take you to the **Configure Screen Scheme** page.

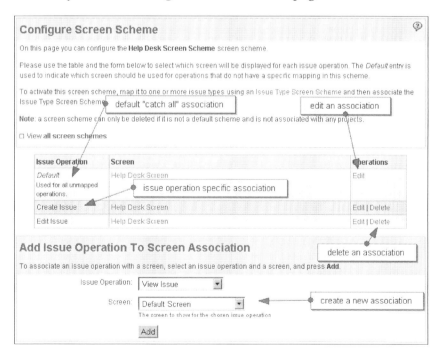

Adding an association

Each issue operation can be associated with one screen, yet each screen can be associated with one or more issue operation.

1. Browse to the **Configure Screen Scheme** page for the screen scheme to be configured.

2. Select the issue operation to be associated from the **Add Issue Operation To Screen Association** section.

3. Select the screen to be associated to the issue operation.

4. Click on the **Add** button to create the association.

Editing/Deleting an association

After you have created an association for an issue operation, JIRA prevents you from creating another association for the same issue operation by removing it from the list of available options. In order to change the association to a different screen, you need to edit the existing association.

1. Browse to the **Configure Screen Scheme** page for the screen scheme to be configured.

2. Click on the **Edit** link for the association you wish to edit. This will take you to the **Edit Screen Scheme Item** page.

3. Select a new screen to associate with the issue operation.

4. Click on the **Update** button to apply the change.

If you decide that one or more existing associations are no longer needed, you can delete them from the screen scheme.

1. Browse to the **Configure Screen Scheme** page for the screen scheme to be configured.

2. Click on the **Delete** link for the association you wish to delete.

Please note that unlike other similar operations, deleting an issue operation association does not prompt you with a confirm page. As soon as you click on the delete link, your association will be deleted immediately.

Issue type screen scheme

Screen schemes group screens together and create associations with issue operations. The next piece of the puzzle is to specify which screen scheme is to be applied for different issue types.

JIRA allows you to have different screen schemes applied to a single project, letting different issue types to have different screens for the same issue operation. This extremely flexible and powerful feature is provided through issue type screen scheme.

1. Log into JIRA as a JIRA Administrator.

2. Click on **Administration** from the top menu bar.

3. Select **Issue Type Screen Schemes** from the left panel to bring up the View Issue Type Screen Schemes page.

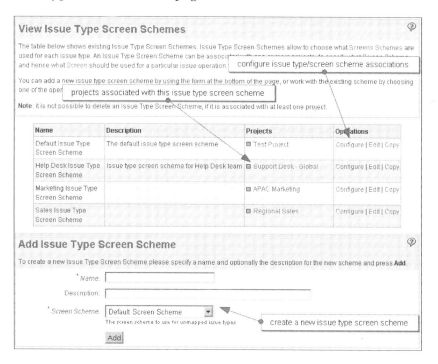

Adding an issue type screen scheme

You would have noticed by now that for any project, all of our issue types have the same screen layout. All projects by default use the default issue type screen scheme. But just like anything else in JIRA, you can create your own schemes and apply them to your projects.

To create a new issue type screen scheme:

1. Browse to the **View Issue Type Screen Schemes** page.
2. Provide a meaningful name for the new issue type screen scheme in the **Add Issue Type Screen Scheme** section.
3. Provide an optional short description for the issue type screen scheme.
4. Select a default screen scheme from the list of screen schemes.
5. Click on the **Add** button to create the issue type screen scheme.

That's right, you guessed it! The new issue type screen scheme is inactive at this stage. It will only become active once it has been applied to one or more projects, which we will look at shortly.

Editing/Deleting an issue type screen scheme

You can make changes to an existing issue type screen scheme's name and descriptions. To change its screen scheme/issue type association details, you need to configure the issue type screen scheme, which will be covered in later sections.

1. Browse to the **View Issue Type Screen Schemes** page.
2. Click on the **Edit** link for the issue type screen scheme you wish to edit. This will take you to the **Edit Issue Type Screen Scheme** page.
3. Update the name and description with new values.
4. Click on the **Update** button to apply the changes.

Just like all other schemes in JIRA, you cannot delete active issue type screen schemes if they are active. You will have to make sure there are no projects using it before JIRA will allow you to delete the scheme.

1. Browse to the **View Issue Type Screen Schemes** page.
2. Click on the **Delete** link for the issue type screen scheme you wish to delete. This will take you to the **Delete Issue Type Screen Scheme** page.
3. Click on the **Delete** button to remove the issue type screen scheme.

Coping an issue type screen scheme

Issue type screen scheme cloning is also available. You can easily make copies of existing issue type screen schemes. One very useful application of this feature is to make backup copies before experimenting with new configurations.

To copy an existing issue type screen scheme:

1. Browse to the **View Issue Type Screen Schemes** page.
2. Click on the **Copy** link for the issue type screen scheme you wish to copy. This will take you to the **Copy Issue Type Screen Scheme** page.
3. Provide a new name and description for the issue type screen scheme.
4. Click on the **Copy** button to copy the selected scheme.

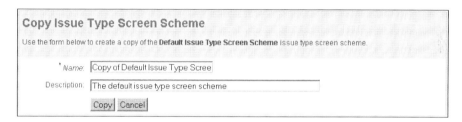

Just like newly created issue type screen schemes are inactive by default, cloned schemes only become active after they have been associated with projects.

Configuring an issue type screen scheme

By creating new issue type screen schemes, we are creating a mapping where we can establish associations between screen schemes and issue types. These associations are what ties projects and issues types to the individual screens.

Each issue type screen scheme needs to be configured separately, and the associations created are specific to the configured scheme.

1. Browse to the **View Issue Type Screen Schemes** page.

2. Click on the **Configure** link for the issue type screen scheme you wish to configure. This will take you to the **Configure Issue Type Screen Scheme** page.

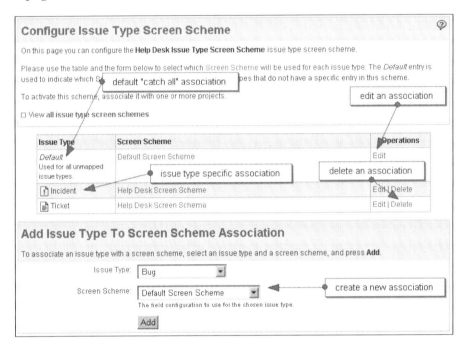

Adding an association

You can tell JIRA which screen scheme to use for different issue types by establishing an association between screen schemes and issue types. Each issue type can have only one screen scheme associated with it. Each screen scheme however, can be associated with more than one issue types.

To add a new association:

1. Browse to the **Configure Issue Type Screen Scheme** page for the issue type screen scheme you wish to configure.

2. Select the issue type to add an association for.

3. Select the screen scheme to be associated with the issue type.

4. Click on the **Add** button to create the association.

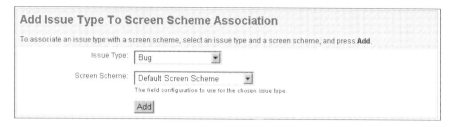

In an issue type screen scheme, each issue type can only be associated with one screen scheme. JIRA will not display associated issue types in the available options.

Editing/Deleting an association

You can update existing associations such as the **Default** association, which is created automatically when you create a new issue type screen scheme.

1. Browse to the **Configure Screen Scheme** page for the screen scheme to be configured.

2. Click on the **Edit** link for the association you wish to edit. This will take you to the **Edit Screen Scheme Item** page.

3. Select a new screen to associate with the issue operation.

4. Click on the **Update** button to apply the change.

You can also delete existing associations for issue types. This means you cannot delete the **Default** association as this is used as a catch-all for issue types that do not have an explicitly defined association. This is important since you may have created associations for all issue types right now, yet you might add new issue types down the line and forget to create associations for them. If we do not have this catch-all default association, JIRA's behavior will become unpredictable.

1. Browse to the **Configure Issue Type Screen Scheme** page for the issue type screen scheme to be configured.

2. Click on the **Delete** link for the association you wish to delete.

Just like associations in screen schemes, you will not be taken to a confirmation page; the association will be deleted immediately.

Activating an issue type screen scheme

In order to activate your new issue type screen scheme, which will display your new screens for the different issue operations, follow the proceeding steps:

1. Log into JIRA as a JIRA Administrator.

2. Click on **Administration** from the top menu bar.

3. Select the project you wish to associate the field configuration scheme with. This will bring up the project administration page.

4. Click on the **Select** link for **Issue Type Screen Scheme**. This will bring up the **Type Screen Scheme Association** page.

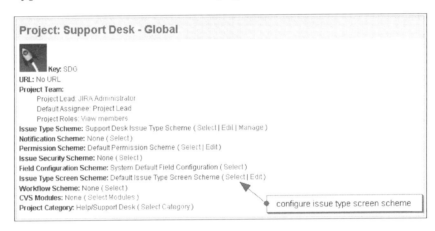

5. Select the issue type screen scheme from the **Scheme** select list.

6. Click on the **Associate** button.

It is time to revisit what we have learned so far and visualize how everything is related to each other. The following diagram illustrates the major components we have covered in the both chapters and their relationships. Workflow will be covered in the next chapter.

How field configurations are applied to projects:

1. Fields are grouped by field configurations.
2. Field configurations are mapped to issue types via field configuration schemes.
3. Field configuration schemes are applied to projects.

How screen configurations are applied to projects:

1. Fields are added to screens.
2. Screens are mapped to issue operations via screen schemes.
3. Screen schemes are mapped to issue types via issue type screen schemes.
4. Issue type screen schemes are applied to projects.

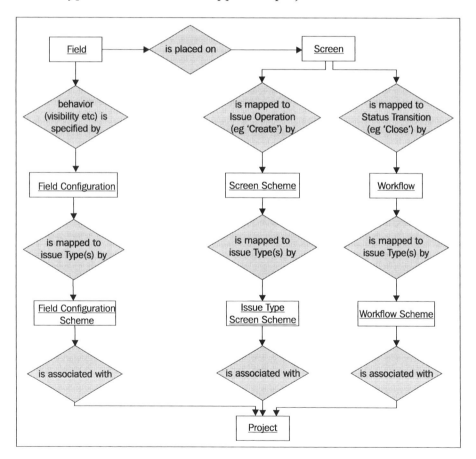

Help Desk Project

Armed with the new knowledge we have gathered in this chapter, together with fields from the last chapter, it is time for us to further customize our JIRA to provide a better user experience through presentation.

What we will customize this time is create new screens and apply them to our Help Desk project. We want to separate out the generic fields from our custom fields designed for escalation. We also want to apply the changes to issues of only the **Incident** type and not affect other issue types. As with any changes to be done on a production system, it is critical that you have a backup of your current data before applying changes. Backup strategy is discussed in *Chapter 10*.

Setting up screens

In *Chapter 4*, *Field Management*, we created a few custom fields specifically designed for our support team. As you have learned, those fields are added to the default screen. The first thing we need to do is to create a couple of screens for our Help Desk project only so we do not affect any other screens used by other projects and teams.

We will be creating three screens. One for creating issues and one for updating issues. We will be sharing the same screen to both creating and viewing issues, as we would like to show our users the same set of information. The third screen will be used for when we transition issues through the workflow. Since workflow is covered in the next chapter, we will just create the screen and come back to it when we discuss workflows.

1. Browse to the **View Screens** page.
2. Name the new screen **Help Desk Create/View Screen**.
3. Provide a helpful description Screen for create/view help desk issues.
4. Click on the **Add** button to create the screen.

The next step is to set up the tabs for our new screen. We would like to have the default fields on the first screen to capture generic issue data, and we will place the new custom fields we have created in *Chapter 4* onto a new tab called **Escalation**.

1. Click on the **Configure** link for our new **Help Desk Create/View Screen**.
2. Rename the default tab to **General**.
3. Create a new tab called **Escalation**.

Now that we have our screen and tabs, it is time to place our fields onto them.

1. Move back to the **General** tab.

2. Add the fields from the **Default** screen onto the tab.

3. Move to the **Escalation** tab.

4. Add the new escalation custom fields onto the tab.

Field	Tab
Summary	General
Issue Type	General
Security Level	General
Priority	General
Due Date	General
Component/s	General
Affects Version/s	General
Fix Version/s	General
Assignee	General
Reporter	General
Environment	General
Description	General
Time Tracking	General
Attachment	General
Escalation List	Escalation
Escalation Level	Escalation
Is Escalation Required	Escalation

Of course, if you are thinking that this can be done much faster by cloning the default screen and moving the escalation fields over to the new tab, you are absolutely correct. However, we are doing it manually this time to go through the process.

We have created and configured our first create/view screen. Our new edit screen is going to look very similar with just a few modifications. We want to take the **Issue Type** field off since we do not want users to change the issue type all the time, and we are going to take the **Escalation Level** field off as it makes little sense to have a non-editable field on the edit screen. Since we are only taking some fields off an existing screen, instead of going to through the entire create and configure process, let's spare ourselves the tedious clicking and copy the screen we just created, since we have already done it once.

1. Browse to the **View Screens** page.
2. Click on the **Copy** link for **Help Desk Create/View Screen**.
3. Name the new screen **Help Desk Edit Screen**.
4. Provide a helpful description Screen to edit help desk issues.
5. Click on the **Copy** button to create the new screen.

Since we have copied the screen, it inherits all of the fields and tabs so there is no need to re-configure them. All we need to do is to remove the fields that we do not need.

1. Click on the **Configure** link for our new **Help Desk Edit Screen**.
2. Delete the **Issue Type** field from the **General** tab.
3. Delete the **Escalation Level** field from the **Escalation** tab.

The last step is to create our third screen, which we will use in the next chapter. This screen will be used during workflow transitions and we would like to allow users to re-assign the issue and also update the **Escalation List** field. Since this is going to be a fairly simple screen, we will create it from scratch.

1. Browse to the View Screens page.
2. Name the new screen **Help Desk Workflow Screen**.
3. Provide a helpful description Screen for transition help desk issues.
4. Click on the **Add** button to create the screen.
5. Click on the **Configure** link for our new Help Desk Workflow Screen.
6. Add **Assignee** and **Escalation** fields to the screen.

Now we have our fully configured screens set up, but they are not in use right now. The next step is to establish the association with their respective issue operations.

Setting up screen schemes

With the screens created and configured, we now need to link them up with issue operations so JIRA will know on which action the new screens should be displayed.

1. Browse to the **View Issue Type Screen Schemes** page.
2. Name the new screen scheme **Help Desk Incident Screen Scheme**.
3. Provide a helpful description Screen scheme for **Help Desk** incidents.
4. Select **Help Desk Create/View Screen** as the default screen.
5. Click on the **Add** button to create the screen scheme.

With our screen scheme in place, it is time to link up our screens with their respective issue operations.

1. Click the **Configure** link for **Help Desk Screen Scheme**.
2. Select **Help Desk Edit Screen** for the **Edit Issue** operation.

Issue Operation	Screen	Operations
Default Used for all unmapped operations.	Help Desk Create/View Screen	Edit
Edit Issue	Help Desk Edit Screen	Edit | Delete

Since we have assigned the **Help Desk Create/View Screen to Default**, the screen will be applied to the un-mapped operations, that is **Create Issue** and **View Issue**. There are no differences if you choose to explicitly set the mappings for the two above operations.

Setting up issue type screen schemes

Now we need to tell JIRA which issue type will be using the screen scheme that we just created. We will be applying our new screens to issues of the type **Incident** initially, since those are usually the type of issues that require immediate attention and appropriate escalation. For future enhancements, we can further customize our design so each issue type will have their own screen design.

The first step is to create a new issue type screen scheme to be used specifically for our project.

1. Browse to the **View Issue Type Screen Schemes** page.
2. Name the new screen scheme **Help Desk Issue Type Screen Scheme**.
3. Provide a helpful description for the Issue type screen scheme.
4. Select **Default Screen Scheme** as the default screen scheme.
5. Click on the **Add** button to create the issue type screen scheme.

With the scheme created, we can establish the associations between screen schemes and issue types.

1. Click on the **Configure** link for **Help Desk Issue Type Screen Scheme**.
2. Select **Incident** for issue type.
3. Select **Help Desk Incident Screen Scheme** for the screen scheme to be associated.
4. Click on the **Add** button to create the association.

This will ensure that issues of the **Incident** type will have our new screens applied while issues of other types will not be affected.

Putting it all together

The last step is to activate all the screens and schemes we have created so far in this chapter and see them in action. Remember there is only one thing we need to do: choose our project and configure it to use our issue type screen scheme.

1. Browse to the **Project Administration** page for our **Help Desk** project.
2. Click on the **Select** link for **Issue Type Screen Scheme**.
3. Select **Help Desk Issue Type Screen Scheme** and click the **Associate** button.

If you are performing this on a live production system, it is recommended that you alert the users of the change and perform this when there are not many users on the system.

This is it, all done! We can now take a look at our hard work, see our custom screens, fields, and tabs all working nicely together to present you with a custom form for collection of user data.

Let's go ahead and create a new incident and see what our newly customized create issue screen will look like in the following screenshot:

As you can see, our new screen is nicely divided into two tabs with our new custom fields on the **Escalation** tab. If you create an issue of the type **Ticket**, you will see that it will not have the tabbed screen design.

Summary

In this chapter, we looked at how JIRA structures its presentation with screens. We also looked at how you can divide your screens into logical part with tabs, and finally, we discussed the relationships between screens, issue operations, and issue types. Together with custom fields that we looked at in the previous chapter, we can now create effective screen designs to streamline our data collection. In the next chapter, we will delve into one of the most powerful features in JIRA, workflows

6
Workflow and Business Process

In the previous chapters, we have learned some of the basics of JIRA and how to customize its look and feel for better data capture and presentation.

In this chapter, we will dive in and take a look at workflows in JIRA and how you can use this powerful feature to adapt your instance of JIRA to your business. By the end of this chapter, you will have learned:

- The life cycle of issues
- What a workflow is and what one consists of
- About the relationship between workflows and screens
- What transitions, conditions, validators, and post functions are
- How to assign a workflow with projects

Mapping business processes

It is often said that a good software system is one that adapts to your business; not one that requires your business to adapt to the software. JIRA is an excellent example of the former. The advantage of JIRA is how easily you can configure it to model after your existing business processes, through the use of workflows.

A business process flow can often be represented as a flow chart. For example, a typical document approval flow might include tasks such as Document Preparation, Document Review, and Document Submission, where the user needs to follow these tasks in a sequential order. You can easily implement this as a JIRA workflow. Each task will be represented as a workflow step, with transitions guiding you how to move from one step to the next.

Now that we have briefly seen what context a JIRA workflow applies to, it is time to take a closer look at the make up of a workflow and how you can create your own.

Workflows

Worrkflows are what JIRA uses to model business processes. They are a flow of states (steps) with paths between them (transitions). All issues in JIRA, based on their issue type and project they are in, have a workflow applied. Issues move through workflows from one step (for example, **Open**) to another (for example, **Closed**). For this reason, it is sometimes referred to as the life cycle of issues.

The preceding diagram shows a very simple workflow in JIRA. The rectangles represent the steps and the arrows represent transitions which links steps together.

Issues in JIRA, starting from when they are created, go through a series of steps such as **In Progress** and **Closed**. These movements are often triggered by user interactions. For example, when a user clicks on the **Start Progress** link, the issue is transitioned to the **In Progress** step.

There is a definitive start to a workflow, when the issue is first created, but the end of a workflow can sometimes be ambiguous. For example, in the default workflow, issues can go from **Open** to **Closed**, to **Re-opened** and back to **Closed** again. By convention, when people talk about the end of a workflow, it usually refers to a step named **Closed** or the step where issues are given a resolution.

Managing workflows

Workflows are controlled and managed centrally from the Administration panel, so you need to be an Administrator to create and configure workflows.

1. Log into JIRA as a JIRA Administrator.
2. Click on **Administration** from the top menu bar.
3. Select **Workflows** from the left panel to bring up the **View Workflows** page.

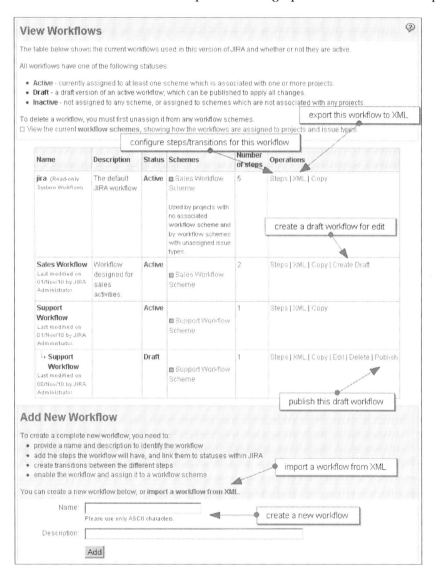

From the **View Workflows** page, you will be able to see a list of all the available workflows. You can also create new workflows and manage existing workflows.

Workflows can have three statuses:

- **Active**: This status means the workflow is currently being used by one or more projects. You cannot make changes directly to an active workflow.
- **Inactive**: This status means the workflow is not being used by any projects. You can update inactive workflows.
- **Draft**: This status means the workflow is an inactive copy linked to the active workflow. You can make changes to a draft workflow (with limitations). Unlike workflows created by the **Copy** operation, draft workflows are linked to the original workflow and changes can be made directly by publishing it.

Workflows can also be associated with one or more workflow schemes (discussed in later sections). When a workflow belongs to a workflow scheme, it cannot be deleted regardless of whether it is in the active, inactive, or draft state.

JIRA comes with a default read-only workflow called **jira**. This workflow is applied to projects that do not have any specific workflows applied. For this reason, you cannot edit or delete this workflow.

Creating a workflow

Creating a new workflow in JIRA is very simple. When you create a new workflow, the workflow is considered to be blank. This means it contains one step (the default open step) and no transitions.

1. Browse to the **View Workflows** page.
2. Provide a meaningful name for the new workflow in the **Add New Workflow** section.
3. Provide an optional short description for the workflow.
4. Click on the **Add** button to create the workflow.

Step Name (id)	Linked Status	Transitions (id)	Operations
Open (1)	Open		Add Transition | Edit | View Properties

Once the new workflow has been created, you will notice that it will have a status of **inactive**. You need to associate it with a workflow scheme for it to become active.

After you have created your new workflow, you can configure it by adding new steps and transitions, which we will look at later in this chapter. One good practice to keep in mind is that it is often a good idea to not have a "dead-end" state in your workflow, for example, allowing closed issues to be re-opened. This will prevent users from accidentally closing an issue and not being able to undo the mistake.

Editing a workflow

You can update a workflow's name and description if the workflow is inactive. It is important to note that editing a workflow does not modify the contents of the workflow itself. The edit option will not be available if the workflow is active.

1. Browse to the **View Workflows** page.
2. Click on the **Edit** link for the workflow you wish to update. This will take you to the **Edit Workflow** page.
3. Update the **Name** and **Description** with new values.
4. Click on the **Edit** button to apply the changes.

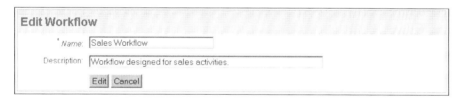

Deleting a workflow

Unused and redundant workflows can be deleted from JIRA. You cannot delete a workflow that is active or a workflow that is associated with a workflow scheme, as this will have an impact on projects that are already configured to use them.

1. Browse to the **View Workflows** page.
2. Click on the **Delete** link for the workflow you wish to remove. This will take you to the **Delete Workflow** page.
3. Click on the **Delete** button to remove the workflow permanently.

Copying a workflow

Workflows are often very complex and creating a new workflow can sometimes be time consuming. In order to expedite the workflow creation process and be more efficient, JIRA allows you to copy existing workflows. Once a workflow has been copied, both workflows will exist as separate entities and you can edit them without affecting one another.

1. Browse to the **View Workflows** page.

2. Click on the **Copy** link for the workflow you wish to copy. This will take you to the **Copy Workflow** page.

3. Provide a new name and description for the workflow.

4. Click on the **Copy** button to copy the workflow.

As with creating a new workflow, the newly copied workflow is inactive until it has been associated.

Importing and exporting a workflow

JIRA allows you to export existing workflows into an XML file which can be imported into another instance of JIRA. This is a useful feature as it allows you to quickly replicate complex workflows across different deployments of JIRA. This is often an ideal solution when workflows developed in a test environment need to be deployed onto a production environment where a full system restore will be inappropriate. There are however, caveats which one will need to look out for while performing workflow imports, which we will discuss later. However, let's first take a look at how to export workflows in JIRA.

To export a workflow:

1. Browse to the **View Workflows** page.

2. Click on the **XML** link for the workflow you wish to export. Depending on your browser setup, you may or may not get a save file dialog prompt.

3. Select the location where you would like to save the exported workflow XML file if you are prompted with the save file dialog.

You can open the exported XML file and edit the workflow directly. A detailed explanation on the contents of the workflow XML file is beyond the scope of this book. JIRA uses the OSWorkflow engine from OpenSymphony. You will be able to find more information online about how you can tweak the XML contents (`http://confluence.atlassian.com/display/JIRACOM/Editing+JIRA+workflow+XML+by+hand`). However, this is only recommended for advanced users.

As we can see, exporting a workflow is quite simple and straightforward. Importing however, takes a bit of planning. When you export a workflow, what you are exporting is not only the workflow entities such as steps and transitions, but also references to other related entities such as statuses linked to the steps, fields used by post functions, and validators. These entities are not exported along with the workflow. If they do not exist in the target system, the import will not work. References that are most likely to be different between systems include:

- Steps and their linked statuses. It is important to note that the statuses need to have the same ID across both systems, not just the names.
- Custom screens referenced by workflow transitions.
- Custom fields referenced by post functions, validators, and conditions.
- Field values such as **Priority** being referenced.

For this reason, it is only recommended to import workflows into a system with an identical setup (such as production and staging). However, often you will need to copy workflows between two JIRA instances that have different setups. For example, when you need to promote a new workflow from the test environment into the production environment, or between two JIRA instances used by different departments.

In cases like this, where the causes of differences between systems are due to introducing new custom fields or statuses as part of a new workflow, it is recommended to carry out the following steps:

1. Create the new entities (custom fields, statuses, and so on) in the target JIRA system.
2. Export the workflow from the base system.
3. Edit the exported XML file and update the referenced IDs with the actual IDs in the target system.
4. Import the workflow into the target system.

Once you have made sure that all the external entities have been created in the target system, you can start import the workflow.

1. Browse to the **View Workflows** page.

2. Click on the **import a workflow from XML** link from the **Add New Workflow** section. This will take you to the **Import Workflow** page.

3. Provide a name for the workflow to be imported. The name must be unique. It cannot be the same as an existing workflow.

4. Provide an optional description for the workflow.

5. Specify the file path of the exported XML file OR cut and paste the XML file content into the Workflow Definition box.

6. Click on the **Import** button to import the workflow.

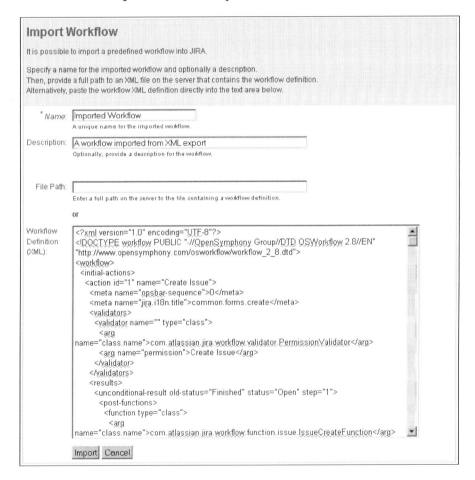

Configuring a workflow

As we have seen, when creating a new workflow, you must add steps and transitions because the workflow starts out completely blank. When your requirements change, you will also need to be able to re-configure a workflow to update its contents.

You cannot configure active workflows directly, as they are read-only. For you to configure an active workflow, you will need to create a draft of the workflow and make your changes on the draft, and when you are done, you can publish the draft, which will apply the changes.

However, there are a few restrictions when editing a draft workflow compared to editing an inactive workflow.

- Existing workflow steps cannot be deleted
- The associated status for an existing step cannot be edited
- If an existing step has no outgoing transitions, it cannot have any new outgoing transitions added
- Step IDs for the existing steps cannot be changed

If you need to make these changes, you will need to either de-activate the workflow by removing the associations of the workflow with all projects or create a copy of the workflow.

You can configure a workflow's content by:

1. Browsing to the **View Workflows** page.
2. Clicking on the **Steps** link for the workflow you wish to configure. This will take you to the **View Workflow Steps** page.

From this page, you get a one-page table view of all the steps and transitions in the current workflow. You can also add new steps and transitions, and manage their properties and configurations. As stated earlier, the default **jira** workflow cannot be changed.

Configuring and publishing a draft

To configure an active workflow, you need to first create a draft. To create a draft workflow:

1. Browse to the **View Workflows** page.

2. Click on the **Create Draft** link for the workflow you wish to configure. This will create a draft and take you directly to the **View Workflow Steps** page of the draft workflow.

After you have finished making changes to the draft, you will need to publish it for the changes to be applied.

1. Browse to the **View Workflows** page.

2. Click on the **Publish** link for the draft workflow you wish to publish. This will take you to the **Publish Draft Workflow** page, where you will be prompted to first create a backup of the original workflow. It is recommended that you create a backup in case of a rollback, and this also and this also allows you to keep a history of changes.

3. Select either **Yes** or **No** to create a backup of the current workflow before applying the changes. This is a handy way to quickly create a backup if you have not made a copy already. If you do choose to create a backup, it is a good idea to name your workflow with a consistent convention (for example, based on version such as Sales Workflow 1.0) to keep track.

4. Click on the **Publish** button to publish the draft workflow and apply changes.

Steps and issue statuses

In a JIRA workflow, a step represents a state in the workflow for an issue. It describes the current status of the issue. If we look at a business process flow chart, the steps will be the rectangles and diamonds in the diagram, indicating the current status of the issue along the process. Just like a task can only be in one stage of a business process, an issue can be in only one step at any given time. For example, an issue cannot be both open and closed at the same time.

There is a one-to-one relationship between workflow steps and issue statuses. Each step is associated with an issue status, also known as **linked status**. In a JIRA workflow, when an issue has been transitioned into a specific step, JIRA updates the issue's status field.

Since you link a step to an issue status, when you view issues, JIRA will display the issue status rather than the step, and when you search issues, you will not search by the workflow's step the issue is in, but rather, you will search by the status that is linked to the step.

Adding a step to a workflow

Each step is unique in a workflow. You can have two steps with exactly the same name in the same workflow, and JIRA will consider them to be different entities.

In a given workflow, if all the issue statuses are mapped, JIRA will not display the **Add New Step** section and you will not be able to add new steps.

1. Browse to the **View Workflow Steps** page.
2. Provide a meaningful name for the new step in the **Add new Step** section. It is often a good idea to name the step after the issue status.
3. Select a linked status.
4. Click on the **Add** button to create the step.

Once the step is created, it will be added to the bottom of the table, and you will be able to use transitions to link existing steps to the new step.

Editing a step

You can edit a step to update its name and its associated linked status. However, as mentioned earlier, if you are configuring a draft workflow, you will not be able to change the step's linked status. Also, if all of your statuses are mapped, you will not be able to change linked status, as the list will only contain free statuses. You will need to create a new status to act as an intermediate buffer.

1. Browse to the **View Workflow Steps** page.
2. Click on the **Edit** link for the step you wish to update.
3. Provide a new value for the name.
4. Select a new linked status if available.
5. Click on the **Update** button to apply the changes.

Deleting a step

You can also delete redundant workflow steps if the workflow is not a draft. For you to delete a step, you have to first make sure that there are no incoming transitions. If there are transitions with a destination to the step you want to delete, JIRA will not display the delete option. To delete a step:

1. Browse to the **View Workflow Steps** page.
2. Click on the **Delete Step** link for the step you wish to remove. This will take you to the **Delete Workflow Step** page.
3. Click on the **Delete** button to remove the step.

Transitions

Steps represent stages in a workflow. The path that takes an issue from one step to the next is known as a transition. A transition links two (and only two) steps together. Transitions cannot exist on their own, meaning they must have a start and finish step, and can only have one of each. This means a transition cannot conditionally split off to different destination steps. Transitions are also only one way. This means if a transition takes an issue from step A to step B, you must create a new transition if you want to go back from step B to step A.

Adding a transition between steps

As we have seen, transitions provide the link between two steps. You can create any number of transitions for a step. You can even create multiple transitions between the same set of steps, although doing so is not encouraged.

When you create a new transition, you start with the originating step. This will be the step from where you can execute your transition.

You then need to provide a name for your transition. This name will be what your users will see when they are presented with all available transitions. It is often a good idea to have your transitions' names start with a command. For example, **Submit Ticket** or **Provide Information**. This way, users will know that they are performing an action.

The next procedure is to determine the destination step. This is your issue's target state once the transition has been successfully executed. While transitions would have different originating and target steps, it is perfectly fine to have the same step for both. Although doing so is not common in a process flow scenario, it can be useful in some situations. For example, you have fields you do not want all users to be able to update via the **Edit Issue** operation. You can create a transition with an intermediate screen with those fields and restrict it to the users who can execute the transition.

The last piece of setting is whether or not the transition will have an intermediate screen. If you select a screen for **Transition View**, when the user clicks on the transition to execute it, the screen will be displayed before it is executed. This allows you to capture additional information that might be relevant for this transition. If you do not select a screen, the transition will be executed as soon as the user clicks on it. To add a transition to a workflow:

1. Browse to the **View Workflow Steps** page.
2. Click on the **Add Transition** link of the step you wish to add a transition for. This will bring you to the **Add Workflow Transition** page.
3. Provide a meaningful name for the new transition. It is often a good idea to have the name start with a verb.
4. Provide an optional description.
5. Select the destination step for the transition.
6. Select a screen if the transition will have an intermediate screen when being executed.
7. Click on the **Add** button to create the transition.

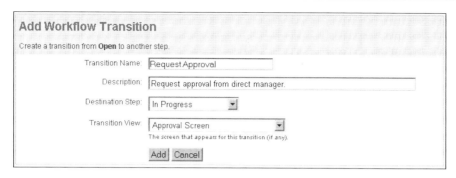

Once you have created the transition, it will be listed under the **Transitions** column for the step which it was created under. You will also see a number in a brackets next to its name. That is the **unique ID** for the transition in the workflow. This can be very useful when you have multiple transitions with the same name (for example, a **Go Back** transition).

Editing a transition

After a transition has been created, you can update its details at any time. Most commonly, you will need to change its destination step or transition screen.

1. Browse to the **View Workflow Steps** page.
2. Click on the transition you wish to edit. This will take you to the **Transition** page.
3. Click on the **Edit** link. This will take you to the **Update Workflow Transition** page.
4. Provide new values for the name and description for the transition.
5. Select a new **Destination Step**.
6. Select a new **Transition View**.
7. Click on the **Update** button to apply the changes.

Deleting a transition

You can also delete transitions from a workflow step. When a transition is deleted, users will no longer see the transition link when viewing issues.

There are two ways of deleting transitions. You can delete a specific transition by going to the **Transition** page:

1. Browse to the **Transition** page for the transition you wish to remove.
2. Click on the **Delete** link. This will take you to the **Delete Workflow Transitions** page.
3. Click on the **Delete** button to remove the transition.

You can also delete multiple transitions that belong to a step:

1. Browse to the **View Workflow Steps** page.
2. Click on the **Delete Transitions** link for the step you wish to delete transitions from. This will bring you to the **Delete Workflow Transitions** page, listing all the transitions belonging to the step.
3. Select the transitions you wish to remove.
4. Click on the **Delete** button to remove all the selected transitions.

Configuring a transition

Transitions are actions in a workflow, so they are more complex than steps. With transitions, you can add three additional components—**Conditions**, **Validators**, and **Post Functions**.

Each of the three components define the behavior of the transitions, allowing you to perform pre- and post-validations on transition execution, and also perform post-execution processing. We will discuss these three components further in the sections.

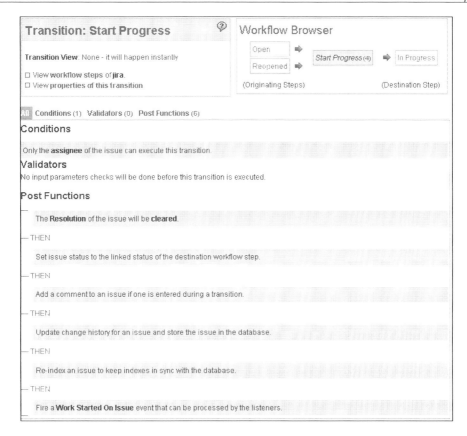

Conditions

Sometimes you will want to have control over who or when a transition can be executed. For example, an authorization transition can only be executed by users in the managers' group so normal employees will not be able to authorize their own requests. This is where conditions come in.

Conditions are prerequisites that must be fulfilled before the user is allowed to execute the transition. If the conditions on transitions are not met, the transition will not be available to the user when viewing the issue. The following table shows a list of default conditions that are shipped with JIRA:

Condition	Description
Only Assignee Condition	Only allows the issue's current assignee to execute the transition.
Only Reporter Condition	Only allows the issue's reporter to execute the transition.
Permission Condition	Only allows users with the given permission to execute the transition.
Sub-Task Blocking Condition	Blocks the parent issue transition depending on all its sub-tasks' statuses.
User Is In Group	Only allows users in a given group to execute the transition.
User Is In Group Custom Field	Only allows users in a given Group Custom Field to execute a transition.
User Is In Project Role	Only allows users in a given project role to execute a transition.

Adding a condition to transition

New transitions do not have any conditions by default. This means anyone who has access to the issue will be able to execute the transition. JIRA allows you to add any number of conditions to the transition. To add a condition to a transition:

1. Browse to the **Manage Transition** page for the transition you wish to add a condition for.
2. Click on the **Conditions** tab.
3. Click on the **Add** link. This will bring you to the **Add Condition To Transition** page, which lists all the available conditions you can add.
4. Select the condition you wish to add.
5. Click on the **Add** button to add the condition.
6. Depending on the condition, you may be presented with the **Add Parameters To Condition** page where you can specify configuration options for the condition.

Add Condition To Transition

Add Condition To Transition

Name	Description
Code Committed Condition	Transition to execute only if code has/has not (depending on configuration) been committed against this issue
No Open Reviews Condition	Transition to execute only if there are no related open Crucible reviews.
Only Assignee Condition	Condition to allow only the assignee to execute a transition.
Only Reporter Condition	Condition to allow only the reporter to execute a transition.
Permission Condition	Condition to allow only users with a certain permission to execute a transition.
Sub-Task Blocking Condition	Condition to block parent issue transition depending on sub-task status.
Unreviewed Code Condition	Transition to execute only if there are no unreviewed changesets related to this issue
User Is In Group	Condition to allow only users in a given group to execute a transition.
User Is In Group Custom Field	Condition to allow only users in a custom field-specified group to execute a transition.
User Is In Project Role	Condition to allow only users in a given project role to execute a transition.

Add | Cancel

Conditions are appended to the end of the existing list of conditions, creating a **condition group**. By default, when there is more than one condition, logical AND is used to group the conditions. This means that all conditions must pass for the entire condition group to pass. If one condition fails, the entire group fails, and the user will not be able to execute the transition. You can switch to use logical OR, which means only one of the conditions in the group to pass for the entire group to pass. This is a very useful feature as it allows you to combine multiple conditions to form a more complex logical unit.

For example, the **User is in Group** condition lets you specify a single group, but with the AND operation, you can add multiple **User is in Group** conditions to ensure the user must exist in all the specific groups to be able to execute the transition. There is one restriction to this however—you cannot use both for the same condition group.

Validators

Validators are similar to conditions in nature. Conditions check for criteria before a transition is performed, validators check criteria after a user has executed a transition. If the one of the validators fail, the transition fails and will be rolled back to its original state. The following table shows a list of validators that come shipped with JIRA.

Validator	Description
Permission Validator	Validates that the user who executed the transitions has permission to do so.
User Permission Validator	Validates that the user has permission, where the OSWorkflow variable holding the username is configurable. This is obsolete.

Adding a validator to transition

Like conditions, transitions do not have any validators associated by default. This means transitions are completed as soon as they are executed. You can add validators to transitions to make sure executions are only allowed to complete when certain criteria are met. To add a validator:

1. Browse to the **Manage Transition** page for the transition you wish to add a condition for.

2. Click on the **Validators** tab.

3. Click on the **Add** link. This will bring you to the **Add Validator To Transition** page, which lists all the available validators you can add.

4. Select the validator you wish to add.

5. Click on the **Add** button to add the validator.

6. Depending on the validator, you may be presented with the **Add Parameters To Validator** page where you can specify configuration options for the validator.

Similar to conditions, when there are multiple validators added to a transition, they form a validator group. But unlike conditions, you can only use logical AND for the group. This means in order for a transition to complete, every validator added to the transition must pass its validation criteria. Transitions cannot selectively pass validations by using logical OR.

Post functions

As their name suggests, post functions are functions that occur after (post) a transition has been executed. This allows you to perform additional processes once you have executed a transition. JIRA heavily uses post functions internally to perform a lot of its functions. For example, when an issue goes through a transition, JIRA uses post functions to update its search indexes so your search results reflect the change in issue status.

This means if a transition has failed to execute (for example, failing validation), post functions attached to the transition will not be triggered. The following table shows a list of post functions that come shipped with JIRA.

Post function	Description
Assign to Current User	Assigns the issue to the current user if the current user has the **Assignable User** permission.
Assign to Lead Developer	Assigns the issue to the project/component lead developer.
Assign to Reporter	Assigns the issue to the reporter.
Create Perforce Job Function	Creates a Perforce Job (if required) after completing the workflow transition.
Update Issue Field	Updates a simple issue field to a given value.

Adding a post function to transition

Transitions by default are created with several post functions. These post functions provide key services to JIRA's internal operations, so they cannot be deleted from the transition. These post functions are:

- Set issue status to the linked status of the destination workflow step
- Add a comment to an issue if one is entered during a transition
- Update change history for an issue and store the issue in the database
- Re-index and issue to keep indexes in sync with the database
- Fire an event that can be processed by the listeners

As you can see, these post functions provide some of the basic functions such as updating search index and setting issue's status after transition execution, which are essential in JIRA. Instead of making users manually add them in and risk the possibility of leaving one or more out, JIRA adds them for you automatically when you create a new transition. To create a new post function:

1. Browse to the **Manage Transition** page for the transition you wish to add a post function for.

2. Click on the **Post Functions** tab.

3. Click on the **Add** link. This will bring you to the **Add Post Function To Transition** page, which lists all the available post functions you can add.

4. Select the post function you wish to add.

5. Click on the **Add** button to add the post function.

6. Depending on the post function, you may be presented with the **Add Parameters To Function** page where you can specify configuration options for the post function.

Just like conditions and validators, multiple post functions form a **post function group** in a transition. After a transition is executed, each post function in the group is executed sequentially as they appear in the list, from top to bottom. If any post function in the group encounters an error during processing, you will receive an error.

Since post functions are executed sequentially and some of them have the abilities to modify values and perform other tasks, often, their sequence of execution becomes very important. For example, if you have a post function that changes the issue's assignee to the current user and another post function that updates an issue field's value with the issue's assignee, obviously the update assignee post function needs to occur first, so you need to make sure it is above the other post function.

You can move the positions of post functions up and down along the list by clicking the **Move Up** and **Move Down** links. Note that not all post functions can be repositioned.

Workflow schemes

While workflows define and model business processes, there still needs to be a way to tell JIRA what situations to apply the to workflows. As with other configurations in JIRA, this is achieved through the use of schemes. As we have seen in previous chapters, schemes act as self-contained, reusable configuration units that associate specific configuration options with projects and optional issue types.

A workflow scheme establishes the association between workflows and issue types. The scheme can then be applied to multiple projects. Once applied, the workflows within the scheme become active.

To view and manage workflow schemes:

1. Log into JIRA as a JIRA Administrator.
2. Click on **Administration** from the top menu bar.
3. Select **Workflow Schemes** from the left panel to bring up the **Workflow Schemes** page.

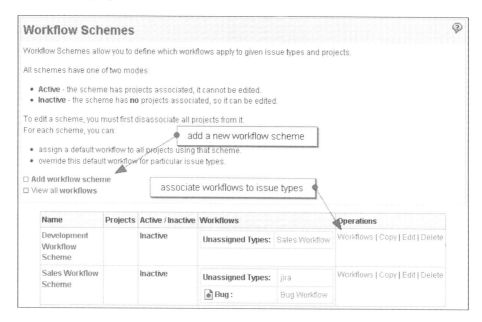

Creating a workflow scheme

JIRA allows you to create new workflow schemes in order to associate workflows to issue types. This allows you to group all your associations into a single re-usable unit (a scheme) that can be applied to multiple projects. To add a new workflow scheme:

1. Browse to the **Workflow Schemes** page.
2. Click on the **Add workflow scheme** link. This will take you to the **Add Workflow Scheme** page.
3. Provide a meaningful name for the new workflow scheme.
4. Provide an optional description.

5. Click on the **Add** button to create the workflow scheme.

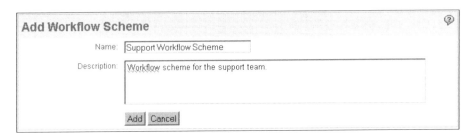

You will be taken back to the **Workflow Schemes** page once the new scheme has been created, and it will be listed in the table of available workflow schemes.

When you first create a new workflow scheme, the scheme is empty. This means it contains no associations of workflows and issue types. What you need to do next is to configure the associations by assigning workflows to issue types.

Configuring a workflow scheme

Workflow schemes contain associations between issue types and workflows. After you have created a workflow scheme, you need to configure and maintain the associations as your requirements change. For example, when a new issue type is added to the project using the workflow scheme, you may need to add an explicit association for the new issue type.

To configure a workflow scheme:

1. Browse to the **Workflow Schemes** page.
2. Click on the **Workflows** link for the workflow scheme you wish to configure. This will take you to the **Configure Workflows for Scheme** page.

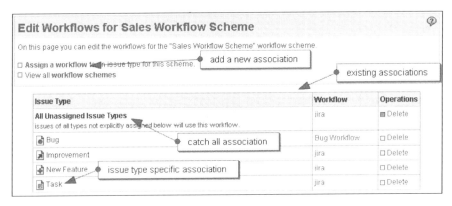

From this page, you will be able to see a list of existing associations, create new associations for issue types, and delete associations that are no longer relevant.

Assigning a workflow to issue type

Issue type and workflow have a many-to-one relationship. This means each issue type can be associated with one, and only one workflow, while one workflow can be associated with multiple issue types. This rule is applied on a per-workflow scheme basis, so you can have a different association of the same issue type in a different workflow scheme.

When you add a new association, JIRA will present you with a list of issue types that have no associations and a list of all available workflows. Once you have assigned a workflow to the issue type, it will not appear in the list again until you remove the original association.

Among the list of issue types, there is an option called **All Unassigned Issue Types**. This option acts as a catch-all option for issue types that do not have an explicit association. This is a very handy feature if all issue types in your project are to have the same workflow. Instead of mapping them out manually one by one, you can simply assign the workflow to all with this option. This option is also important as new issue types are added and assigned to a project. They will automatically be assigned to the catch-all workflow. If you do not have an **All Unassigned Issue Types** association, new or unassigned issue types will be assigned to use the default basic **jira** workflow. As with normal issue types, you can have only one catch-all association.

To add a new workflow association:

1. Browse to the **Configure Workflows for Scheme** page for the workflow you wish to configure.
2. Click on the **Assign a Workflow** link. This will take you to the **Add Workflow to Scheme** page.
3. Select the issue type to add an association for.
4. Select the workflow to associate to the issue type.
5. Click on the **Add** button to create the association.

Once an association has been added, you will be taken back to the **Configure Workflows for Scheme** page, and the new association will be listed in the table of associations.

Editing/Deleting an association

Once you have associated an issue type to a workflow in a scheme, you cannot add a new association for the same issue type. There is also no edit option to change the association. What you need to do is to delete the existing association and create a new one. To do so, follow these steps:

1. Browse to the **Configure Workflows for Scheme** page for the workflow you wish to configure.

2. Click on the **Delete** link for the association you wish to remove. This will take you to the **Delete Workflow Scheme Entity** page.

3. Click on the **Delete** button to confirm the removal.

Once an association is deleted, you will be able to create a new one for the issue type. If you do not assign a new workflow to the issue type, it will be given either the catch-all workflow (if present), or use the default **jira** workflow.

Editing a workflow scheme

You can maintain your workflow scheme's details by updating its name and description. Often a name that makes sense at one time may not few months later. JIRA allows you to make changes to the name and description of your workflow schemes if they are inactive. To edit an existing workflow scheme:

1. Browse to the **Workflow Schemes** page.

2. Click on the **Edit** link for the workflow scheme you wish to update. This will take you to the **Edit Workflow Scheme** page.

3. Update the name and description with new values.

4. Click on the **Update** button to apply the changes.

Deleting a workflow scheme

Unused workflow schemes can be deleted from JIRA. Workflow schemes can only be deleted if they are not being used by projects. You cannot delete workflow schemes if they are being used by one or more projects.

1. Browse to the **Workflow Schemes** page.
2. Click on the **Delete** link for the workflow scheme you wish to update. This will take you to the **Delete Workflow Scheme** page.
3. Click on the **Delete** button to remove the workflow scheme.

When you delete a workflow scheme, you are removing the associations from the system. The issue types and workflows are not affected.

Copying a workflow scheme

You can also make copies of existing workflow schemes. When you make a copy, all of the original scheme's associations will be copied over. Once copied, both copies exist as separate entities.

1. Browse to the **Workflow Schemes** page.
2. Click on the **Copy** link for the workflow scheme you wish to copy.

Unlike most other copy operations in JIRA, you will not be prompted with the **Copy** page asking for a new name and description of the new workflow scheme. Instead, JIRA will create a copy of the workflow scheme immediately, with a pre-defined name. For example, if you copied the workflow named jira, the copy would be called Copy of jira.

Copying workflow schemes can become really handy when you need to make configuration changes. As we have seen, you cannot configure or edit existing workflow schemes if they are active. Normally, this means you have to remove all the associations between projects and the workflow scheme one by one, before you can make your changes. As we will see later in the chapter, changing workflow associations can sometimes be rather disruptive.

A better approach is to first make a copy of the workflow scheme you wish to change, and apply your changes to the copy first. You then update the projects to use the new workflow scheme. This approach still requires you to update the projects one by one, but it offers the following advantages:

- Less disruptive to the users as the projects are not modified until the workflow scheme changes are ready

- An easier transition when updating projects to the new workflow scheme (as we will see later in this chapter)

- Provides you with a "sand pit" to experiment without risk, breaking the existing configurations

- Allows you to have a versioning system with the old and new workflow scheme (for example, the copied scheme can be named **Development Workflow Scheme 2.0**), letting you easily find and roll back to the old scheme

Activating a workflow scheme

Workflow schemes are inactive after they are created, by default. This means there are no projects in JIRA using the workflow scheme. To activate a workflow scheme, you need to select the scheme and apply it to a project.

When assigning a workflow scheme to a project, you need to go through a three-page process:

1. Select the project(s) that will be using the workflow scheme.

2. Click on the **Select** link for **Workflow Scheme**. This will bring up the **Associate Workflow Scheme to Project** page.

3. Select the workflow scheme to be used.

4. Click on the **Associate** button. This will bring up the association confirmation page.

On the confirmation page, depending on the differences between the current and new workflow, you will be prompted to make migration decisions for existing issues. For example, if the current workflow has a step called **Reopened** and the new workflow does not (or it has something equivalent but with a different ID), you need to specify the new step to place the issues that are currently in the **Reopened** step. Once mapped, JIRA will start migrating existing issues to the new step.

1. Select new workflow steps for existing issues that are in steps that do not exist in the new workflow.

2. Click on the **Associate** button to start the migration.

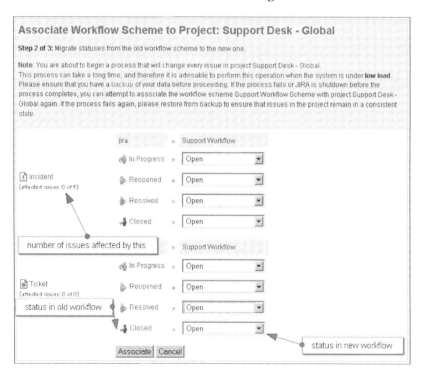

Once the migration starts, JIRA displays a progress bar showing you the progress. Depending on the number of issues that need to be migrated, this process may take some time. It is recommended to allocate a time frame to perform this task as it can be quite resource-intensive for large instances.

Help Desk Project

We have seen the power of workflow and how we can enhance the usefulness of JIRA by adapting to everyday business processes. With our Help Desk project, as with most support-oriented systems, it is often the case that our help desk staff will require more information from the business user who has submitted the support ticket to help further diagnose and finally solve the problem. Our requirements for the business process would then include:

- Ability for support staff to request more information from the business user
- Allowing business users to re-assign the ticket back after the request information is supplied

Furthermore, as a bonus, it will be ideal to automate certain aspects of this process. For example, whenever our help desk staff requests for information, he/she will not need to decide who to assign the ticket to, but rather, let the system work it out. The same can be applied to the business user so when he/she re-submit the ticket, it will be re-assigned accordingly. As we will see in the next chapter, this level of automation not only enhances the user experience, it is also very useful when facilitating communication between parties involved.

Setting up issue status

The first task while setting up our workflow is to make sure we have the issue statuses prepared so we can map them to steps. From our requirements, we need to create a new step, which represents waiting for additional information from the business users, so we will need to create the issue status for this.

We learned how to manage issue statuses from *Chapter 2, Project Management*, so if you have skipped or forgotten some of the steps, now will be a good time for a refresh. To set the issue status up, follow these steps:

1. Log in to JIRA as a JIRA Administrator.
2. Click on **Administration** from the top menu bar.
3. Select **Statuses** from the left panel to bring up the **View Statuses** page.
4. Name our new status **Waiting for Info**.
5. Provide a helpful description like **The issue is waiting for additional information from users**.
6. Choose `/images/icons/status_needinfo.gif` for **Icon URL**.
7. Click on the **Add** button to create the new status.

Now that we have our status, we can use that as the linked status for our workflow step.

Setting up the workflow

Now it is time to create our new workflow. Since our requirements state that we need to have an extra step that will allow our help desk team to re-assign the issue back to the business user (reporter), instead of creating a workflow from scratch, we will make a copy of the existing workflow as a template, and modify its configuration. This is usually the preferred approach as it saves you the time to set up some of the common transitions.

The first step is to create a workflow for the help desk team:

1. Log into JIRA as a JIRA Administrator.
2. Click on **Administration** from the top menu bar.
3. Select **Workflows** from the left panel to bring up the **View Workflows** page.
4. Click on the **Copy** link for the **jira** workflow.
5. Name the new workflow **Help Desk Workflow**.
6. Provide a helpful description like **Workflow for the help desk team**.
7. Click on the **Copy** button to create our workflow.

The next step is to add in the extra steps we have.

1. Click on the **Steps** link for **Support Workflow**.
2. Name our new step **Waiting for Info**.
3. Select **Waiting for Info** for the **Linked Status**.
4. Click the **Add** button to create the workflow step.

Now that we have our step added to our workflow, we need a way for our help desk team to get there, and the answer is to add a new transition. What we need is to be able to ask users for more information once our team has started working on the issue, and once the business users provide the information, the issue can then be handed back to the help desk team. What we need to do is to add a new transition to the **In Progress** step that will link to the new **Waiting for Info** step.

1. Click on the **Add Transition** link for the **In Progress** step. This will bring up the **Add Workflow Transition** page.
2. Name the new transition **Request for Info**.
3. Provide a helpful description like **Request the business user for additional information**.
4. Select **Waiting for Info** as the **Destination Step**.
5. Select **No view for transition**.
6. Click on the **Add** button to create the transition.

We will also need to add another transition that will link the issue back to **In Progress** when the business users have provided the requested information.

1. Click on the **Add Transition** link for the **Waiting for Info** step.
2. Name the new transition **Re-submit**.
3. Provide a helpful description like **Re-submitting the ticket back to support**.
4. Select **In Progress** as the **Destination Step**.
5. Select **No view for transition**.
6. Click on the **Add** button to create the transition.

With this setup, our team can continue to request for information if required. Now we will want to make sure that only the currently assigned help desk team member can request business user for more information, and to automatically re-assign the issue back to the business user (reporter) so he/she will be notified. This means we need to add a condition and a post function to our transition.

1. Click on the **Request for Info** transition link for the **In Progress** step.
2. Click on the **Conditions** tab.
3. Click on the **Add** link to bring up the **Add Condition To Transition** page.
4. Select **Only Assignee Condition**.
5. Click on the **Add** button to add the condition.
6. Click on the **Post Functions** tab.
7. Click on the **Add** link.
8. Select **Assign to Reporter**.
9. Click on **Add** to add the post function to the transition.

Now, only the team member who is the currently assigned the ticket will be able to request the business user for information, and when they do, the ticket will be automatically re-assigned back to the business user. We will also need to do the same for the **Re-submit** transition, so when the business user provides the requested information, the issue will be re-assigned back to the help desk team.

1. Click on the **Re-submit** transition link for the **In Progress** step.
2. Click on the **Post Functions** tab.
3. Click on the **Add** link to bring up the **Add Post Function To Transition** page.
4. Select **Assign to Lead Developer**.
5. Click on **Add** to add the post function to the transition.

Setting up a workflow scheme

Without a workflow in place and set up, JIRA will not know which issue types need to use our new workflow, so we need to create a new workflow scheme.

1. Browse to the **Workflow Schemes** page.
2. Click on the **Add workflow scheme** link
3. Name the new workflow scheme **Help Desk Workflow Scheme**.
4. Provide a helpful description like **Workflow Scheme for the support desk team**.
5. Click on the **Add** button to create the workflow scheme.

We now need to associate our new support workflow with the appropriate issue type:

1. Click on the **Workflows** link for **Support Workflow Scheme**.
2. Click on the **Assign a workflow** link to bring up the **Add Workflow to Scheme** page.
3. Select **Incident** for **Issue Type**.
4. Select **Help Desk Workflow** for **Workflow**.
5. Click on **Add** to create the association.
6. Repeat this for **Ticket issue type**.
7. Create another association for **All Unassigned Issue Types**. This time, select **jira** as the workflow.

This associates our new workflow with the issue types specifically for our help desk team project and uses the default workflow for the others.

Putting it all together

We have created statuses, workflows, and workflow schemes. All we have to do now is to tell our project to use them all, and this is the easiest part.

1. Browse to the **Project Administration** page for our **Help Desk** project.
2. Click on the **Select** link for **Workflow Scheme**.
3. Select **Help Desk Workflow Scheme** and click on the **Associate** button.
4. Click on the **Associate** button again in the next screen for JIRA to migrate all existing issues to use the new workflow.

Wait for JIRA to finish migrating the existing issue and that's it, all done! We can now create a new ticket and start testing our implementation. Since we need to simulate a scenario where a business user submits a ticket to the help desk team, we need to create a new business user. We will look at user management and security in *Chapter 8, Securing your JIRA*. For now, we will simply add a new user to our system.

1. Log into JIRA as a JIRA Administrator.
2. Click on **Administration** from the top menu bar.
3. Select **User Browser** from the left panel to bring up the **User Browser** page.
4. Click on the **Add User** link to bring up the **Create New User** page.
5. Name the new user **john.doe (John Doe)**.
6. Set the password and e-mail for this new user.

7. Uncheck the **Send Password Email** option.

8. Click on the **Create** button to create the user.

Now log into JIRA as our new business user, **john.doe** and create a new incident. After you have created the incident issue, you will notice that you cannot execute any transitions. This is because the issue is not currently assigned to you. You need to be the assignee of the issue (member of the help desk team) to start working on the issue. Log out and log back in as a member of the team (admin).

Once logged in, you will see that familiar transitions such as **Start Progress** and **Resolve Issue** are once more available. If you click on the **Workflow** drop-down box, you will also see that our new **Request for Info** transition is listed.

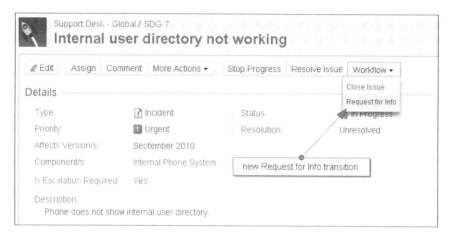

Executing that transition will place the issue in the **Waiting for Info** status and the **Assignee** automatically changed to **John Doe**, the reporter of the issue.

Try re-submitting the issue as the business user and you will see that the issue will be re-assigned back to the Administrator.

You will notice right now, even as a member of the help desk team, you are able to re-submit the issue, which is not ideal. As an exercise, add a validation rule so that only the business user will be able to re-submit the issue back.

Summary

In this chapter, we looked at how JIRA can be customized to adapt to your organization. In the heart of this powerful feature is a robust workflow system that allows you to model JIRA workflows based on existing business processes. We also looked at the various components within a workflow and how to perform validations, as well as post processing, which provides a level of process automation. In the next chapter, we will look at how we can combine the power of workflow and its event-driven system to facilitate communication through JIRA's notifications and e-mail system.

7
E-mail and Notification

So far, we have learned how to use and interact with JIRA directly from its web interface through a web browser. However, you are not restricted only to a web browser; you can communicate with JIRA through e-mails.

One powerful feature of JIRA is its ability to update the users of their issue's progress automatically through e-mails, as well as the ability to create and comment on issues through e-mails sent from the user. This provides you with a whole new option of how you and your users can interact with JIRA. By the end of the chapter, you will have learned:

- How to set up a mail server in JIRA
- About mail handlers
- How to create issues and comments by sending e-mails to JIRA
- About events, and how they are related to notifications
- How to configure JIRA to send out notifications based on events

JIRA and E-mail

E-mail has become one of the most important communication tools in today's world. Businesses and individuals rely on e-mails to send and receive information around the world almost instantly. It should come as no surprise that JIRA comes fully equipped and integrated with e-mail support.

JIRA's e-mail support comes in several flavors. First, JIRA can send out e-mails to users to notify them of actions being performed on their issues, to keep them updated with their issues progress. Second, JIRA can also poll mailboxes for e-mails and create issues and comments based on their contents. The third feature is the ability for users to create and subscribe filters to set up feeds in JIRA (we will discuss filters in *Chapter 9*). These features open up a whole new dimension on how users can interact with JIRA.

In the following sections, we will look at what you need to do to enable JIRA's powerful e-mail support and also explore the tools and options at your disposal to configure JIRA to "e-mail it" your way. The following diagram shows how JIRA interacts with various mail servers:

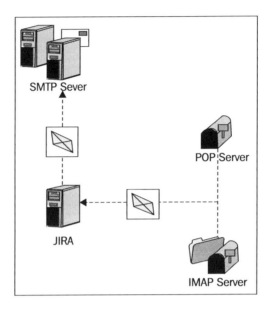

Mail servers

In order for JIRA to communicate through e-mails, you need to configure or register your mail servers in JIRA. There are two types of mail servers you need to configure:

- SMTP: This is the mail server used to send e-mails.
- POP/IMAP: This is the mail server that JIRA uses to retrieve e-mails.

JIRA will only let you to set up one SMTP mail server which will be used as the primary mail server to send out e-mails. You can configure any number of POP/IMAP mail servers. This allows JIRA to pick up e-mails from multiple sources.

Mail server configuration details are maintained by the JIRA administrator.

1. Log into JIRA as a JIRA Administrator.
2. Click **Administration** from the top menu bar.
3. Select **Mail Servers** from the left panel to bring up the **Mail Servers** page.

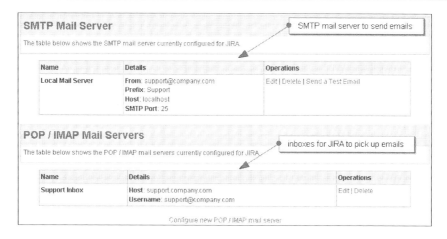

The page lists all the mail servers that are currently registered in JIRA.

Adding an SMTP mail server

There are two ways to add an SMTP mail server in JIRA, but regardless of which option you take, there are first some common configuration parameters you will need to fill in. The following table shows those parameters in italics:

Field	Description
Name	A name for this mail server.
Description	A brief description for the mail server.
From address	The e-mail address that outgoing mails will appear to have come from.
Email prefix	The prefix that will appear in all e-mails sent from JIRA. This allows your users to set up filter rules in their mail clients. The prefix will be added to the beginning of the e-mail's subject.
Host Name	The host name of your mail server (for example, smtp.example.com).
SMTP Port	The port number your mail server is running on. This is optional; if left blank, default port number 25 will be used.
Username	Username used to authenticate against the mail server, if required. Note: Mail servers may require authentication to relay mail to non-local users.
Password	Password for the user to authenticate against the mail server, if required.
JNDI Location	The JNDI lookup name if you already have a mail server configured for your application server. Please refer to the following section for details.

For the rest of the parameters, depending on which option you take to set up your mail server, you only need to fill in the ones that are appropriate.

The first option is to specify the mail server's details such as its host name and port number directly in JIRA. This is usually the approach that most people will use as it is simple and straightforward. With this approach, the administrator fills in the mail server's host information. To configure the mail server's details:

1. Browse to the **Mail Servers** page.

2. Click on the **Configure new SMTP mail server** link under the **SMTP Mail Server** section. This will bring you to the **Add SMTP Mail Server** page.

3. Fill in the details of your mail server including the host name, port number, username, and password.

4. Click on the **Add** button to register the mail server.

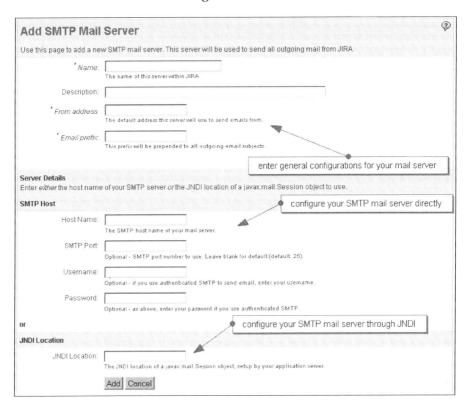

The second option is to use JNDI. This approach is slightly more complicated as this requires configuration on the application server itself (which is different per application server), and sometimes require a restart of the application server.

If you are using the standalone distribution which uses Tomcat, the JNDI location will be `java:comp/env/mail/JiraMailServer`. You will also need to specify the mail server details as a JNDI resource in the `server.xml` file in the `JIRA_INSTALL/conf` directory.

A sample declaration for Apache Tomcat is shown below. You will need to substitute your mail server's details in the parameters' values. If you are using a different application server such as IBM WebSphere, you will need to consult your user manual.

```
<Resource name="mail/JiraMailServer"
    auth="Container"
    type="javax.mail.Session"
    mail.smtp.host="mail.server.host"
    mail.smtp.port="25"
    mail.transport.protocol="smtp"
    mail.smtp.auth="true"
    mail.smtp.user="username"
    password="password" />
```

You will need to restart JIRA after you have saved your changes.

Enabling SMTP over SSL

To increase security, you can encrypt the communication between JIRA and your mail server if SSL is supported by your mail server. There are two steps involved in enabling SMTP over SSL in JIRA.

The first step is to import your mail server's SSL certificate into Java's trust store. You can do this with Java's keytool utility. On a Windows machine, run the following command in a command prompt:

```
Keytool -import -alias mail.yourcompany.com -keystore $JAVA_HOME/jre/lib/
security/cacerts -file yourcertificate
```

The second step is to configure your application server to use SSL for mail communication. The declaration below is for Apache Tomcat which is used by JIRA Standalone. We use the same configuration file and only need to add two additional parameters.

```
<Resource name="mail/JiraMailServer"
    auth="Container"
    type="javax.mail.Session"
    mail.smtp.host="mail.server.host"
    mail.smtp.port="25"
    mail.transport.protocol="smtp"
```

```
mail.smtp.auth="true"
mail.smtp.user="username"
password="password"
mail.smtp.atarttls.enabled="true"
mail.smtp.socketFactory.class="javax.net.ssl.SSLSocketFactory" />
```

Once you have imported your certificate and configured your mail server, you will have to restart JIRA.

Sending a test e-mail

It is always a good idea to send a test e-mail after you have configured your SMTP mail server to make sure the server is running and you have set it correctly in JIRA. To do this, follow these steps:

1. Browse to the **Mail Servers** page.

2. Click on the **Send a Test Email** link for SMTP mail server. This will take you to the **Send Mail** page.

3. Click on the **Send** button to send the e-mail. JIRA should auto-fill the **To address** based on your user profile.

If everything is correct, you should see a confirmation message in the **Mail log** section and receive the e-mail in your inbox. If there are errors such as with the mail server connection, the **Mail log** section will display the problems.

Mail queue

E-mails in JIRA are not sent immediately when an operation is performed. Instead, e-mails are placed on a mail queue, which JIRA empties periodically (every minute). This is very similar to the real-life scenario where mail is placed in the post boxes and picked up every day. There are two advantages with this approach.

Viewing the mail queue

Normally you do not need to manage the mail queue. JIRA automatically places e-mails into the queue and sends them out periodically. However, as an administrator, there may be times when you wish to inspect the current queue and check if there are e-mails that are "stuck" and cannot be sent. E-mails can become stuck for a number of reasons. For example, if the configured SMTP mail server is not accessible, JIRA will automatically retry.

To view the mail queue and the e-mails it contains:

1. Log into JIRA as a JIRA Administrator.
2. Click on **Administration** from the top menu bar.
3. Select **Mail Queue** from the left panel to bring up the **Mail Queue** page.

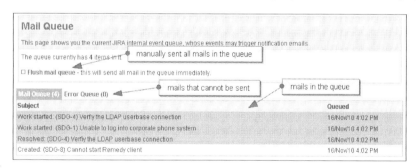

This page provides you with a one-page view of the current e-mails in the queue waiting to be delivered. There are two queues, the main mail queue and the error queue.

The main mail queue contains all the e-mails that are pending to be delivered. If JIRA is able to successfully deliver the e-mails, they will be removed from the queue. Items listed in red are e-mails that JIRA has attempted unsuccessfully to send. JIRA will retry ten times, if still unsuccessful, these items will be moved to the error queue.

The error queue contains e-mails that cannot be delivered by JIRA. You can choose to resend or delete all the failed items in the error queue.

Flushing the mail queue

While JIRA automatically flushes the mail queue, you can also manually flush it if the queue gets stuck or you need to send out e-mails immediately. When you manually flush the queue, JIRA will attempt to send out all e-mails in it.

To manually flush the mail queue:

1. Browse to the **Mail Queue** page.
2. Click on the **Flush mail queue** link.

If JIRA is successful at sending the e-mails, you will see the queue shrink and the items disappear. If for some reason some e-mails fail to be delivered, those items will be highlighted in red.

Events

JIRA is an event-driven system. What this means is that when an action occurs, for example, when an issue is created, JIRA fires off a corresponding event. This event is then picked up by components that are designed to listen for the event. Not surprisingly, they are called **listeners**. When a listener picks up an event, it will perform its duty, such as keeping issues up to date with changes or sending an e-mail to users watching the issue.

This mechanism allows JIRA to process operations asynchronously. The advantage of this model is operations such as sending e-mails are separated to JIRA's core functions like issue creation. If there is a problem with the mail server for example, you will not want this problem to prevent your users to log issues.

There are two types of events in JIRA:

- **System event**: Internal events used by JIRA, usually representing the main functionalities in JIRA. They cannot be added, edited, or deleted.
- **Custom event**: Events that are created by users. They can be added and deleted and are fired via a workflow's post functions.

The following table lists all the system events in JIRA and what they are used for.

Event	Description
Issue Created	An issue has been created in JIRA.
Issue Updated	An issue has been updated (for example, changes to its fields).
Issue Assigned	An issue has been assigned to a user.
Issue Resolved	An issue has been resolved (usually applied to the **Resolve** workflow transition).
Issue Closed	An issue has been closed (usually applied to the **Closed** workflow transition).
Issue Commented	A comment has been added to an issue.
Issue Comment Edited	A comment has been edited.
Issue Reopened	An issue has been reopened (usually applied to the **Re-open** workflow transition).
Issue Deleted	An issue has been deleted from JIRA.
Issue Moved	An issue has been moved (to a different or the same project. The latter is sometimes used to change the issue's type).
Work Logged On Issue	Time has been logged on this issue (if time tracking has been enabled).
Work Started On Issue	The assignee has started working on this issue (usually applied to the **Start Progress** workflow transition).
Work Stopped On Issue	The assignee has stopped working on this issue (usually applied to the **Stop Progress** workflow transition).
Issue Worklog Updated	Worklog has been updated (if time tracking has been enabled).
Issue Worklog Deleted	Worklog has been deleted (if time tracking has been enabled).
Generic Event	A generic event that can be used by any workflow post function.
Custom Event	Events created by user to represent arbitrary events generated by business processes.

As an administrator, you will be able to get a one-page view of all the events in JIRA.

1. Log into JIRA as a JIRA Administrator.
2. Click on **Administration** from the top menu bar.
3. Select **Events** from the left panel to bring up the **View Events** page.

Like most other entities in JIRA such as screens, events can be either **active** or **inactive**. New events are inactive by default and they need to be associated with a notification scheme or workflow post function to become active. While you cannot edit or delete system events, you can inactivate them by removing their association with notification schemes and workflow post functions.

Each event is associated with a template, referred to as a **mail template**. These templates contain the base e-mail contents when notifications are sent. For the system events, you cannot change their templates (you can change the template files, however). For custom events, you can choose to use one of the existing templates or create your own mail template.

Adding a mail template

Mail templates are physical files that you create and edit directly via a text editor. Each mail template is made up of three files:

- **Subject**: This file contains the template used to generate the e-mail subject.
- **Text template**: This file contains the template used by JIRA when the e-mail is sent as plain text.
- **HTML template**: This file contains the template used by JIRA when the e-mail is sent as HTML.

Mail templates are stored in the `<JIRA_INSTALL>/atlassian-jira/WEB-INF/classes/templates/email` directory. Each of the three files listed above are placed in their respective directories called `subject`, `text`, and `HTML`.

When creating new mail templates, it is good practice to name your template files after the issue event. This will help future users understand the purpose of the templates.

Mail templates use Apache Jakarta's Velocity template language. For this reason, creating new mail templates will require some understanding of HTML and template programming.

If your templates only contain static text, you can simply use standard HTML tags for your template. However, if you need to have dynamic data rendered as part of your templates, such as the issue key or summary, you will need to use Velocity syntax. A full explanation of Velocity is beyond the scope of this book. The following section provides a quick introduction to creating simple mail templates for JIRA. You can find more information on Velocity and its usage in the JIRA mail templates at:

`http://confluence.atlassian.com/display/JIRA/Customising+Email+Content`.

In a Velocity template, all text will be treated as if they are normal. Anything that starts with a dollar sign ($) such as `$issue` is a Velocity statement. The $ sign tells Velocity to reference the item after the sign, and when combined with a period (.), you are able to retrieve the value specified. For example, the following snippet will get the issue key and summary from the current issue, separated by a "-" character.

```
$issue.key - $issue.summary
```

JIRA provides a range of Velocity references you can use for creating mail templates. You can find a comprehensive list at:

```
http://confluence.atlassian.com/display/JIRA/Velocity+Context+for+Ema
il+Templates.
```

Now that we have a brief understanding of how Velocity works, we first need to create a template for the mail subject. The snippet below shows a typical subject template.

```
$eventTypeName: ($issue.key) $issue.summary
```

When the template is processed, JIRA will substitute in the actual values for the event type (for example, **Issue Created**), issue key, and issue summary. For example, "Issue Escalated: HD-11 – Database server is running very slow".

We then need to create a template for the actual e-mail content. We need to create both a text and HTML version. The following snippet shows a simple example of text-based template which displays the key for the escalated issue.

```
Hello,

The ticket $issue.key has been escalated and is currently being
worked on.  We will contact you if we require more information.

Regards
Support team.
```

When JIRA sends out the e-mail, all text will be preserved as-is, with the issue key substituted in at where `$issue.key` is.

After you have created your mail templates, you must register them with JIRA. To register your new templates, locate and open the `email-templates-id-mappings.xml` file from the `<JIRA_INSTALL>/atlassian-jira/WEB-INF/classes` directory in a text editor. Add a new entry to the end of the file before the closing `</templatemappings>` tag, as shown in the following snippet:

```
<templatemapping id="10001">
    <name>Example Custom Event</name>
    <template>examplecustomevent.vm</template>
    <templatetype>issueevent</templatetype>
</templatemapping>
```

Here we have registered a new custom mail template entry. The following table explains the parameters in the file:

Parameter	Description
ID	The unique ID for the template.
Name	A human-readable name for JIRA to display.
Template	The mail template file names for subject, text, and html. All three template files must be named as specified here.
Type	Template type. For events generated from an issue, the value will be **issueevent**.

After you have created your templates and registered them in the mapping file, you will have to restart JIRA for the changes to be picked up.

Adding a custom event

JIRA comes with a comprehensive list of system events focused around issue-related operations. However, there will be times when you will need to create custom-designed events that represent specialized business operations, or you may simply need to use a custom e-mail template.

To add a new custom event:

1. Browse to the **View Events** page.
2. Provide a meaningful name for the new event in the **Add New Event** section.
3. Provide an optional description.
4. Select the mail template for the new event.
5. Click on the **Add** button to create the new event.

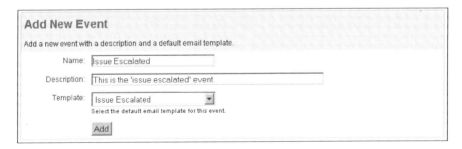

New events are inactive by default. Associating them with a notification scheme or workflow post function will activate them.

Firing a custom event

Unlike system events, with custom events you need to tell JIRA when it should fire.

Custom events are mostly fired by workflow transitions. If you recall from *Chapter 6, Workflow and Business Process*, you can add post functions to workflow transitions. Almost all of JIRA's transitions will have a post function that fires an appropriate event. It is important to understand that just because an event is fired it does not mean there needs to be something to listen for it.

If you have skipped *Chapter 6* or still do not have a good understanding of workflows, now would be a good time to go back and revisit the chapter.

To fire a custom event from a workflow post function:

1. Browse to the **View Workflows** page.
2. Create a **draft** of the workflow if it is active or click on the **Steps** link if the workflow is inactive.
3. Click on the transition that will fire the event when executed.
4. Click the **Post Functions** tab.
5. Click on the **Edit** link for the post function that reads **Fire a <event name>** event that can be processed by the listeners.

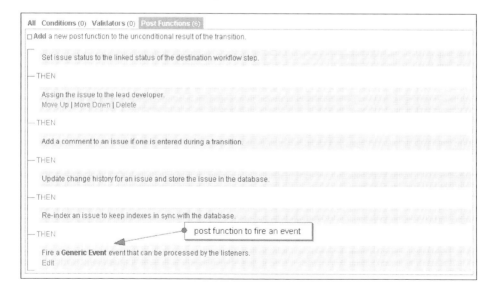

6. Select the custom event from the drop-down list.
7. Click on the **Update** button to apply the change to the post function.

8. Publish the workflow.

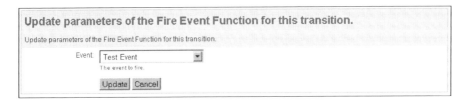

Now, whenever the workflow transition is executed, the post function will run and fire the selected event. Each transition can only fire one event, so you cannot have both **Issue Created** and **Issue Updated** events being fired from the one transition.

Notifications

Notifications associate events (both system and custom) to e-mail recipients. When an event is fired and picked up, e-mails will be sent out. Notification recipients are defined by notification types. For example, you can set them to only send e-mails to a specific user or all members from a given user group. You can add multiple notifications to a given event.

JIRA ships with a comprehensive list of notification types that will cover almost all of your needs. The following table lists all the notification types available and how they work.

Notification type	Description
Current Assignee	The current assignee of the issue.
Reporter	The reporter of the issue (usually the person who originally created the issue).
Current User	The user who fired the event.
Project Lead	Lead of the project that the issue belongs to.
Component Lead	Lead of the component the issue belongs to.
Single User	Any user that exists in JIRA.
Group	All users that belong to the specified group.
Project Role	All users that belong to the specified project role.
Single Email Address	Any e-mail address.
All Watchers	All users that are watching this issue.

Notification type	Description
User Custom Field Value	The users specified in the user type custom field. For example, if you have a user picker custom field called **Recipient**, the user selected in the custom field will received notifications if he/she has access to the issue.
Group Custom Field Value	All users that belong to the group in the group type custom field. For example, if you have a group picker custom field called **Approvers**, all users from the group (with access to the issue) selected in the custom field will receive notifications.

As you can see, the list includes a wide range of options, ranging from issue reporters to values contained in custom fields. Basically, anything that can be represented as a user in JIRA can have notifications set up.

If a user belongs to more than one notification for a single event, JIRA will make sure that only one e-mail will be sent so the user does not receive duplicates. In order for a user to receive notifications, the user must have permission to view the issue. The only exception to this is when using the **Single Email Address** option (we will discuss security in *Chapter 8, Securing your JIRA*). If the user does not have permission to view the issue, JIRA will not send a notification e-mail.

We will look at how you can add notifications to events so users can start receiving e-mails, but before that, we need to first take a look at what links them together, a **notification scheme**.

Notification schemes

A notification scheme is a reusable entity that links events with notifications. In other words, it contains the associations between events and their respective e-mail recipients.

1. Log into JIRA as a JIRA Administrator.

2. Click on **Administration** from the top menu bar.

3. Select **Notification Schemes** from the left panel to bring up the **Notification Schemes** page.

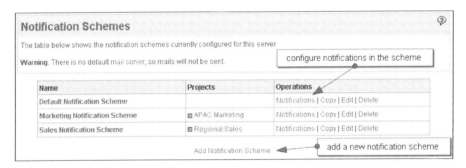

From this screen, you can see a list of all the notification schemes and what projects are currently using them.

JIRA comes with a generic **Default Notification Scheme**. The default scheme is set up with notifications set for all the system events. This allows you to enable notifications in JIRA quickly. The default setup has the following notifications:

*   Current Assignee
*   Reporter
*   All Watchers

You can modify the default notification scheme to add your own notification rules, but it is a better idea to create a new scheme from scratch or copy the default scheme and make your modifications.

Adding a notification scheme

As with all other aspects in JIRA, you are not forced to use the default configurations provided. JIRA allows you to create your own custom notification schemes to set up customized notification rules that can be applied to your projects.

To create a new notification scheme:

1. Browse to the **Notification Schemes** page.
2. Click on the **Add Notification Scheme** link. This will bring you to the **Add Notification Scheme** page.
3. Provide a meaningful name for the new notification scheme.
4. Provide an optional description that will help explain the purpose and usage of the new scheme.
5. Click on the **Add** button to create the notification scheme.

When you create a new notification scheme, you are creating a blank scheme in which you can later configure and add your own notification rules. It is important that after you create a new notification scheme to configure its notification rules before applying the scheme to projects, otherwise no notifications will be sent out. We will look at how to configure notification rules later in this chapter.

Editing a notification scheme

You can keep your notification scheme's name and description up-to-date through editing. Do not confuse this with updating the scheme's configuration. Just like other schemes, a notification scheme's name and description details are kept and managed separately from its configuration details.

To edit a notification scheme:

1. Browse to the **Notification Schemes** page.
2. Click on the **Edit** link for the notification scheme you wish to update. This will bring up the **Edit Notification Scheme** page.
3. Provide new name and description.
4. Click on the **Update** button to apply the changes.

You can make updates to the notification scheme at any time regardless of whether it is being used by projects.

Deleting a notification scheme

Unlike most other schemes such as workflow schemes, JIRA allows you to delete notification schemes even when they are being used by projects. However, JIRA does prompt you with a warning when you attempt to delete a notification scheme that is in use.

To delete a notification scheme:

1. Browse to the **Notification Schemes** page.
2. Click on the **Delete** link for the notification scheme you wish to remove. This will bring up the **Delete Notification Scheme** page.
3. Click on the **Delete** button to remove the notification scheme.

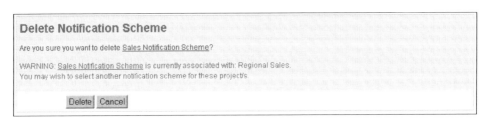

Once you have deleted a notification scheme, the projects that were previously using the scheme will have no notification schemes, so you will have to reapply other schemes individually.

When you delete a notification scheme, you are removing all the notifications you have set up in the scheme. It is always a good idea to have a backup (for example, by making a clone of the scheme) before deleting the scheme.

Copying a notification Scheme

It is always a good idea to make a backup copy of your notification schemes before making changes or deleting them. This allows you to quickly roll back your changes if problems are detected. Another benefit of copying an existing notification scheme is the amount of time it can save. As we have seen, when you create a new notification scheme from scratch, it will contain no notifications. Most of the time, it will be more efficient to use the default notification scheme provided by JIRA as a base and modify the notification rules accordingly.

Whatever the reason, you will find the ability to make copies of existing notification schemes to be handy from time to time. To copy a notification scheme:

1. Browse to the **Notification Schemes** page.
2. Click on the **Copy** link for the notification scheme you wish to copy. A copy of the notification scheme will be made immediately with name **Copy of** appended to the beginning of the original notification scheme's name.

Once you have copied the notification scheme, you can edit its name and description to better describe its purpose, and configure its notifications as explained in the next sections.

Managing a notification scheme

Notification schemes contain notifications that are set on events in JIRA.

To configure a notification scheme:

1. Browse to the **Notification Schemes** page.

2. Click on the **Notifications** link for the notification scheme you wish to configure. This will bring you to the **Edit Notifications** page.

This page lists all the existing events in JIRA and their corresponding notification recipients. If you are configuring a new notification scheme, there will be no notifications set for the events.

Adding a notification

There are two ways you can add a new notification. You can add a notification for a specific event, or you can add a notification for multiple events.

To add a new notification:

1. Browse to the **Edit Notifications** page for the notification scheme you wish to configure.

2. Click on the **Add notification** link or the **Add** link for the event you wish to add a notification for. This will bring you to the **Add Notification** page. If you click on the **Add** link, the **Events** select list will preselect the event for you.

3. Select the notification type from the available options.

4. Click on the **Add** button.

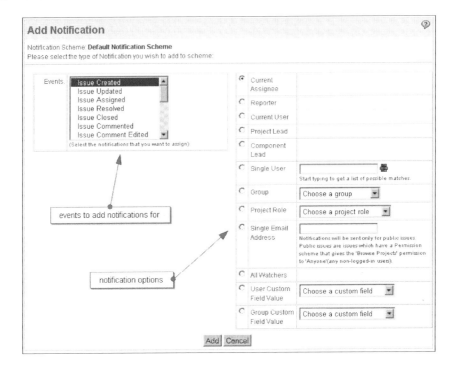

Once added, the notification will be listed against the events selected. You can continue to add notifications for the events by repeating the same steps.

Deleting a notification

When notifications are no longer required for certain events, you can also have them removed. To remove notifications, you will need to do it one by one, per event, by following these steps:

1. Browse to the **Edit Notifications** page for the notification scheme you wish to configure.

2. Click on the **Delete** link for the notification you wish to remove. This will bring you to the **Delete Notification** page.

3. Click on the **Delete** button to remove the notification for the event.

After you have removed a notification, users affected by that notification will stop receiving e-mails from JIRA. However, you need to pay attention to your configurations as there might be other notifications for the same event that will continue to send e-mails to the same user. For example, if you have created two notifications for the event **Issue Created**, one set to **Single User admin** (who belongs to the jira-administrator group), and another set to **Group** (jira-administrator). If your goal to is prevent e-mails being sent to the user admin, you will need to remove both notifications from the event instead of simply the **Single User** option.

Assigning a notification scheme

Notification schemes need to be assigned to projects for their notifications to be used. There are two ways you can assign a notification scheme to a project.

The first way is when a project is being created. When you create a project, you have the option to select a notification scheme. By default, the project will have no notification scheme. This means no e-mail notifications will be sent out for activities that happen within the project.

Then second option is going to the project administrator page to update the notification scheme.

1. Select the project that will be using the notification scheme.

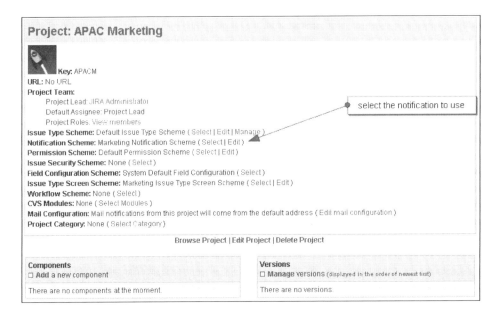

2. Click on the **Select** link for **Notification Scheme**. This will bring up the **Associate Notification Scheme to Project** page.

3. Select the notification scheme to use.
4. Click on the **Associate** button.

As soon as a notification scheme is applied to the project, it will take effect immediately and you will see e-mails being sent out for the events that have been configured in the scheme.

Like any other schemes in JIRA, notification schemes can be assigned to multiple projects to share the same notification behavior.

Receiving E-mails

We have seen how you can configure JIRA to send e-mails to notify users of updates on their issues, but this is only half of the story when it comes to JIRA's e-mail support.

You can also set up JIRA for it to periodically poll mailboxes for e-mails and create issues based on the email's subject and content. This is a very powerful feature as it:

- Hides the complexity of JIRA from business users so they can log issues more efficiently and leave the complexity to your IT team.

- Allows users to create issues even if JIRA can only be accessed within the internal network. Users can send e-mails to a dedicated mailbox for JIRA to poll.

Adding a POP/IMAP mail server

For JIRA to retrieve e-mails and create issues from them, you need to add POP/ IMAP mail servers to JIRA. POP and IMAP are mail protocols used to retrieve e-mails from a server. E-mail clients such as Microsoft Outlook and Mozilla Thunderbird can use one of these protocols to retrieve your e-mails.

Unlike SMTP mail servers, JIRA allows you to add multiple POP/IMAP mail servers. This is because while you only need one mail server to send e-mails, you might have multiple mail servers or multiple mail accounts (on the same server) that people will send e-mails to. For example, you might have one dedicated to support and another one for sales. It is usually a good idea to create separate mail accounts so they do not get mixed up. Adding POP/IMAP mail servers can be thought of as adding multiple mail accounts in JIRA.

To add a POP/IMAP mail server:

1. Browse to the Mail Servers page.
2. Click on the **Configure POP/IMAP mail server** link under the **POP/IMAP Mail Servers** section. This will bring you to the **Add POP/IMAP Mail Server** page.
3. Provide a meaningful name for the mail server.
4. Provide an optional description.
5. Specify the host name of the POP/IMAP server.
6. Enter the username/password credentials for the mail account.

7. Click on the **Add** button to create the POP/IMAP mail server.

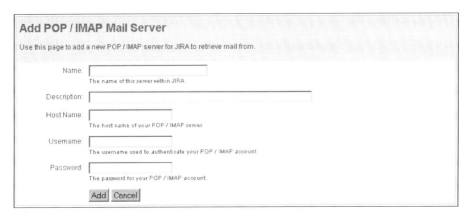

You can repeat this and add additional POP/IMAP mail servers.

Mail handlers

This is sometimes referred to as **services**, as these are periodic functions that JIRA runs to perform specific functions. To view the services that are currently running:

1. Log into JIRA as a JIRA Administrator.
2. Click on **Administration** from the top menu bar.
3. Select **Services** from the left panel to bring up the **Services** page.

JIRA is shipped with a number of mail handlers, each with their own features. In the following sections, we will discuss each of the handlers in detail.

Creating an issue handler

As the name suggests, the **Create Issue Handler** creates issues from e-mails. It is the most basic mail handler available in JIRA, other built-in handlers add additional features such as allowing users to add comments to existing issues.

Parameter	Description
project	The project key for the project to create issues in. For example, **project=HD**.
issuetype	The ID of the issue type to use to create the issue. You can find issue type IDs by going to the **Manage Issue Types** page and clicking on the **Edit** link for each issue type. The URL will display the ID with **?id=1**. For example, **issuetype=1**.
reporterusername	Username of the user to be set as the reporter if the sender cannot be recognized by JIRA (for example if the sender does not exist in the JIRA database). The username set here must also be a valid user in JIRA. For example, **reporterusername=admin**.
createusers	If the e-mail is sent from an unknown address, JIRA will create a new user based on the e-mail's sender and randomly generate a password. An e-mail will be sent to the from-address informing the new JIRA account. This option overrides **reportusername** option if both are present. For example, **createusers=true**.
notifyusers	If **notifyusers** is set to false, JIRA will not sent out confirmation e-mails to users created by the **createusers** parameter. For example, **notifyuser=false**.
catchemail	Specifies if JIRA is to only handle e-mails that are sent to the specified address. For example, **catchemail=example@company.com**.
ccassignee	JIRA will assign the issue to the user specified in the **To** field first. If no user can be matched from the **To** field, JIRA will then try the users in the **CC** field. For example, **ccassignee=true**.
ccwatcher	JIRA will add users in the **CC** list (if they exist) as watchers of the issue. For example, **ccwatcher=true**.

Parameter	Description
bulk	This specifies how to handle auto-generated e-mails, such as those generated by JIRA. It is possible to create a loop if JIRA sends e-mails to the same mailbox where it also picks up e-mails. In order to prevent this, you can specify for JIRA to: • **ignore**: Ignore these mails • **forward**: Forward these mails to another address • **delete**: Delete these mails altogether For example, **bulk=forward**.

When setting handler parameters, each parameter is separated by a comma. For example,

```
project=HD, issuetype=1, catchemail=example@company.com,
createusers=true
```

The configuration above will pick up e-mails sent to example@company.com and create issues of type **Bug** (1) in the Support Desk (SD) project. Users will also be created if they do not exist in JIRA.

Create or comment handler

The Create or Comment handler is similar to the Create Issue handler, but it can also add comments to existing issues if the incoming e-mail's subject contains a matching issue key. If the subject does not contain a matching issue key, a new issue is created.

It has the same set of parameters as the Create Issue handler plus one additional parameter: stripquotes.

Parameter	Description
stripquotes	If present in the parameters, quoted text from the e-mail will not be added as part of the comment.

Full Comment Handler

The Full Comment Handler extracts text from an e-mail's content and adds it to issues with a matching issue key a comment. The author of the comment is taken from the from-address of the e-mail.

It has a similar set of parameters as the Create Issue handler.

Non-quoted comment handler

This is very similar to the Full Comment handler, but only extracts non-quoted texts and adds them as comments. Texts that starts with ">" or "|" are considered to be quoted.

It has a similar set of parameters as the Create Issue handler.

Regex comment handler

This is a more powerful version of the comment handlers. It uses the regex expressions to extract text from e-mail contents and add it to the issue.

Parameter	Description
splitregex	The regex expression to use to extract contents. There are two rules for the regex expression: • It must start and end with a delimiter character, usually / • It cannot contain commas for example, /-{}{}{}{}{}{}\s*Original Message\s*{}-/ or /_____*/

Adding a mail handler

You can add multiple mail handlers. It is recommended that you create dedicated mail servers for each project you wish to allow JIRA to create issues from e-mails for. For each account, you will then need to create a mail handler. The mailbox you set up needs to be accessible via POP or IMAP.

To add a mail handler:

1. Browse to the **Services** page.
2. Click on the **Built-in Services** link in the **Add Service** section. A list of available services will be displayed. The services we are interested in are **Create issues from POP** and **Create issues from IMAP**.
3. Provide a meaningful name to the new service.
4. Select either **Create issues from POP** or **Create issues from IMAP**, depending on your mailbox.
5. Specify how long JIRA should wait to poll the mailbox for new e-mails (in minutes).

6. Click on the **Add Service** button.

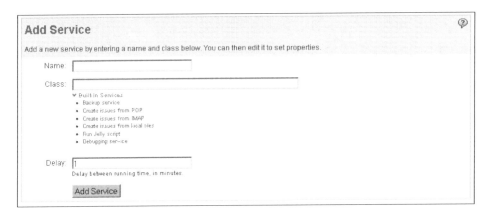

After you have added the service, you will be taken to the **Edit Service** page where you can adjust further configuration options. It is from this page that you can choose what type of mail handler you would like to use, and its relevant parameters.

Parameter	Description
Handler	The type of mail handler to add.
Handler Parameters	Parameters used to configure the handler.
Forward Email	The e-mail address to forward e-mails that cannot be handled to.
Uses SSL	Whether or not SSL needs to be used to access the mailbox.
Server	The POP/IMAP server configured from the Mail Servers section.
Port	The port to connect to for the mail server.
Delay	The interval between polling, in minutes.

The Handler parameters are configured as a set of comma separated values. For example,

```
Project=HDG, issuetype=1,createuser=true
```

Editing and deleting a mail handler

You can update the details of your mail handlers at any time. You will often need to tune your handler's parameters a few times until you get your desired results. To update a mail handler:

1. Browse to the **Services** page.
2. Click the **Edit** link for the mail handler service you wish to update. This will bring up the **Edit Service** page.
3. Update the configure options.
4. Click on the **Update** button to apply the changes.

Once updated, the updated configurations will be immediately applied and JIRA will use the new handler parameters for the next polling run.

You can also delete mail handlers that are no longer required at any time.

1. Browse to the **Services** page.
2. Click on the **Delete** link for the mail handler service you wish to remove.

You will not be prompted with a confirmation page. The mail handler will be removed immediately, so think carefully before you delete it.

Help Desk Project

Users will often want to get constant progress updates on their issues after they have logged them. Instead of getting them to send e-mails asking for updates, we will proactively update them through our newly acquired knowledge, JIRA notifications.

In *Chapter 4* we added a custom field called **Escalation List**. What this field will do is allow users to add others who will receive notifications along with the issue's reporter and assignee.

Another customization we made is to the workflow in *Chapter 6* with new transitions. We need to make sure those transitions will fire appropriate events and also send out notifications. In summary, what we need to do is:

1. Send out notifications for our new custom events fired by our custom workflow transitions.

2. Send out notifications to users specified in our Escalation List custom field.

While you can achieve both by using other JIRA features such as adding users as watchers to the issue and reusing existing JIRA system events, this exercise will explore the options available to you, and as you will see in later chapters, there are other criteria to consider when deciding on the best approach.

Setting up mail servers

The first step to enable e-mail communication, is to register mails servers in JIRA. If you are using the standalone distribution of JIRA, it is recommended that you add your mail server by entering the host information.

1. Log into JIRA as a JIRA Administrator.

2. Click on **Administration** from the top menu bar.

3. Select **Mail Servers** from the left panel to bring up the **Mail Servers** page.

4. Click on the **Configure new SMTP mail server** link under the **SMTP Mail Server** section.

5. Fill in your mail server information.

After you have added your mail server, you can try sending yourself a quick test e-mail to see if JIRA is able to access your server successfully.

Setting up custom events

In *Chapter 6*, we created two new workflow transitions. One is for the help desk staff to request additional information from the business user, and another for the business user to supply the requested information. What we need to do now is to create the custom events for the transitions when they are executed.

1. Log into JIRA as a JIRA Administrator.
2. Click on **Administration** from the top menu bar.
3. Select **Events** from the left panel to bring up the **View Events** page.
4. Name the new event **Info Requested**.
5. Provide a description for the event, **This is the request information event**.
6. Select the **Issue Updated** template.
7. Click on the **Add** button to create the new event.

With our event created, we now need to update our workflow so our transitions can fire the correct event.

1. Browse to the **View Workflows** page.
2. Create a **draft** of the **Help Desk Workflow**.
3. Click on the **Request for Info** transitions.
4. Update the post function to use fire our **Info Requested** event rather than the **Generic Event**.

In this case, we can reuse the **Issue Updated** event and it will work just as fine. However, there are advantages of having your own custom events as it helps to distinguish exactly what the nature of the update is. When you have listener components in JIRA, having specialized events help to distinguish the origin and act accordingly.

Setting up a notification scheme

Now we need to have our own notification scheme so we can start adding notifications to our events. We will be basing our notification scheme on the default scheme to help us get things set up quickly.

1. Log into JIRA as a JIRA Administrator.
2. Click on **Administration** from the top menu bar.
3. Select **Notification Schemes** from the left panel to bring up the **Notification Schemes** page.

4. Click on the **Copy** link for the **Default Notification Scheme**. A new notification scheme named **Copy of Default Notification Scheme** will be created.

5. Click on the **Edit** link of the **Copy of Default Notification Scheme**.

6. Rename it to **Help Desk Notification Scheme**.

This will create a new notification scheme with the basic notifications pre-populated. All we need to do now is modify the events and add our own notification needs.

Setting up notifications

There are two rules we need to add for our notifications. First, we need to add notifications for our custom events so e-mails will be sent out when they are fired. Second, we want users specified in the **CC List** custom field to also receive e-mails along with the assignee and reporter of the issue. To accomplish this:

1. Click on the **Notifications** link for **Help Desk Notification Scheme**.

2. Click on the **Add notification** link.

3. Select all the event types.

4. Select **User Custom Field Value** for notification type and select **CC List** from the drop-down list.

5. Click on the **Add** button.

Nice and easy. With just a few clicks, JIRA has allowed us to add a new notification to not only all the system events, but also our new custom events.

Putting it together

The last step, as always, is to associate our scheme with projects for activation.

1. Browse to the **Project Administration** page for our **Help Desk** project.

2. Click on the **Select** link for **Notification Scheme**.

3. Select **Help Desk Notification Scheme**.

4. Click on the **Associate** button.

With just a few clicks, you have enabled JIRA to automatically send out e-mails to update users with their issue's progress. Not only that, we have tied in the custom fields we created from earlier chapters to manage who, along with the issue assignee and reporter, will also get the notifications. Let's put this to the test!

1. Create a new issue in the **Help Desk** project.

2. Select one or more users for the **Escalation List** custom field. It is a good idea not to select yourself since the reporter will get notifications by default. Also make sure the user selected has a valid e-mail address.

3. Execute the **Request for Info** transition on the new issue.

4. You should receive an e-mail from JIRA within minutes.

5. If you do not receive an e-mail from JIRA, check your mail queue and see if the mail is being generated.

Summary

In this chapter, we looked at how JIRA can "stay in touch" with your users with the use of e-mail. With today's new gadgets like smart phones and tablets, being able to keep users up to date via e-mail is a very powerful feature, and JIRA has a very flexible structure in place to define the rules which determine who will receive notifications.

We have also very briefly mentioned some of the security rules surrounding who can receive notifications. JIRA performs security checks prior to sending out notifications for two very good reasons: one, there is no point sending out an e-mail to a user who cannot view the issue, and two, you will not want users not authorized to view the issue to receive updates that they should not know about.

In the next chapter, we will look into the security aspects of JIRA and how you can secure your data to prevent unauthorized access.

8
Securing your JIRA

In the previous chapters, we have learned how to store data in JIRA by creating issues. As we can see, as an information system, JIRA is all about data. It should come as no surprise to you that security plays a big role in JIRA not only to ensure that only the right people get access to the data, but also to maintain data integrity by preventing accidental changes.

By the end of the chapter, you will have learned:

- How to utilize user management features in JIRA
- About JIRA's permission hierarchy
- About general access control in JIRA
- How to manage fine-grained permission settings

Before we delve into the deep end of how JIRA handles security, let's first take a look at how user memberships are managed.

Users

In any information system, for users to access the system, they need to have an account. In JIRA, each user needs to have their own user account for them to access the data. Each user is identified by their username, which cannot be changed after account creation.

User Browser

JIRA administrators can manage users centrally from the **User Browser**.

1. Log into JIRA as a JIRA Administrator.
2. Click on **Administration** from the top menu bar.
3. Select **User Browser** from the left panel to bring up the **User Browser** page.

From the **User Browser**, you will be able to see a list of all the users in JIRA. The **User Browser** also provides you with search capabilities. You will be able to search for users that fit criteria such as **username**, **full name**, **e-mail address**, and **group association**. By default, the results will be paginated to show twenty users per page, but you can change this setting to show up to one hundred users per page. When dealing with large deployments with hundreds of users, these options will become extremely useful to quickly find the users you need to manage.

Other than the ability for you to effectively search for users, the **User Browser** also serves as the portal for you to add new users to JIRA, and manage user's group/role associations.

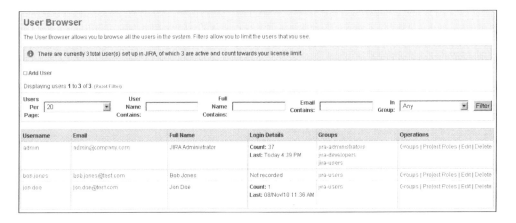

Adding a user

There are two ways for new user accounts to be created in JIRA. The first option is to have centralized management where only the JIRA administrators can create and maintain user accounts. This option is applicable to most private JIRA instances designed to be used by an organization's internal users.

The second option is to allow users to sign up for accounts themselves; this is most useful when you are running a public JIRA instance where manually creating user accounts is not feasible because of the volume of work. We will be looking at how to enable public signup options in later sections, for now we will examine how administrators can create user accounts manually.

1. Browse to the **User Browser** page.

2. Click on the **Add User** link. This will bring you to the **Create New User** page.

3. Provide a unique username for the new user. The username cannot be changed once it is set.

4. Specify the password, full name, and e-mail address for the user.

5. Optionally check the **Send Password Email** option if you have a SMTP server configured for JIRA (see *Chapter 7*). If checked, JIRA will send an e-mail to the user with a link for them to reset their password.

6. Click on the **Create** button to create the new user.

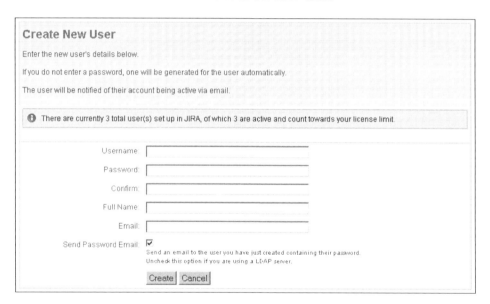

Enabling public signup

If your JIRA instance is public, for example, as a public support system, creating user accounts individually as explained earlier will become a very demanding job for your administrator. For this type of JIRA setup, you can enable public signup to allow users create accounts themselves.

To enable public signup in JIRA:

1. Log into JIRA as a JIRA Administrator.
2. Click on **Administration** from the top menu bar.
3. Select **General Configuration** from the left panel to bring up the **General Configuration** page.
4. Click on the **Edit Configuration** link at the bottom of the page.
5. Select **Public** for the **Mode** field.
6. Click on the **Update** button to apply the setting.

Once you have set JIRA to run in the **Public** mode, users will be able to sign up and create their own accounts from the login page.

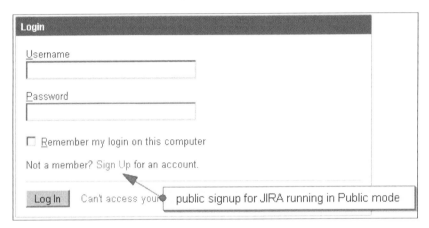

As we will see in the later section, *Global Permissions*, once a user has signed up for a new account, he/she will automatically join groups with JIRA users' global permission.

If you have set JIRA to run in **Private** mode, only the administrator will be able to create new accounts.

Enabling CAPTCHA

If you are running JIRA in **Public** mode, you run the risk of having automated spam bots creating user accounts on your system. To counter this, JIRA provides the CAPCHA service where potential users will be required to type in a word represented in an image into a text field. To enable CAPTCHA service:

1. Browse to the **General Configuration** page.
2. Click on the **Edit Configuration** link at the bottom of the page.
3. Select **On** for **CAPTCHA** on signup.
4. Click on the **Update** button to apply the setting.

Now when someone tries to sign up for an account, JIRA will present them with a CAPTCHA challenge that must be verified before the account is created.

Groups

Groups are a common way of managing users in any information system. A group often represents a collection of users, usually based on their positions and responsibilities within the organization. In JIRA, groups provide an effective way to apply configuration settings to users, such as permissions and notifications.

Groups are global in JIRA, which is something that should not be confused with **Project Roles** (discussed later). This means if you belong to the **jira-administrators** group, you will always be in that group regardless of which project you are accessing. We will see in later sections how this is different from project roles and their significance.

One important point to keep in mind is that a group association does not cascade in JIRA. For example, just because a user is in the **jira-developers** group does not mean he/she will have the privileges of the **jira-users** group.

Group Browser

JIRA administrators can manage groups centrally from the **Group Browser**.

1. Log into JIRA as a JIRA Administrator.
2. Click on **Administration** from the top menu bar.
3. Select **Group Browser** from the left panel to bring up the **Group Browser** page.

Similar to the **User Browser**, the **Group Browser** allows you to search, add, and configure groups within JIRA.

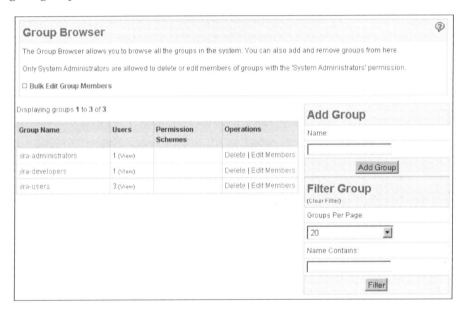

JIRA comes with three default groups. These groups are created automatically when you install JIRA.

Group	Description
jira-administrators	Administrators of JIRA.
jira-developers	Usually developers or people that will work on issues.
jira-users	Normal users in JIRA.

Out of the three groups, **jira-administrators** and **jira-users** are of most significance. As we will see later in this chapter, by default, **jira-administrators** are given the global permission to administer JIRA while **jira-users** are only given permission to access JIRA. You can, as we will learn, change this default behavior so your custom groups have the same permissions.

Adding a group

Other than the three groups that come by default with JIRA, you can create your own groups. It is important to note that once you have created a group, you cannot change its name. Make sure you think about the name of the group carefully before you create it.

1. Browse to the **Group Browser** page.
2. Specify a unique name of the new group in the **Add Group** section.
3. Click on the **Add Group** button to create the new group.

After a group has been created, it is empty and will have no members. It will also have no configuration settings such as the permissions applied.

Editing group membership

It is often that people move around within an organization, and JIRA needs to be kept up-to-date with the movement.

From the **Group Browser**, there are two ways to manage group membership. The first option is to manage the membership on per-group level, and the second option is to manage several groups at the same time. Both options are actually very similar, so we will be covering both at the same time.

To manage individual groups:

1. Browse to the **Group Browser** page.
2. Click on the **Edit Members** link for the group you wish to manage the member for. This will bring you to the **Bulk Edit Group Members** page.

To manage multiple groups:

1. Browse to the **Group Browser** page.
2. Click on the **Bulk Edit Group Member** link. This will bring you to the **Bulk Edit Group Members** page.

You will notice that both options will take you the same page. The difference is if you have chosen the individual group option, JIRA will auto select the group to update, and if you have chosen the bulk edit option, no groups will be selected. However, regardless of which option you have chosen, you can still select one or all of the groups to apply your changes to.

To update the membership in one or more groups:

1. Browse to the **Bulk Edit Group Members** page.
2. Select one or more groups to update.
3. Select users from middle box and click on the **Leave** button to take users out of the groups.
4. Specify users (by typing usernames) in the right-hand box and click on the **Join** button to add users into the groups.

Deleting a group

If a group has become redundant, you can remove it from JIRA.

1. Browse to the **Group Browser** page.
2. Click on the **Delete** link of the group you wish to remove. This will take you to the **Delete Group** page.
3. Click on the **Delete** button to permanently remove the group.

Once you have removed the group, it will automatically remove all the users who previously belonged to it.

Project roles

As we have seen, groups are collections of users and are applied globally. JIRA offers another way of grouping users, which is applied on the project level only.

Project role	Description
Administrators	Project role that represents the administrator of the project (for example, project manager).
Developers	Project role that represents the developer of the project.
Users	Project role that represents the user of the project (for example, tester).

Project role browser

Similar to users and groups, project roles are maintained centrally by the JIRA administrator through the **Project Role Browser**. There is a slight difference however, since project roles are specific to projects, JIRA administrators only define what roles are available in JIRA and their default members. Each project's administrators (discussed in later sections) can further define each role's membership for their own projects, overriding the default assignment. We will first look at what JIRA administrators can control through the **Project Role** browser and then look at how project administrators can fine-tune the membership assignment later.

To access the **Project Role Browser**:

1. Log into JIRA as a JIRA Administrator.
2. Click on **Administration** from the top menu bar.
3. Select **Project Role Browser** from the left panel to bring up the **Project Role Browser** page.

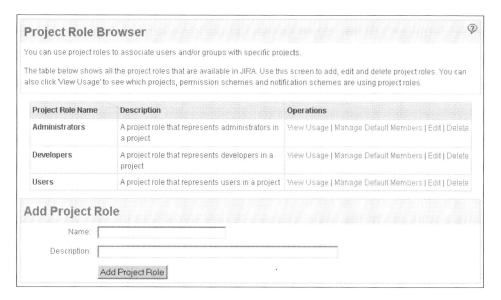

Adding a project role type

The list of project roles is managed by the JIRA administrator. As an administrator, you can create new role types which can then be used by project administrators for their projects.

To create a new project role:

1. Browse to the **Project Role Browser** page.
2. Specify a unique name for the new project role in the **Add Project Role** section.
3. Specify an optional description.
4. Click on the **Add Project Role** button to create the project role.

Once you have added a new project role, it will appear for all the projects.

Editing a project role

You can update a project role's name and description.

1. Browse to the **Project Role Browser** page.
2. Click on the **Edit** link for the project role you wish to update. This will take you to the **Edit Project Role** page.
3. Specify a new name and description.
4. Click on the **Update** button to apply the changes.

Deleting a project role

Existing project roles can be deleted if they are no longer used.

1. Browse to the **Project Role Browser** page.
2. Click on the **Delete** link of the project role you wish to remove. This will bring up the **Delete Project Role** page.
3. Click on the **Delete** button to remove the project role.

Managing default members

As new projects are created in JIRA, often those projects share a similar security requirement. It becomes desirable to have default members assigned to the project roles when new projects are created.

For example, by default, users in the **jira-administrators** group will have the **Administrators** project role. This increases the efficiency of security setup by creating a baseline for new projects, but also offers the flexibility to allow modifications to the default setup to cater for unique requirements.

To set default members for a project role:

1. Browse to the **Project Role Browser** page.

2. Click on the **Manage Default Members** link for the project role you wish to remove. This will take you to the **Edit Default Members for Project Role** page.

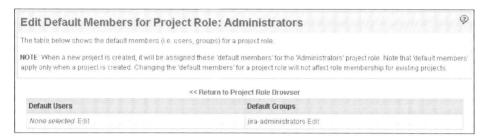

From this page, you will see all the default members assigned to the selected project role. Default members can be logically assigned project roles based on group setup. Users can be useful when you have exceptional cases, such as a lead developer who should have the **Developers** role in all software development projects.

To add a default user/group for the project role:

1. Click on the **Edit** link for the default member option (either user or group).

2. Use the user picker/group picker function to select the users/groups you wish to assign to the project role.

3. Click on the **Add** button to assign the role.

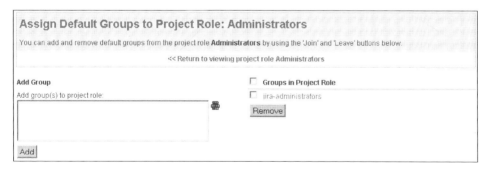

Once added, any new project created will have the specified users/groups assigned to the project role. It is important to note that after you have set default members, only new projects will have the settings applied. Existing projects will not retrospectively have the default members applied.

Default members is an efficient way for JIRA administrators to assign project role members automatically without having to manually manage it for each new project as they come in. After a project has been created, it becomes the responsibility of the project administrator to maintain the project's role membership, which we will be looking at in the next section.

Assigning project role members

JIRA allows you to assign default members to projects when they are created. This might be sufficient for most projects when they start, but changes will often need to be made due to staff movements throughout the project life cycle. It is possible for the JIRA administrator to continue maintaining each project's membership, but it can easily become an overwhelming task. In most cases, since project roles are specific to each project, it makes sense to delegate this responsibility to the owner of each project.

In JIRA, an owner of a project is someone with the **Administrators Projects** permission. By default, members of the **Administrators project** role will have this permission. We will see how to manage JIRA's permissions in the later sections.

As a project administrator, you will be able to assign members to the various project roles for your project. You can assign roles from the project administration page.

1. Log into JIRA as a user with Administrators project role for one or more projects. (By default, members of the **jira-administrators** group will have this role).

2. Click on **Administration** from the top menu bar.

3. Select the project you wish to manage the role members for. This will bring you to the **Project Administration** page.

4. Click on the **View Members** link next to **Project Roles**. This will bring you to the **Manage Project Role Membership** page.

5. Click on the **Edit** link for either **Users** or **Groups** for the project role you wish to configure. This will take you to the **Assign Users/Groups to Project Role** page.

6. Use the user/group picker to search and select users/groups to assign to the project role.

7. Click on the **Add** button.

The users and groups assigned to the project role will be for the current project only. You will have to reconfigure the members again for other projects. This way, project role members are maintained separately for each project.

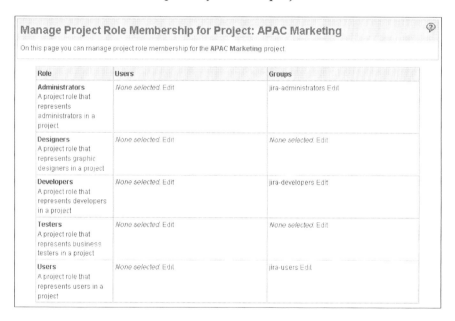

JIRA permission hierarchy

JIRA manages its permissions in a hierarchical manner. Each level is more fine-grained than the one above it. For a user to gain access to a resource, for example, to view an issue, he/she needs to satisfy all three levels of permission (if they are all set on the issue in question).

- **JIRA Global Permission**: Controls overall access rights to JIRA. For example, who can access JIRA.

- **Project Level Permission**: Controls project level permissions.

- **Issue Level Security**: Controls view access on a per issue level.

We will look at each of the permission levels and how you can configure them to suit your requirements, starting from the most coarsely grained permission level—**Global Permissions**.

Global Permissions

Global permissions, as the name suggests, is the highest permission level in JIRA. These are permissions applied globally across JIRA, controlling broad security levels such as ability to access JIRA and administer configurations.

Since they are not very specific permissions, global permissions are applied to user groups rather than users. The following table lists all the permissions and what they control in JIRA.

Global Permission Level	Description
JIRA System Administrators	Permission to perform all JIRA administration functions. This is akin to root or god mode in other systems.
JIRA Administrators	Permission to perform most JIRA administration functions that are not related to system-wide changes. (for example, configure SMTP server, export/restore JIRA data).
JIRA Users	Permission to log into JIRA. Newly created users will automatically join the groups with this permission.
Browse Users	Permission to view list of JIRA users and groups. This permission is required if the user needs to use the user/group picker function.
Create Shared Object	Permission to share filters and dashboards with other users.
Manage Group Filter Subscriptions	Permission to manage group filter subscriptions. Filters will be discussed in *Chapter 9*.
Bulk Change	Permission to perform bulk operations, including: <ul><li>Bulk Edit</li><li>Bulk Move</li><li>Bulk Delete</li><li>Bulk Workflow Transition</li></ul>

JIRA System Administrator versus JIRA Administrator

For people who are new to JIRA, it is often confusing when it comes to distinguishing between JIRA System Administrator and JIRA Administrator. For the most part, both are identical, in that they can carry out most of the administrative functions in JIRA.

The difference is that a JIRA Administrator cannot access functions that can affect the application environment or network while a JIRA System Administrator has access to everything.

Although it is not necessary to have a separate role for both, it is sometimes useful to have one person overlooking general JIRA administrative tasks while have another with the ability to configure system-wide settings such as SMTP mail service, which is a system resource outside of the JIRA application. By default, the **jira-administrators** group has both JIRA System Administrators and JIRA Administrators permission.

The following list shows system operations that are only available to people with JIRA System Administrators permission.

- Configure SMTP server details
- Configure CVS source code repository
- Configure listeners
- Configure services
- Configure where JIRA stores index files
- Import data into JIRA from an XML backup
- Export data from JIRA to an XML backup
- Configure where attachments are to be stored on the file system
- Access JIRA license details
- Grant/revoke JIRA System Administrators global permission
- Delete users with JIRA System Administrators global permission

Configuring Global Permissions

Global permissions are configured and maintained by JIRA administrators and JIRA system administrators (to grant JIRA System Administrator global permission).

1. Log into JIRA as a JIRA Administrator.

2. Click on **Administration** from the top menu bar.

3. Select **Global Permissions** from the left panel to bring up the **Global Permissions** page.

Granting global permission

Global permissions can only be granted to groups. For this reason, you will need to organize your users into logical groups for global permissions to take effect. For example, you will want to have your internal users who will use JIRA to be placed in the jira-users group (the default group given the JIRA Users global permission).

1. Browse to the **Global Permissions** page.

2. Select the **Permission** you want to assign from the **Add Permission** section.

3. Choose the **Group** to be given the permission.

4. Click on the **Add** button to add the assignment.

The **Group** drop-down list will list all the groups in JIRA. It will also have an extra option called **Anyone**. This option includes users who are not logged in. You cannot select this option when granting JIRA Users permission, as JIRA Users is required to user to login and **Anyone** refers to users who are not logged in. For a production system, it is recommended not to grant any global permission to **Anyone** as this can lead to security and privacy concerns.

Revoking global permission

Global permissions can also be revoked. However, there are a few rules and restrictions you need to be aware of. They are as follows:

*   Both JIRA System Administrators and JIRA Administrators can revoke global permissions, but JIRA Administrators **cannot** revoke a JIRA System Administrator's global permission.

*   If you revoke JIRA Users permission, you are effectively disallowing the affected users from accessing JIRA (they will not be able to log into JIRA).

*   You will not be able to grant additional JIRA Users permission if you have exceeded the number of users permitted by your license.

To delete a global permission from a group:

1. Browse to the **Global Permissions** page.

2. Click on the **Delete** link for the group you wish to remove from the global permission. This will take you to the **Delete Global Permission** page.

3. Click on the **Delete** button to remove the global permission.

JIRA has validation rules built-in to prevent you from accidentally locking yourself out by accidentally removing the wrong permissions. For example, JIRA will not let you delete the last group from JIRA System Administrators global permission, as doing so will effectively prevent you from adding yourself back, as only members of JIRA System Administrators can assign/revoke global permissions.

Project permissions

As we have seen, global permissions are rather coarse in what they control and are applied globally. Since they can only be applied to groups, it is rather inflexible when it comes to decide whom to grant the permissions to.

To provide a more flexible way of managing and designing permissions, JIRA allows you to manage permissions on the project level, which allows each project to have its own distinctive permission settings. Furthermore, JIRA allows you to grant permissions to users through a range of options, including:

- **Reporter**: The user who submitted the issue
- **Group**: All users that belong to the specified group
- **Single User**: Any user in JIRA
- **Project Lead**: Lead of the project
- **Current Assignee**: The user currently assigned to the issue
- **User Custom Field Value**: User specified in a custom field of type **User** custom field
- **Project Role**: All users that belong to the specified role.
- **Group Custom Field Value**: Users within the specified group in a **Group** custom field

The list of permissions is also more fine-grained and designed more around controlling permissions on a project level. The only catch to this is the list is final; you cannot add new permission types.

Permission	Description
Administer Project	Permission to administer a project. Users with this permission are referred to as project administrators. Project administrators are able to edit project role membership, components, versions, and general project details such as name and description.
Browse Project	Permission for users to browse and view the project and its issues. If a user does not have browse project permission for a given project, the project will be hidden from him/her and notifications will not be sent.
View Version Control	Permission to view version control system configured for this project (usually for software development projects).
Create Issues	Permission for users to create issues.
Edit Issues	Permission for users to edit issues.

Permission	Description
Schedule Issues	Permission for users to set and update due dates for issues.
Move Issues	Permission for users to move issues.
Assign Issues	Permission for users to assign issues to different users.
Assignable User	Users that can be assigned to issues.
Resolve Issues	Permission for users to resolve an issue and set values for the **Fix For Version** field.
Close issues	Permission for users to close an issue.
Modify Reporter	Permission for users to change the value for the **Reporter** field.
Delete issues	Permission for users to delete an issue.
Link Issues	Permission for users to link issue together (if issue linking is enabled).
Set Issue Security	Permission for users to set issue security levels to enable issue level security.
View Voters and Watchers	Permission to view voters and watchers on issues.
Manage Watchers	Permission to manage the list of watchers on an issue.
Add Comments	Permission for users to add comments to issues.
Edit All Comments	Permission for users to edit comments made by all users.
Edit Own Comments	Permission to edit own comments.
Delete All Comments	Permission to delete all comments.
Delete Own Comments	Permission to delete own comments.
Create Attachments	Permission to add attachments to issues (if attachments are enabled).
Delete All Attachments	Permission to delete all attachments on issues.
Delete Own Attachments	Permission to delete attachments on issues added by the user.
Work On Issues	Permission to log work done on issues (if time tracking is enabled).
Edit Own Worklogs	Permission to edit worklogs made by the user.
Edit All Worklogs	Permission to edit all worklogs.
Delete Own Worklogs	Permission to delete worklogs made the user.
Dele All Worklogs	Permission to delete all worklogs.

Even though the list cannot be modified, JIRA provides you with a very comprehensive list of permissions that will cover almost all of your permission needs.

As you probably have guessed, with this many permissions, it will be highly inefficient if you have to create them individually for each project you have. JIRA lets you define your permissions once and apply them to multiple projects, with permission schemes.

Permission scheme

Permission schemes, like other schemes such as notification schemes, are collections of associations between permissions and users or a collection of users. Each permission scheme is a reusable self-contained entity that can be applied to one or more projects.

Like most schemes, permission schemes are applied at the project level. This allows you to apply finely-tuned permissions for each project. Just like project roles, JIRA administrators oversee the creation and configuration of permission schemes, and it is up to each project's administrators to choose and decide which permission scheme to use. This way, it encourages administrators to design their permissions that can be reused based on common needs of an organization. With meaningful scheme names and descriptions, project administrators will be able to choose the scheme that will fit their needs the most, instead of requesting a new set of permissions to be set up for each project.

We will first look at how JIRA administrators manage and configure permission schemes and then how project administrators can apply them in their projects.

To start managing permission schemes:

1. Log into JIRA as a JIRA Administrator.
2. Click **Administration** from the top menu bar.
3. Select **Permission Schemes** from the left panel to bring up the **Permission Schemes** page.

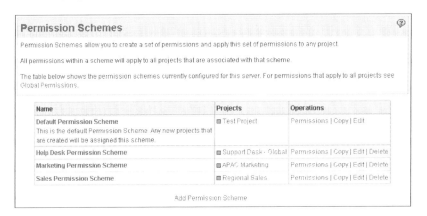

On the **Permission Schemes** page, you will see a list of all the permission schemes. From here, you will be able to create new schemes, edit and delete existing schemes, as well as configure each scheme's permission settings.

Adding a permission scheme

JIRA comes with a preconfigured permission scheme called **Default Permission Scheme**. This scheme is suitable for most simple software development projects. However, it is often not enough and it is usually a good practice to not modify the **Default Permission Scheme** directly, so you should create your own permission schemes.

1. Browse to the **Permission Schemes** pages.
2. Click on the **Add Permission Scheme** link. This will take you to the **Add Permission Scheme** page.
3. Provide a meaningful name for the new permission scheme.
4. Provide an optional description.
5. Click on the **Add** button to create the permission scheme.

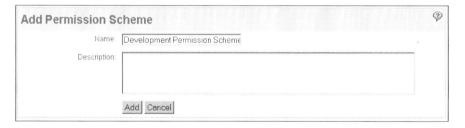

For new permission schemes, all of the permissions will have no user associations. This means if you start using your new scheme without further configuring its permission settings, you will wind up with a project that nobody can access. We will look at how to configure permissions in later sections.

Editing a permission scheme

You can keep a permission scheme's name and description up-to-date. You will often need to do this after you have made a copy of an existing permission scheme. As we will see in the following section, when you copy a permission scheme, JIRA automatically generates a name for your new scheme.

1. Browse to the **Permission Schemes** pages.

2. Click on the **Edit** link for the permission scheme you wish to update. This will take you to the **Edit Permissions Scheme** page.

3. Update the name and description with new values.

4. Click on the **Update** button to apply the changes.

Deleting a permission scheme

Unlike some other types of schemes, you can delete permission schemes even if they are being used by projects.

1. Browse to the **Permission Schemes** page.

2. Click on the **Delete** link for the permission scheme you wish to remove. This will take you to the **Delete Permission Scheme** page.

3. Click on the **Delete** button to remove the permission scheme

If you are deleting a permission scheme that is being used by one or more projects, JIRA will prompt you with the list of projects that are currently using the scheme. If you delete it, all the projects will be automatically updated to use the **Default Permission Scheme**. You cannot delete the **Default Permission Scheme**.

Copying a permission scheme

It is not always desirable to create permission schemes from scratch, as there are around thirty permissions you will need to set for a new permission scheme. JIRA allows you to easily clone existing permission schemes with the copy function.

1. Browse to the **Permission Schemes** pages.

2. Click on the **Copy** link for the permission scheme you wish to clone. This will immediately create a copy of the permission scheme with the name with **Copy of** appended to the front of the original scheme's name.

One good use of the copy function is to create a backup of an existing permission scheme before you make changes. It is sometimes good practice to name your permission schemes with a version number and every time you need to make a change, create a copy and increase the version number in the name. This way, it helps you to keep track of your changes and help you to roll back your changes if things do not work out as planned.

Configuring a permission scheme

Just like most other schemes in JIRA, you need to further fine-tune your permission scheme to make it useful.

1. Browse to the **Permission Schemes** page.

2. Click on the **Permissions** link for the permission scheme you wish to configure. This will take you to the **Edit Permissions** page.

From this page, you will be presented with a list of project-level permissions available, along with short descriptions for each, and the users, groups, roles, and so on that are linked to each of the permissions. You will notice that for the **Default Permission Scheme**, most of the permission options have default users linked to them through project roles. If you are looking at a new permission scheme, there will be no users linked to any of the permissions. This is your one page view of permission settings for projects and you will also be able to add and delete users.

Unlike some other schemes such as a notification scheme, which allows you to add additional options (through custom events), you cannot define new permissions for a permission scheme.

Granting a permission

Like a notification scheme, JIRA offers you a range of options to specify which users should have certain permissions. You can specify users through some of the most common options such as groups, but you can also utilize some advanced options such as selecting users specified in a custom field.

Again, you have two options to grant permissions to a user. You can add a specific permissions or multiple permissions at once. Both options will present you with the same interface and there is no difference between the two.

1. Browse to the **Edit Permissions** page for the permission scheme you wish to configure.
2. Click on the **Grant permission** link or the **Add** link for specific permission. This will take you to the **Add New Permission** page.
3. Select the permissions you wish to grant to the user.
4. Select the user option to specify whom to grant the permission to.
5. Click on the **Add** button to grant the selected permission.

An option like **User Custom Field Value** is a very flexible way of allowing the end-users control access. For example, you can have a custom field called **Editors**, and set up your **Edit Issues** permission to allow users specified in the custom field to be able to edit issues.

The custom field does not have to be placed on the usual view/edit for the permission to be applied. For example, you can set the custom field to appear on a workflow transition called **Submit to Manager**, and once the user has selected the manager, only the manager will have permission to edit the issue.

Revoking a permission

You can easily revoke a permission given to a user.

1. Browse to the **Edit Permissions** page for the permission scheme you wish to configure.
2. Click on the **Delete** link for the permission you wish to revoke. This will take you to the **Delete Permission** page.
3. Click on the **Delete** button to revoke.

When you are trying to revoke permission to prevent users from gaining certain access, you need to make sure that there are no other user options granted to the same permission that might be applied to the same user. For example, if you have both **Single User** and **Group** options set for the **Browse Projects** permission, you will need to make sure to revoke the **Single User** option and also make sure that the user does not belong to the **Group** selected, so that the user does not have access via their group's permission setting.

Applying a permission scheme

We have gone over how permission schemes can be selected by project managers to set permissions for their projects. Now we will look at how to apply the scheme to your projects. The process will feel familiar; permission schemes are applied to projects in the same way as notification and workflow schemes.

1. Log into JIRA as a project administrator.
2. Select the project(s) that will be using the permission scheme.
3. Click on the **Select** link for **Permission Scheme**. This will bring up the **Associate Permission Scheme to Project** page.
4. Select the permission scheme to be used.
5. Click on the **Associate** button.

Permission schemes are applied immediately and you will be able to see the permissions take effect.

Issue security

We saw how JIRA administrators can restrict general access to JIRA with **Global Permissions**, and what project administrators can do to place permissions on individual projects through **Permission Schemes**. JIRA allows you to go down yet another level to allow ordinary users to set security level on the issues they are working with, with **Issue Security**.

Issue Security allows users to set view permission (not edit) on issues by selecting one of the pre-configured issue security levels. This is a very powerful feature as it allows the delegation of security control to the end users and empowers them (to a limited degree) to decide who can view their issues.

On a high level, issue security works in a similar way as permission schemes. A JIRA administrator will start by creating and configuring a set of issue security schemes with the security level set. Project administrators can then apply one of these schemes to their projects, which finally allow the users (with **Set Issue Security** permission) to select the security levels within the scheme and apply that to individual issues.

Issue security scheme

As explained earlier, the starting point of using **Issue Security** is the **Issue Security Scheme**. This is the responsibility of the JIRA administrator to create and design the security levels so they can be re-used as much as possible.

1. Log into JIRA as a JIRA Administrator.
2. Click **Administration** from the top menu bar.
3. Select **Issue Security Schemes** from the left panel to bring up the **Issue Security Schemes** page.

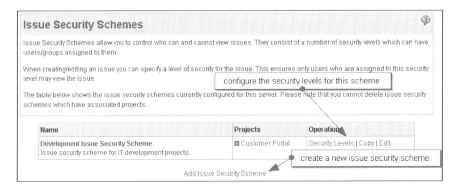

Adding an issue security scheme

JIRA does not come with any predefined issue security schemes, so you will have to create your own from scratch. To create a new issue security scheme:

1. Browse to the **Issue Security Schemes** page.
2. Click on the **Add Issue Security Scheme** link. This will bring up the **Add Issue Security Scheme** page.
3. Provide a meaning name for the new scheme.
4. Provide an optional description.
5. Click on the **Add** button to create the new issue security scheme.

Since an issue security scheme does not define a set of security levels like a permission scheme, you will need to create your own set of security levels right after you have created your scheme.

Configuring an issue security scheme

Unlike permission schemes that have a list of predefined permissions, with issue security schemes you are in full control over how many options you would like to add to the schemes.

The options within an issue security scheme are known as **Security Levels**. They represent the levels of security that users need to meet before JIRA will allow them access to the requested issue. Please note that even though they are called security levels, this does not mean there are any forms of hierarchy amongst the set of levels you create.

To configure an issue security scheme:

1. Browse to the **Issue Security Schemes** page.
2. Click on the **Security Levels** link for the issue security scheme you wish to configure. This will bring up the **Edit Issue Security Levels** page.

From here, you can create new security levels and assign users to existing security levels.

Adding a security level

Since issue security schemes do not define any security levels, the first step to configure your scheme would be to create a set of new security levels.

1. Browse to the **Edit Issue Security Levels** page for the issue security scheme you wish to configure.

2. Provide a meaningful name for the new security level in the **Add Security Level** section.

3. Provide an optional description.

4. Click on the **Add Security Level** button.

You can add as many security levels as you like in a scheme. A good practice is to design your security levels based on your team or project roles.

Assigning users to a security level

Similar to permission schemes, once you have your security levels in place, you will then need to assign users to each of the levels. Users assigned to the security level will have permission to view issues with the specified security level.

1. Browse to the **Edit Issue Security Levels** page.

2. Click on the **Add** link for the security level you wish to assign users to. This will bring up the **Add User/Group/Project Role to Issue Security Level** page.

3. Select the users you wish to assign to the security level.

4. Click on the **Add** button to assign the users.

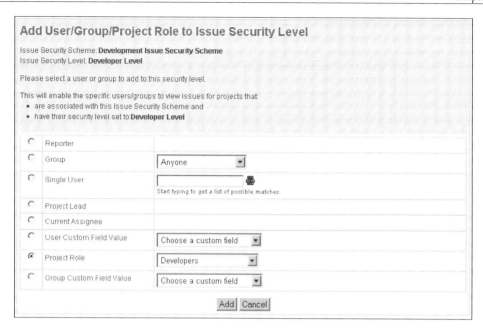

While it may be tempting to use the **Single User** option to add individual users, it is a better practice to use other options such as **Project Role** and **Group** as this is more flexible by not tying the permission to individual users and allows you to control permission with options such as group association.

Setting a default security level

You can set a security level to be the default option for issues if none is selected. This can be a useful feature for projects with high security requirements to prevent users (with **Set Issue Security** permission) from forgetting to assign a security level for their issues.

1. Browse to the **Edit Issue Security Levels** page.
2. Click on the **Default** link for the security level you wish to set as default.

Once set as default, the security level will have **Default** next to its name. Now, when the user creates an issue and does not assign a security level, the default security level will be applied.

Deleting a security level

You can revoke users assigned to security levels or remove the security level completely. When you revoke a user, he/she will no longer have access to the issue unless there is another user setting which the user also belongs to, applied to the same security level.

To revoke a user from a security level:

1. Browse to the **Edit Issue Security Levels** page.
2. Click on the **Delete** link for the **Users/Groups/Project Roles** you wish to remove. This will take you to the **Delete Issue Security** page.
3. Click on the **Delete** button to revoke the user.

When you delete a security level, you will be affecting all the issues that are currently set to that security level. JIRA allows you to update those issues to use a different security level (if one is available), or have no security level applied.

1. Browse to the **Edit Issue Security Levels** page.
2. Click on the **Delete** link for the security level you wish to remove. This will take you to the **Delete Issue Security Level** page. If there are issues set to the security level, JIRA will list the issues and also ask you to change their security level settings.
3. Select a new security level for the issues affected.
4. Click on the **Delete** button to remove the security level.

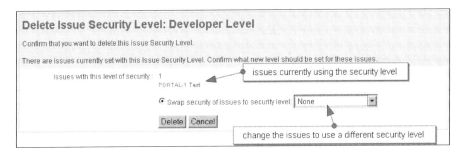

Applying an issue security scheme

Just like permission schemes, the project administrators apply issue security schemes to projects. Applying an issue security scheme is similar to when you apply a workflow scheme, there is an intermediate migration step involved. This is to ensure existing issues with issue security levels set can be successfully migrated over to the new security levels in the scheme.

1. Log into JIRA as a project administrator.
2. Select the project(s) that will be using the issue security scheme.
3. Click on the **Select** link for **Issue Security Scheme**. This will bring up the **Associate Issue Security Scheme to Project** page.
4. Select the permission scheme to use.
5. Click on the **Next** button to move to step 2 of the process.
6. Select the new security level to apply to the existing issue that might be affected by this change.
7. Click on the **Associate** button to apply the new issue security scheme.

Workflow security

Security features that we have looked at up until now are not applied to workflows. When securing JIRA, you will also need to consider who will be allowed to perform certain workflow transitions. For example, only users in the managers group will be able to execute the Authorize transition on issues. For you to enforce security on workflows, you will have to set it on each of the transitions you have, by adding workflow conditions. Please refer to *Chapter 6*, which discusses workflows and conditions in more detail.

Help Desk Project

In the previous chapters, we have configured JIRA to capture data with customized screens and fields, and process the captured data through workflows. What we need to do now is to secure the data we have gathered to make sure only the authorized users can access and manipulate issues.

Since our Help Desk Project is used by our internal team, what we really need to do is to secure our issues to ensure the data they hold do not get modified by other users, usually by mistake. This allows us to mitigate human errors by handling access accordingly.

To achieve this, we have the following requirements:

- We need to be able to tell who belongs to the help desk team.
- Restrict issue assign operation to only the user who has submitted the ticket and members of the help desk team.
- Not to allow tickets to be moved to other projects.
- Limit the assignee of tickets to the reporter and members of the help desk team.

Of course, there are a lot of other permissions we can apply here. The above four requirements will be a good starting point for us to build on further.

Setting up groups

The first thing we need to do is to set up a new group for our help desk team members, this will help us distinguish normal JIRA users from our help desk staff.

1. Browse to the **Group Browser** page.
2. Name the new group **help-desk-team** in the **Add Group** section.
3. Click on the **Add Group** button.

We can create more groups for other teams and departments, for our scenario here, since anyone can log a ticket in our project, there is no need to make that distinction.

Setting up user group association

With our group setup, we can start assigning members of our team to the new group.

1. Browse to the **Group Browser** page.
2. Click on the **Edit Members** link for the **support-desk-team** group.

3. Select users with the user picker or simply type in the usernames separated by a comma. This time, let's add our **admin** user to the group.

4. Click on the **Join** button.

Setting up a permission scheme

The next step is to set up permissions for our Help Desk project, so we need to have our own permission scheme. As always, it is more efficient to copy the **Default Permission Scheme** as a base and make our modifications on top, since we are only making a few changes here.

1. Browse to the **Permission Schemes** pages.

2. Click on the **Copy** link for **Default Permission Scheme**.

3. Click on the **Edit** link for the new **Copy of Default Permission Scheme** created.

4. Name the new permission scheme **Help Desk Permission Scheme**.

5. Change the description to **Permission scheme** designed for Help Desk team projects.

Now we have our base permission scheme set up, we can start on the fun part: interpreting requirements and implementing them in JIRA.

Setting up permissions

The first thing we need to do when we start setting up permissions is to try to match up existing JIRA permissions to our requirements. In our case, we want to restrict the following:

- Who can assign issues
- Who can be assigned to an issue
- To disable issues from being moved

Looking at the existing list of JIRA permissions, we can see that we can match up the requirements with the **Assign Issues**, **Assignable Users**, and **Move Issues** permissions, respectively.

Once we have worked out what permissions we need to modify, the next step is to work out a strategy to specify which users that should be given the permissions. Restricting **Move Issue** options is simple. All we have to do is remove the permission from everyone, thus effectively preventing anyone from moving issues in our project.

The next two requirements are similar, as they are both granted to the reporter (user that submitted the ticket), and our new **help-desk-team** group.

1. Browse to the **Permission Schemes** pages.
2. Click on the **Permissions** link for **Help Desk Permission Scheme**.
3. Click on the **Grant permission** link.
4. Select both **Assign Users** and **Assignable Users permissions**.
5. Select the **Reporter** option.
6. Click on the **Add** button.
7. Repeat the steps and grant the **help-desk-team** group both permissions.

By selecting both permissions in one go, we have quickly granted multiple permissions to users. Now we need to remove all the users granted with the **Move Issues** permission. There should be only one granted at the moment, **Project Role** (Developer), but if you have more than one granted, you will need to remove all of them.

1. Browse to the **Permission Schemes** pages.
2. Click on the **Permissions** link for **Help Desk Permission Scheme**.
3. Click on the **Delete** link for all the users that have been granted **Move Issues** permission.

And that's it! We have addressed all of our permission requirements with just a few clicks.

Putting it together

Last but not least, we can now put on our project administrator's hat and apply our new permission scheme to our Help Desk project.

1. Browse to the **Project Administration** page for our **Help Desk** project.
2. Click on the **Select** link for **Permission Scheme**.
3. Select **Help Desk Permission Scheme**.
4. Click on the **Associate** button.

By associating the permission scheme with our project, we have applied all of our permission changes. Now if we create a new issue or edit an existing issue, you will notice that the list of assignees will no longer include all users in JIRA.

Summary

In this chapter, we covered JIRA's user management options with groups and project roles. While both are very similar, groups are global while project roles are specific to each project.

We have also learned in detail how JIRA hierarchically manages permissions at each permission level and how one can manage them.

In the next chapter, we will take a different approach and look at another powerful use of JIRA: getting your data out through reporting.

9
Searching, Reporting, and Analysis

From *Chapter 2* to *Chapter 5*, we looked at how JIRA can be used as an information system to gather data from users. In *Chapter 5* and *Chapter 6*, we discussed some of the features JIRA provides to add values to the gathered data through workflows and notifications. In this chapter, we will look at the other half of the equation, getting the data out and presenting it as useful information back to the users.

By the end of this chapter, you will have learned:

- How to utilize the search interface in JIRA
- About different search options available in JIRA
- About filters and how you can share search results with other users
- How to generate reports in JIRA
- How to share information with dashboards and gadgets

Search interface and options

As an information system, JIRA comes fully-loaded with features and options when it comes to searching for data. JIRA allows you to search for issues quickly through simple text-based searches, or more refined searches by specifying criteria that must be fulfilled based on issue fields, and more advanced search through JIRA's own searches language.

However, before we start looking into the in-depth details of all the search options JIRA provides, let's first take a look at the main search interface you will be using in JIRA when you perform your searches.

Issue Navigator

The **Issue Navigator** is the primary location where you will be performing all of your searches in JIRA. The **Issue Navigator** is roughly divided into three major sections. The first part is where you specify all of your search criteria such as the project you want to search in and the issue type you are interested in. The second part is a table that lists the search results brought back. The last part includes operations you can perform on the search results, such as exporting them in a different format.

To access the **Issue Navigator**:

1. Click on the **Issues** link from the top menu bar. This will take you to the **Issue Navigator**.

When you access the **Issue Navigator** for the first time, you will be in **Simple Search** mode (we will discuss different search options in more details later in this chapter). If you have previously visited Issue Navigator and chosen to use a different search option such as **Advanced Search**, JIRA will remember this and open up **Advanced Search** instead.

The following screenshot shows **Issue Navigator** in **Simple Search** mode. In **Simple Search**, you specify your search criteria to your left, and the results will be displayed to your right.

On top of allowing you to search through issues, JIRA includes a few additional features that will help you to work with your search results.

- Toggle between simple and advanced searches
- Export search results into different views
- Select the columns you want to see for the issues in the results
- Create and manage filters

Customizing issue navigator

JIRA lets you configure the columns in the **Issue Navigator** to specify which fields are to be displayed when showing your search results. In JIRA, you can customize your **Issue Navigator** on a global level, which will affect all searches, giving each search query its own **Issue Navigator** column layout.

To customize your global **Issue Navigator** column layout:

1. Browse to the **Issue Navigator** page.
2. Bring up the **Tools** drop-down menu from top right-hand corner.
3. Select the **Configure Columns** option. This will bring you to the **Issue Navigator Columns** page.

From the **Issue Navigator** columns page, you can add new columns to the navigator layout, remove existing columns, and re-order them. There is also an option to hide the **Actions** column, which is always the last column and shows some shortcut links for actions you can perform on issues directly from the navigator.

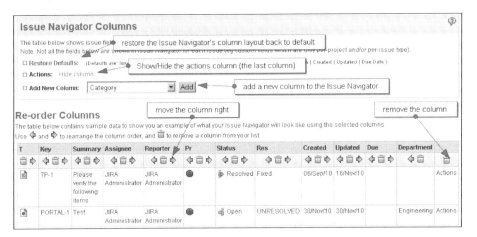

Once you have updated the column layout of the **Issue Navigator**, the layout will be used for all future searches you perform. If you want to have dedicated layouts for searches, you need to create named searches called **filters** and configure the column layout on the filters. We will look at filters in later sections of this chapter.

Simple search

While a quick search along with well-chosen search terms is able to cover a lot of your search requirements, it is still rather coarse-grained. Users often need to narrow down their search criteria and bring back only the issues that fit the requirements, or issues with specific field values (often custom fields), rather than a blanket text search across entire JIRA, and this is where **Simple Search** comes in.

Simple Search is probably the most used search facility in JIRA. It is simple, as the name suggests, but also powerful. It is called simple search because the users search by selecting and filling in fields provided by the interface. The interface provides some additional features such as auto-completion and date selection to help users correctly fill in the fields.

The simple search interface is divided into several sections:

- **Project and Issue Type**: Specify the context of the search (is it going to be global?)
- **Text Search**: Perform a simple text search in the **Summary**, **Description**, **Comments**, and/or **Environment** fields (if you check them).
- **Issue Attributes**: Includes fields that are not custom fields.
- **Dates and Times**: Issue attributes that are of type, date, and time, for example, issue creation date.
- **Actual vs. Estimated Work Ratio**: Search by time tracking criteria.
- **Custom Fields**: All custom fields.

To execute a simple search:

1. Click on the **Issues** link from the top menu bar. This will take you to the **Issue Navigator**.
2. Select and fill in the fields from the simple search interface. If you just click on **Search** without select any search parameters, JIRA will bring back all issues.
3. Click on the **View** button to execute the search.

After you have executed the search, JIRA will bring back the results and display them on the right-hand side of the page, next to the search interface. JIRA will also remember the search parameters you have selected before so you can fine-tune your search to narrow down what you are looking for.

Advanced search (JQL)

Simple search is useful and will fulfill most of the user's search needs. However, there are still some limitations. One of these limitations is that simple search allows you to perform searches based on **OR** logic, but not **NOT** logic. For example, if you need to search for issues in all but one project, with simple search you will have to select every project except for the one to exclude, since the simple search interface does not let you specify exclusions. It is because of limitations such as this that Atlassian decided to add the new and more powerful **Advanced Search** option.

With **Advanced Search**, instead of using a field selection-based interface as in **Simple Search**, you will be using what is known as the **JIRA Query Language** or **JQL** for short. JQL is a custom query language developed by Atlassian. If you are familiar with the **Structured Query Language** or **SQL**, you will notice that it has a similar syntax. However, JQL is not the same as SQL.

One of the most notable differences between JQL and SQL is that JQL does not start with a `SELECT` statement. A JQL query consists of a field, followed by an operator, and then by a value or a function (which will return a value). You cannot specify what fields to return from a query with JQL, which is different than SQL. You can think of a JQL query as the part that comes after the **WHERE** keyword in a normal SQL **SELECT** statement.

Each JQL search is essentially made up of one or more queries. A basic query consists of the following three elements:

- **Field**: This can be an issue field (for example, **status**) or a custom field.
- **Operator**: This defines the comparison logic (for example, = or >) that must be fulfilled for an issue to be returned in the result.
- **Value**: This is what the operator is to be compared to. This can be a literal value expressed as text (for example, **Bug**) or a function that will return a value.

Queries can then be linked together to form a more complex query with either logical AND or OR. For example, a basic query to get all issues with a status of `Resolved` will look like:

```
status = Resolved
```

A more complex query to get all issues with a status of `Resolved`, issue type `Bug`, and assigned to the currently logged in user will look like (where `currentUser()` is a JQL function):

```
issuetype = Bug and status = Resolved and assignee = currentUser()
```

Discussing each and every one of JQL's functions and operators is out of the scope of this book, but you can get a full reference by clicking on the **Query syntax** link from the **Advanced Search** interface.

You can access the advanced search interface from the **Issue Navigator**.

1. Click on the **Issues** link from the top menu bar. This will take you to the **Issue Navigator**.
2. Click on **Switch to advanced searching** link from top left-hand corner. You can click on the **Switch to simple searching** link to go back to **Simple Search**.
3. Type in the JQL query.
4. Click on the **Search** button.

As JQL can be complex and take some time to get familiar with, the advanced search interface has some very useful features to help you construct your query. The interface has an auto-complete feature (which can be turned off) that can help you pick out keywords, values, and operators to use. It also validates your query in real time and informs you if your query is invalid. You can also click on the **Query syntax** link from top-right corner to get help if you are stuck.

If there are no syntax errors with your JQL query, JIRA will display the results in a table below the JQL input box. The full JQL syntax reference can be found at `http://confluence.atlassian.com/display/JIRA/Advanced+Searching`.

Quick search

JIRA provides a **Quick Search** function, which allows you to perform quick and simple searches based on text contained in the issue's **summary**, **description**, or **comments**. This allows you to perform quick text-based searches on all issues in JIRA.

The **Quick Search** function has several additional features to let you perform more specialized searches with minimal typing, through **smart querying**. JIRA has a list of built-in queries which you can use as your quick search terms to pull up issues with a specific issue type and/or status. Some useful queries include:

Smart Query	Result
Issue Key (for example, **HD-12**)	Takes you directly to the issue with the specified issue key.
Project Key (for example, **HD**)	Displays all issues in the project specified by the key in **Issue Navigator**.
My or my open bugs	Displays all issues that are assigned to the currently logged in user.
Overdue	Displays all issues that are due before today.
Issues with a particular Status (for example, **open**)	Displays all issues with the specified status.
Issues with a particular Resolution (for example, **resolved**)	Displays all issues with the specified resolution.

You can combine these queries together to create quick and powerful searches in JIRA. For example, the following query brings back all resolved issues in the HD project.

```
HD resolved
```

As you can see, the goal of **Quick Search** is to allow you to find what you are looking for in the quickest possible way. With smart queries, you are able to perform more than just simple text-based searches.

Exporting search results

From the **Issue Navigator**, JIRA allows you to export your search results in a variety of formats, such as Microsoft Word or Excel. In JIRA, this is called **views**. JIRA is able to present your search results in different views such as XML or a printer-friendly page. When you select views such as Microsoft Word, JIRA will generate the appropriate file and let you download it directly.

To export your results to a different format:

1. Browse to the **Issue Navigator** page.
2. Execute a search.
3. Bring up the **Views** drop-down menu from top right-hand corner.
4. Select the view you wish to see your search results in.

Depending on the view you select, some views will be onscreen (printable), while others will prompt you with a download dialog (Microsoft Word).

Filters

After you have performed a query, sometimes it will be useful to save the query for later use. For example, you might have created a query to list all open bugs and new features in a project that are to be completed by a certain date in several projects, so you can keep an eye on their progress. Instead of recreating this search query every time you want to check on the statuses, you can save the query as a **filter**, which can be reused at a later stage. You can think of filters as named search queries that can be reused.

Other than being able to quickly pull up a report without having to recreate the queries, saving search queries as filters provide you with other benefits including:

- Share saved filters with other users
- Use the filters as a source of data to generate reports

- Display results on a dashboard as a gadget
- Subscribe to the search query to have results e-mailed to you automatically

We will explore all of the advanced operations you can perform with filters and explain some of the new terms and concepts such as dashboard and gadgets in later sections, but first let's look at how we can create and manage filters.

Creating a filter

To create a new filter, you will first have to construct and execute your search query. You can do this with any of the three available search options provided in JIRA, but please note that the search result must bring you to the **Issue Navigator**. If you are using the **Quick Search** option and the **Search by Issue** key, you will not be able to create a filter. Once you have executed your query, regardless of whether it brings back any result, you will be able to create a new filter based on the executed search.

1. Construct and execute a search query in JIRA. This needs to take you to the **Issue Navigator**.
2. Click on the **Save it as a filter** link on the left-hand side. This will bring you to the **Save Current Filter** page.
3. Provide a meaningful name for the filter.
4. Provide an optional description for the filter.
5. Select whether or not the new filter should be a favorite filter for you (for easy access).
6. Select if you wish to share the filter with anyone.
7. Click on the **Save** button to create the filter.

Once you have created the filter, all your search parameters will be saved. In the future, when you re-run the saved filter, JIRA will retrieve updated results based on the same parameters.

Managing filters

As the number of saved filters grow, you will need a centralized location to manage and maintain them.

There are two ways to access the **Manage Filters** page. You can access the page through the **Issue Navigator**:

1. Browse to the **Issue Navigator**.

2. Click on the **Manage** tab from the left-hand side. This will bring you to the **Manage Filters** page.

You can also access the **Manage Filters** page by going through the top navigator bar:

3. Bring up the drop-down menu from **Issues**.

4. Click on the **Manage Filters** option at the bottom of the list.

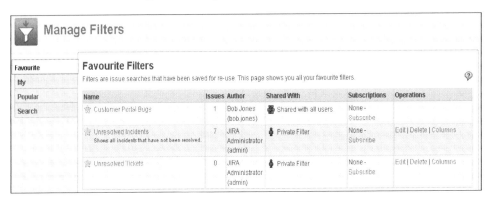

The **Manage Filters** page displays the filters that are visible to you in four main categories, as tabs to the left, along with the option to search for existing filters.

- **Favourite**: Filters with a golden star next to their names. These filters will be listed from the **Issues** drop-down menu. You can mark a filter as **Favourite** by clicking on the **Start** button directly.

- **Popular**: Lists the top 20 filters that have the most number of people marking them as **Favourite**.

- **My**: Lists the filters that are created by you.

- **Search**: Searches for existing filters that are shared by other users.

Editing and sharing a filter

After you have created a filter, you can update its details such as name, description, sharing permission, and search parameters.

1. Browse to the **Manage Filters** page.

2. Click on the **Edit** link for the filter you wish to edit. This will bring you to the **Edit Current Filter** page.

3. Update the details of the filter.

4. Select the group/project role to share the filter with.

5. Click on the **Update** button to apply the changes.

For you to be able to share a filter, you will also need to have the **Create Shared Object** global permissions (please refer to *Chapter 8* for more information on global permissions).

After you have shared your filter, other users will be able to search and subscribe to it. However, they will not be able to make changes to your filter. Only the owner of the filter is able to make changes to its search parameters. Filter ownership cannot be passed from one user to the other.

Subscribing to a filter

We saw in *Chapter 7, E-mail and Notification*, that JIRA is able to send out e-mails when certain events occur to keep the users updated. With filters, JIRA takes this feature one step further by allowing you to subscribe to a filter.

When you subscribe to a filter, JIRA will run a search based on the filter and send you the results in an e-mail. You can specify the schedule of when and how often JIRA should perform this. For example, you can set up a subscription to have JIRA send you the results every morning before you come in to work, so when you open up your mail inbox, you will have a full list of issues that require your attention.

To subscribe to a filter, you will need to be able to see the filter (either created by you or shared with you by other users).

1. Browse to the **Manage Filters** page.

2. Locate the filter you wish to subscribe to.

3. Click on the **Subscribe** link for the filter. This will take you to the **Filter Subscription** page.

4. Select the recipient of the subscription. Normally, this will be you (**Personal Subscription**). But you can create subscriptions for other people by selecting a group.

5. Check the **Email zero results** option if you wish to have an e-mail sent to you even if there are no results returned from the filter. This can be useful to make sure that the reason you are not getting e-mails is not due to other errors.

6. Specify the frequency and time when JIRA should send you the e-mails.

7. Click on the **Subscribe** button. This will create the subscription and take you to the **Subscription Summary** page.

8. Click on the **Run Now** link to test out your new subscription.

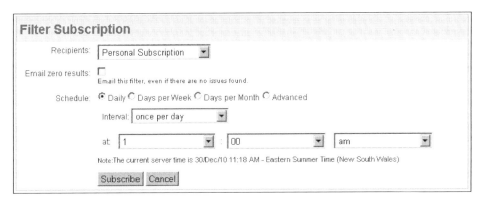

Deleting a filter

You can delete a filter when it is no longer needed. However, since you can share your filters out to other users and they can create subscriptions, you need to keep in mind that if you are deleting a shared filter, you might impact other users. Luckily, when you delete a filter, JIRA will inform you if other people are using the filter. To proceed with deleting a filter:

1. Browse to the **Manage Filters** page.

2. Click on the **Delete** link for the filter you wish to remove. This will bring up the **Delete Filter** confirmation dialog.

3. Make sure the removal will not impact other users.

4. Click on the **Delete** button to remove the filter.

In our preceding example, the **Unresolved Incidents** filter is shared and there is one user subscribing for it. JIRA informs you that and by clicking on the **1** link, you will be taken to the **View Subscription** page where you can see a list of users that are subscribed to the filter. You can then decide either to proceed with deleting the filter and letting the other users know, or leaving the filter in JIRA.

Reports

Searches with JQL and filters are powerful to extract data from JIRA.

Most reports in JIRA are designed to report on issues from a specific project, however, there are some reports that can be used globally across multiple projects, with the use of filters. The following table shows all the reports that come with JIRA out of the box.

Report type	Description
Workload Pie Chart Report	Shows the relative workload for assignees of all issues in a particular project or issue filter.
User Workload Report	Shows how much work a user has been allocated, and how long it should take.
Version Workload Report	Shows how much outstanding work there is (per user and per issue) before a given version is complete.
Version Time Tracking Report	Shows progress towards completing a given version, based on issues' work logs and time estimates.
Single Level Group By Report	Shows the search results from an issue filter, grouped by a field of your choice.
Created vs. Resolved Issues Report	Shows the number of issues created vs. number of issues resolved over a given period of time.
Resolution Time Report	Shows the average time taken to resolve issues.

Report type	Description
Pie Chart Report	Shows the search results from a specified issue filter (or project) in a pie chart, based on a statistic of your choice.
Average Age Report	Shows the average age (in days) of unresolved issues.
Recently Created Issues Report	Shows the rate at which issues are being created in the current project.
Time Since Issue Report	Shows the number of issues for which your chosen date field (for example, **Created**) was set on a given date.

Creating a report

All JIRA reports are accessed from the **Browse Project** page of a specific project, regardless of whether the report is project-specific or global. The difference between the two types of reports is that a global report will let you choose a filter as a source of data, while a project-specific report will have its source of data predetermined based on the project you are in.

When generating a report, you will often need to supply several configuration options. For example, you might have to select a filter, which will provide the data for the report, or select a field to report on. The configuration options vary from report to report, but there will always be hints and suggestions to help you work out what each option is.

To create a report, you will first need to get to a project's browse page.

1. Bring up the drop-down menu from **Projects**.
2. Select the project you wish to report on, or **View All Projects** if the project does not show up in the list.
3. Bring up the drop-down menu from **Reports** from the **Browse Project** page.
4. Select the report you wish to create. This will bring you to the **Report Configuration** page.
5. Specify the configuration options for the report.
6. Click on the **Next** button to create the report.

In the following example, we are creating a pie chart report. We first select the type of report we will be generating by selecting it from a list of available report types that come with JIRA. We then configure the necessary report parameters. In this case, we need to specify if we are generating a report based on a project or an existing filter. We also need to specify which issue field we will be reporting on.

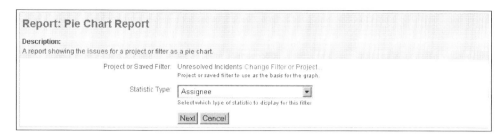

Once we have configured the report and clicked on the **Next** button, JIRA will generate the report and present it on screen.

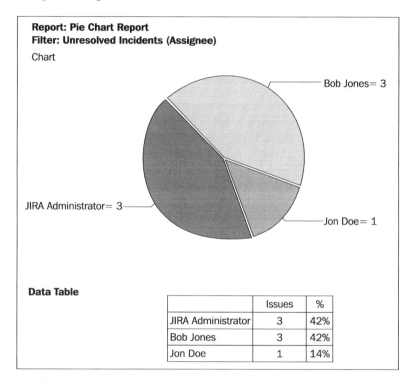

The report type determines the report's layout. Some reports have a chart associated with it (for example, **Pie Chart Report**), while other reports will have a tabular layout (for example, **Single Level Group By Report**). Some reports would even have an option for you to export its content into formats such as Microsoft Excel (for example, **Time Tracking Report**).

Dashboard

The dashboard is the first page you see when you access JIRA. Dashboards host "mini-applications" known as **Gadgets**, which provides various data and information from your JIRA instance. The dashboard acts as a portal which provides users with a quick one-page view on information that is relevant or of interest to them.

Managing dashboards

When you first install JIRA, the dashboard you see is called the **System Dashboard**, and it is preconfigured for your convenience. You can have more than one dashboard in JIRA, and each dashboard functions and are configured independently.

1. Bring up the drop-down menu from **Dashboards**.

2. Select the **Manage Dashboards** option. This will bring you to the **Manage Dashboards** page.

From this page, you can edit and maintain dashboards created by you, search dashboards created and shared by others, and mark them as **Favourite** so they will be listed as tabs for easy access.

When a dashboard is marked as **Favourite** (which is done by clicking on the star icon in front of its name), the dashboard will be accessible when you click on the **Dashboards** link from the top menu bar. If you have more than one favorite dashboard, each will be listed in tabs and you can select which one to display.

Creating a dashboard

The default **System Dashboard** cannot be changed by users, so if you want to have a personalized dashboard displaying information that is specific to you, you will need to create a new dashboard.

To create a new dashboard:

1. Bring up the drop-down menu from **Tools**.

2. Select the **Create Dashboard** option. This will bring you to the **Create New Dashboard** page.

3. Provide a meaningful name for the new dashboard.

4. Provide an optional description.

5. Select if you wish to copy from an existing dashboard or start with a blank one.

6. Select whether or not the new dashboard should be a **Favourite** dashboard (for easy access).

7. Select whether you wish to share the dashboard with anyone.

8. Click on the **Save** button to create the dashboard.

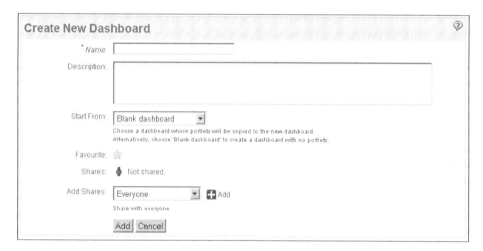

Once you have created the new dashboard, you immediately be taken to it. As the owner of the new dashboard, you will be able to edit its layout and add gadgets. We will be looking at these configuration options in the next section.

Editing and sharing a dashboard

For dashboards created by you, you can edit the name and description, and choose to share it with other users so they will be able to access the dashboard by choosing them as favorite.

1. Browse to the **Manage Dashboards** page.
2. Click on the **Edit** link for the dashboard you wish to edit. This will bring you to the **Edit and Share Dashboard** page.
3. Update the details of the dashboard.
4. Select the group/project role to share the dashboard with.
5. Click on the **Update** button to apply the changes.

For you to be able to share a dashboard, you will also need to have the **Create Shared Object** global permissions (please refer to *Chapter 8* for more information on global permissions).

Deleting a dashboard

Dashboard creators can also delete dashboards they have created. However, it is important to note that if you have shared out the dashboard, by removing it from JIRA, all other users that have added it as favorite will be affected.

1. Browse to the **Manage Dashboards** page.
2. Click on the **Delete** link for the dashboard you wish to remove. This will bring up the **Delete Dashboard** confirmation dialog.
3. Click on the **Delete** button to remove the dashboard.

The **Delete Dashboard** dialog will alert you if there are users who have added the dashboard as favorite.

Configuring a dashboard

All custom created dashboards can be configured once they have been created. As the owner, there are two aspects of a dashboard you can configure:

- **Layout**: How the dashboard page should be divided
- **Contents**: The gadgets that are to be added to the dashboard

Setting a layout for a dashboard

You have to be the owner of the dashboard to change the layout. Setting a dashboard's layout is quite simple and straightforward. If you are the owner, you will have the **Edit Layout** option at the top right-hand corner when you are viewing the dashboard.

JIRA comes with five layouts you can choose from. These layouts differ in how the dashboard page's onscreen real estate is divided. By default, new dashboards have the second layout, which divides it into two columns of equal sizes.

1. Bring up the drop-down menu from **Dashboards**.
2. Select the dashboard you wish to edit the layout for.
3. Click on the **Edit Layout** option from the top right-hand corner. This will bring up the **Edit Layout** dialog.
4. Select the layout to change to.

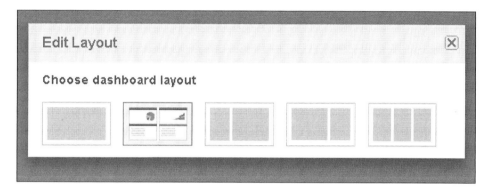

Once you have selected a layout from the dialog, it will immediately be applied to the dashboard. Any existing contents will automatically have their size re-adjusted to fit within the new layout.

After you have decided on your dashboard's layout, you can start adding contents onto your dashboard. But before we get to that, let's first take a brief look at gadgets.

Gadgets

If you are familiar with the personalized Google homepage (iGoogle), you should be fairly familiar with gadgets by now. As a matter of fact, JIRA gadgets and iGoogle gadgets are built on the same technology.

Gadgets are mini-applications that live on a dashboard in JIRA. Each gadget has its own unique interface and behaviors, for example, the **Pie Chart** gadget displays data in a pie chart while the **Assigned to Me** gadget lists all unresolved issues that are assigned to the current user in a table.

Prior to JIRA 4.0, gadgets are known as **portlets** (they are actually two different technologies). Starting with JIRA 4.0, Atlassian has included the OpenSocial technology, to make JIRA a more collaborative and social application. This allows JIRA to use gadgets that are available from other vendors such as Google, and also lets other OpenSocial-compliant services such as iGoogle use gadgets that are shipped with JIRA. With gadgets, you can now add a weather gadget from Google onto your JIRA dashboard or display your JIRA issues on your iGoogle page.

To discuss the in-depth details of gadgets and OpenSocial is beyond the scope of this book, but there is a lot of information on this topic available on the Internet if you are interested in creating your own gadgets to use with JIRA. A good place to start is the Atlassian documentation: `http://confluence.atlassian.com/display/ GADGETDEV/Getting+Started+with+Gadget+Development`.

Adding a gadget

To add a gadget to your dashboard:

1. Bring up the drop-down menu from **Dashboards**.
2. Select the dashboard you wish to add a gadget to.
3. Click on the **Add Gadget** option from the top right-hand corner. This will bring up the **Gadget Directory**.
4. Click on the **Add it Now** button for the gadget you wish to add.
5. Click on the **Finish** button to return to the dashboard.

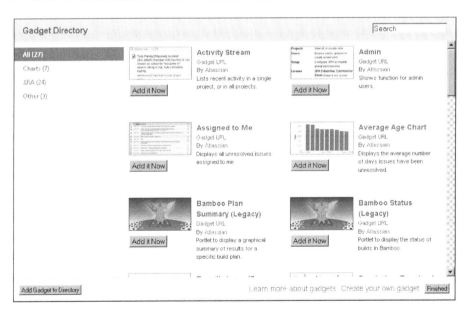

Depending on the gadget you have selected, it may require additional options to be configured. For gadgets that require configuration, you will be presented with their configuration screen on the dashboard. Fill in the options and click on the **Save** button.

Moving a gadget

When you are adding a gadget, they are usually added to the first available spot on the dashboard. This sometimes may not be where you want the gadget to display, and in other cases, you might want to move existing gadgets around from time to time. As the owner of the dashboard, you can easily move gadgets on a dashboard, through a simple drag-and-drop interface. To move gadgets on a dashboard:

1. Browse to the dashboard that has gadgets you wish to move.
2. Click on the gadget and drag it to the new position on the dashboard.

As soon as you drop the gadget to its new location (releasing your mouse button), the gadget will be moved permanently until you decide to move it again. You can also move a gadget to a different dashboard with drag-and-drop. Simply drag the gadget over the target dashboard's name and the gadget will be moved over to the new dashboard.

Editing a gadget

You can edit existing gadgets to update their configuration details or even their look and feel.

1. Browse to the dashboard that has gadgets you wish to delete.
2. Click on the down arrow button on the top right hand corner of the gadget. This will bring up the gadget configuration menu.
3. Click on the **Edit** option.

   This will change the gadget into its configuration mode.
4. Update the configuration options.
5. Click on the **Save** button to apply the changes.

Deleting a gadget

You can remove existing gadgets from the dashboard when they are no longer needed. When you remove a gadget from a dashboard, please note that all other users who have access to your dashboard will no longer see it.

1. Browse to the dashboard that has gadgets you wish to delete.
2. Click on the down arrow button on the top right-hand corner of the gadget. This will bring up the gadget configuration menu.
3. Click on the **Delete** option.
4. Confirm the removal when prompted.

Once removed, the gadget will disappear from the dashboard. If you choose to re-add the same gadget again at a later stage, you will have to configure the gadget again.

Help Desk Project

In the previous chapters and exercises, we have built and customized our JIRA to collect data from JIRA users. What we need to do now is to process and present this data back to the users. The goal we are trying to achieve in this exercise is to setup a portal page for our Help Desk team that will have useful information such as statistics and issue listings that can help our team members to better organize themselves to provide better services to other departments.

Setting up filters

The first step is to create some useful filters that can be shared with other members of the team and also act as a source of data to feed into our gadgets. We will be using the advanced search to construct our search.

1. Browse to the **Issue Navigator**.
2. Click on the **Switch to advanced searching** link to bring up the JQL interface.
3. Type in the following JQL search query.

   ```
   project = HD and issuetype = Incident and status != Resolved and
   status != Closed order by priority
   ```

4. Click on the **Search** button to execute the search.
5. Click on the **Save it as a filter** link to bring up the **Save Current Filter** page.
6. Name the filter **Unresolved Incidents**.
7. Mark the filter as **Favourite**.

8. Share the filter with **help-desk-team** group setup from *Chapter 8*.

9. Click on the **Save** button to create the filter.

This filter searches and returns a list of unresolved issues of type **Incident** from our Help Desk project. The search results are then ordered by their priority so users can determine the urgency. As you will see in later steps, this filter will be used as the source of data for our gadgets to present information on our dashboard.

Setting up dashboards

The next step is to create a new dashboard for our help desk team. What we need is a dashboard specifically for our team so we can share information easily. For example, we can have the dashboard displayed in a large overhead projector showing all high priority incidents that need to be addressed.

1. Bring up the drop-down menu from **Tools**.

2. Select the **Create Dashboard** option. This will bring you to the **Create New Dashboard** page.

3. Name the new dashboard **Help Desk**.

4. Select **Blank dashboard** as our base.

5. Tick the new dashboard as favourite.

6. Share the filter with the **help-desk-team** group.

7. Click on the **Save** button to create the dashboard.

In our example, we will be using the default two column layout for our new dashboard. You are free to experiment with other layouts and find one that best suits your needs.

Setting up gadgets

Now that we have set up our portal dashboard page and shared it with other members of the team, we need to start adding some useful information onto it. One example would be to have the dashboard display all unresolved incidents that are waiting to be processed. JIRA has the **Assigned to Me** gadget which shows all issues that are assigned to the currently logged in user, but what we need is a global list which does not filter by the assignee of the incident.

Luckily, JIRA also has the **Filter Results** gadget, which will display search results based on a search filter. Since we have already created a filter that returns all unresolved incidents in our Help Desk project, the combination of both will nicely solve our problem.

1. Browse to the **Help Desk** dashboard we just created.

2. Click on the **Add Gadget** option from the top right hand corner. This will bring up the **Gadget Directory**.

3. Click on the **Add it Now** button for the **Filter Results** gadget.

4. Click on the **Finish** button to return to the dashboard.

5. Select the **Unresolved Incidents** filter we have created.

6. Select **Default Columns** and any additional fields you wish to add.

7. Set the **Refresh Interval** to **15 minutes**.

8. Click on the **Save** button.

This will add a new **Filter Results** gadget to our new dashboard, using our filter as the source of data. The gadget will auto-refresh its contents every 15 minutes, so you will not need to refresh the page all the time. You can add some other gadgets to the dashboard to make it more informative and useful. Some other useful gadgets include the **Activity Stream** and **Assigned to Me** gadgets.

Putting it together

This is all you have to do to set up and share a dashboard in JIRA. After you have added gadgets, you will be able to see it in action. The great thing is that since you have shared the dashboard with others in the team, they will be able to see the dashboard too. Members of the team will be able to search for our new dashboard, and mark it as **Favourite** to add it to their list of dashboards.

You do have to keep in mind that if you are using a filter as a source of data for your gadget, you have to share the filter with other users too, or they will not be able to see anything from the gadget.

Summary

We have covered how users can search and report on the data they have put into JIRA, which is an essential component for any information system. JIRA provides a robust search facility by offering users with many different search options, including **Quick**, **Simple**, and **Advanced**. You can save and name your searches by creating filters which can be re-run at later dates to save you from re-creating the same search over and over again.

JIRA also allows you to create adhoc reports on projects or results brought back from search filters. Information can be shared with others through a dashboard, which acts as a portal for users to quickly get a glance of the data kept in JIRA.

In the next chapter, we will round up our discussions by looking at various other features and administration options such as the backup/restore utility and automated services in JIRA which can further help in setting up a more robust installation.

10
General Administration

JIRA is a very powerful and flexible application. We have seen how you can customize its functionalities by building new fields, screens, workflows, notifications, and permission rules. Apart from the major areas we have already covered, there are some other useful features that you can customize.

You can change the appearance of JIRA so that its look and feel will be more consistent with other web applications you have in your organization. You can also select the language JIRA will use to display text in, as well as perform quick backups and restores with the built-in tools. Finally, we will take a look at how you can extend the power of JIRA through custom **Plugins**.

By the end of the chapter, you would have learned:

- How to customize JIRA's look and feel
- About general administration options in JIRA
- How to back up and restore data in JIRA
- How to keep the search index in sync with data
- How to extend JIRA's functionalities through custom plugins

Look and feel

While the default appearance that is configured with JIRA upon installation is sufficient for most purposes, organizations often require their applications and websites to be branded and to have a standardized look and feel. JIRA allows for this level of flexibility by allowing you to configure its colors, date representations, and even letting you add a logo to it.

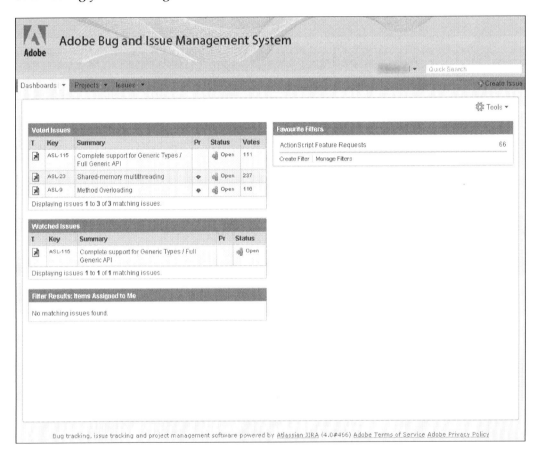

As an example, the preceding screenshot shows a branded version of JIRA that may be used for a department in the Adobe company.

Since appearance is something that is global across JIRA, you will need to be a JIRA Administrator or System Administrator to configure these settings.

1. Log into JIRA as a JIRA Administrator.
2. Click on **Administration** from the top menu bar.
3. Click on **Look and Feel** from the left-hand side panel. This will bring up the **Look and Feel Configuration** page.

From this page, you will be able to customize the color, logo, and date format settings of your JIRA instance.

Logo

People often say a picture is worth a thousand words; a logo is usually the first thing to come to mind when it comes to a brand's website. JIRA lets you assign a logo which will be displayed on top of every page in JIRA.

1. Browse to the **Look and Feel Configuration** page.
2. Click on the **Edit Configuration** link at the bottom of the page. This will allow you to edit the look and feel settings.
3. Specify the URL or the file path of your logo image under the **Logo** section.
4. Specify the width and height of the image.
5. Click on the **Update** button to set your logo.

Once you have set your logo, JIRA will display the logo in the preview section with your specified dimensions. The logo will be applied immediately at the top left-hand corner.

Colors

JIRA divides up its user interface into a number of elements and each can be assigned its own color. For example, you can set a different color for the top navigation bar and another for. This allows you to have flexibility to configure the color of JIRA to be more consistent with your organization's branding standards.

1. Browse to the **Look and Feel Configuration** page.
2. Click on the **Edit Configuration** link at the bottom of the page. This will allow you to edit the look and feel settings.

3. Specify the colors for each of the component/section under the **Colors** section. You can either specify the **hexadecimal** color code directly or use the **color picker** to select the color you want.

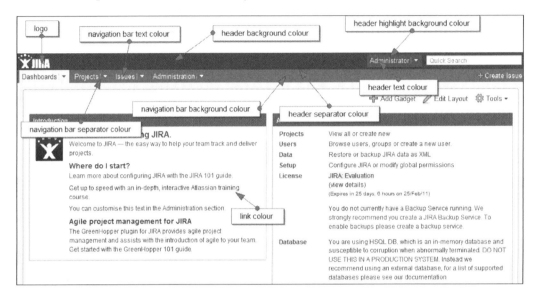

The preceding image shows a breakdown of the different sections in JIRA and what color setting to change for each.

Color Option	Description
Header Background Color	The background color of the top bar (where the logo image is).
Header Highlight Background Color	The background color of the text that sits inside the top bar when highlighted (hovered over).
Header Text Color	The color of the text that sits inside the top bar.
Header Text Highlight Color	The color of the text that sits inside the top bar when highlighted.
Header Separator Color	The color of the horizontal line between the top bar and the navigation bar.
Navigation Bar Background Color	The background color of the bar that contains the navigation links such as **Dashboard** and **Administration**.
Navigation Bar Text Color	The color of text links in the navigation bar.
Navigation Bar Separator Color	The color of the vertical dotted line between each menu item in the navigation bar.
Link Color	The color of text links in JIRA.
Link Active Color	The color of text links in JIRA when selected.
Heading Color	The color of the text headings in JIRA.

Gadget colors

In *Chapter 9, Searching, Reporting, and Analysis*, we introduced dashboards and gadgets in JIRA. A gadget's color, look, and feel is independent from JIRA. As a matter of fact, JIRA allows the administrator to create a set of colors for users to pick from. To create your custom color set:

1. Browse to the **Look and Feel Configuration** page.

2. Click on the **Edit Configuration** link at the bottom of the page. This will allow you to edit the look and feel settings.

3. Specify the colors for your gadgets under the **Gadget Colours** section. The first colour (Color 1) will be the default color for all gadgets without a color selected.

4. Click on the **Update** button.

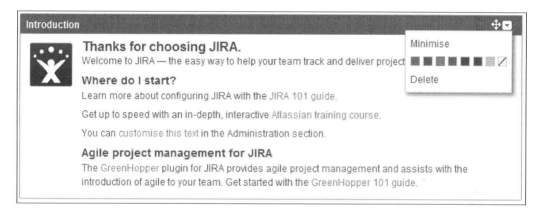

Once you have saved your set of gadget colors, they will be made available for users to select from. For gadgets that do not have a color selected, the default color will be applied automatically.

Date/Time format

Another aspect of JIRA's look and feel that can be customized is how dates are displayed and entered. Different countries display dates differently. For example, some countries display dates in the *month/day/year* format while other use the *day/month/year* format. JIRA allows you to set how you would like dates to be handled to better suit your environment.

JIRA follows the date format set by Java, the technology that JIRA is built on. You can find the full explanation of the format at: http://download.oracle.com/javase/6/docs/api/java/text/SimpleDateFormat.html.

1. Browse to the **Look and Feel Configuration** page.

2. Click on the **Edit Configuration** link at the bottom of the page.

3. Click on the **Update** button to set your logo.

Date/Time Formats

These time and date formats are used throughout JIRA. To specify them, use the format described at http://java.sun.com/j2se/1.4.2/docs/api/java/text/SimpleDateFormat.html.

	Format	Example
Time Format	h:mm a	5:02 PM
Day Format	EEEE h:mm a	Tuesday 5:02 PM
Complete Date/Time Format	dd/MMM/yy h:mm a	25/Jan/11 5:02 PM
Day/Month/Year Format	dd/MMM/yy	25/Jan/11
Date Picker Format (javascript format)	d/MMM/yy (%e/%b/%y)	25/Jan/11
Date Time Picker Format (javascript format)	dd/MMM/yy h:mm a (%e/%b/%y %I:%M %p)	25/Jan/11 5:02 PM
Use ISO8601 standard in Date Picker	OFF	

After you have updated the date/time format settings, all **date** and **datetime** fields in JIRA, such as **due date**, will adopt the new format to display dates, and users will be required to enter dates in the new format.

General configurations

In the past few chapters, we have been focusing on how to customize JIRA's issue management features and options. As an application, there are also several system configuration options that can be changed. These include the maximum failed login attempts allowed before locking the user out, setting the default language used by JIRA, and other miscellaneous options.

JIRA groups these options under the **General Configurations** so that you can fine-tune these settings.

1. Log into JIRA as a JIRA Administrator.

2. Click on **Administration** from the top menu bar.

3. Click on **General Configuration** from the left-hand side panel. This will bring up the **JIRA General Configuration** page.

From here, you will be able to set configuration settings for options that are not related to JIRA projects and issues.

Settings

The **Settings** section contains several system-wide configurations that control some generic behaviors of JIRA.

Setting	Description
Title	Name of your JIRA instance. This name will appear in the Introduction Gadget on the dashboard.
Mode	This option lets you decide if JIRA will allow users to sign up/create an account on JIRA.
	Public: Anyone can create an account by signing up.
	Private: Only the JIRA administrator can create new accounts.
Maximum Authentication Attempts Allowed	The number of failed login attempts allowed before the CAPTCHA challenge is required. This is helpful to prevent brute force login attacks, where malicious users continuously attempt to log into an account by trying and guessing password combinations.
CAPTCHA on signup	To enable/disable CAPTCHA challenge when users sign up for new accounts. Useful to prevent bots from signing up.
Base URL	The base URL of your JIRA application. This is usually the URL used by users to access your JIRA instance. For example, the base URL in our example will be `http://localhost:8080/jira`. This is often used by JIRA internally for operations such as sending links in e-mails from notifications or gadgets. It is important that this is set correctly.
Email from	The **From:** header used by JIRA when sending out notifications.
Introduction	A short introduction to be displayed on the dashboard in the Introduction gadget.

Internationalization

The Internationalization section lets you set the language JIRA will be using when displaying its contents. JIRA comes with a wide range of languages to choose from. If the language you are looking for is not available, you can check the **Atlassian Plugin Exchange** to see if someone has created a translation that you can use. We will discuss plugins and plugin exchange in more details in later sections.

Setting the default language

To set the default language for JIRA:

1. Browse to the **General Configuration** page.

2. Select the default language under **Internationalization**.

3. Click on the **Update** button to set the default language.

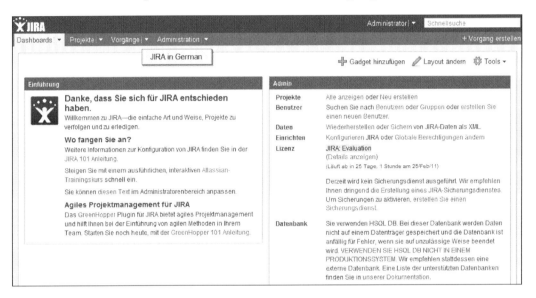

Once you have chosen the default language, the change will be applied immediately. The selected default language will be used by JIRA for users that have not set up a personal language preference. The preceding screenshot shows JIRA in German, one of the languages shipped with JIRA.

Setting the user language

For multinational organizations, sometimes a single JIRA instance is used by teams across the globe. In these cases, it becomes desirable to be able to have different languages available to users depending on where the user comes from. This is where user-based language settings come in. JIRA lets each user select the language of their choice, which will take precedence over the default language setting applied by the administrator. This selection needs to be done by each user individually. To select a language:

1. Log into JIRA.

2. Click on your username at the top right corner of the page. This will bring up your **User Profile** page.

3. Click on the edit icon for the **Preferences** section. This will bring up the **Update User** Preference page.

4. Select the language you wish to use.

5. Click on the **Update** button to apply the change.

Once selected, the change will be applied immediately and you should see JIRA displayed in the language of your choice.

Options

The **Options** section contains a list of settings that allow you turn certain features of JIRA on or off. JIRA comes with sensible default settings for these options. However, it is quite common for users to change these settings to better suit their environment.

Options	Description
Allow users to vote on issues	Enable/disable voting in JIRA.
Allow users to watch issues	Enable/disable issue watching in JIRA.
Allow unassigned issues	When enabled, issues can be set to **unassigned**. If disabled, issues MUST have assignees.
External user management	When enabled, this tells JIRA that you are using an external application to manage users (for example, LDAP Atlassian Crowd). JIRA will disable user management features so you will not be able to create, edit, or delete users/groups from within itself.
External password management	When enabled, this tells JIRA that you are using an external application to manage user passwords. JIRA will not allow users to change their password and remove the **Forgot Password** link on the login screen.
Logout confirmation	Controls if a confirmation prompt will be displayed when users log out.
Use gzip compression	Controls if compression should be applied when JIRA sends pages to the browser.

Options	Description
Accept remote API calls	Controls if JIRA will accept web service calls (XML-RCP or SOAP). This needs to be enabled if other applications attempt to access/integrate JIRA with these services.
User email visibility	Controls if users' e-mail addresses will be be viewable.
Comment visibility	Determines the options available when users restrict their comment visibility.
Exclude email header "Precedence: bulk"	Controls whether to prevent the **Precedence: Bulk** header on JIRA notification e-mails.
Issue Picker Auto-complete	Enable/disable auto-completion of issue keys in the Issue Picker popup screen.
User Searching By Full Name	Enable/disable auto-completion feature when searching users by their full name instead of username.
JQL Auto-complete	Enable/disable auto-completion feature when constructing JQL queries.
Internet Explorer MIME Sniffing Security Hole Workaround Policy	Enable cross-site scripting vulnerabilities present in Internet Explorer 7 and earlier. <ul><li>Insecure: Inline display of attachments—allows all attachments to be displayed inline. Least secure option.</li><li>Secure: Force download of all attachments for all browsers. Most secure option, but less convenient.</li><li>Work around Internet Explorer security hold—Force download attachments that IE would mistakenly detect as an HTML file. This is the preferred and default option.</li></ul>

Announcement banner

There will often be times when you need to make a change to the system where you need to take JIRA down for a period of time. In a production environment where there is a high reliance on the uptime, this can lead to an unnecessary disruption to the users if not planned and communicated accordingly. JIRA recognizes this and provides a facility to help by letting administrators place an announcement banner on every page in JIRA. Together with traditional methods such as e-mail alerts, day-to-day business disruptions caused by system downtime can be minimized.

To put up an announcement banner in JIRA:

1. Log into JIRA as a JIRA Administrator.

2. Click on **Administration** from the top menu bar.

3. Click on **Announcement Banner** from the left hand panel. This will bring up the **Edit Announcement Banner** page.

4. Specify the announcement. This can be simple text, valid HTML markup, CSS, or JavaScript.

5. Select if you want this announcement to be **public** where everyone will be able to see it or **private** where only logged-in users can see.

6. Click on the **Set Banner** button to put up the announcement.

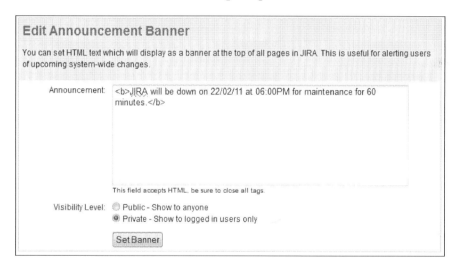

The preceding screenshot shows an announcement banner created with HTML markup. Once you have set the announcement banner, it will be visible on every page in JIRA until you remove it.

Backing up and restoring

For any applications running in a production environment, it is critical that its data is backed up regularly so that it can be restored in case of a disaster.

The first thing you will need is to have a disaster recovery plan in place. This plan should outline the details of the strategy in place to back up JIRA's data, where the backups should be stored, and the recovery process of restoring the data. In JIRA, there are typically two items you will need to back up.

- **Database**: This is where JIRA stores most of its critical data such as issues and configuration settings. It is recommended to use the native database backup tools available for your database (for example, `mysqldump` for MySQL).
- **JIRA_HOME**: This is where JIRA stores other important files such as attachments and third-party plugin extensions. Since this is a directory on the field system, you will need a native tool to back up the files (for example, **Scheduled Tasks** in Windows).

JIRA also comes with an XML backup/restore function which will back up data from a database into an XML file. However, this utility is not designed to be used for large JIRA instances (for example, with 300 thousand issues or more). It is important to note that data kept in `JIRA_HOME` is not backed up.

Create an XML backup

JIRA comes with a simple backup utility that lets you back up your data into an XML file which can be later imported back in to restore JIRA. However, you must keep in mind that you should **not** rely on this utility as your sole backup strategy as this option has several limitations.

- It cannot be used to back up large JIRA installations. JIRA is unable to restore backup files that are 2GB or greater in size.
- It does not back up data on the file system, such as attachments.

Nonetheless, this can still be very handy when you need a quick way to perform a once-off backup before you make some systemwide changes such as an upgrade, or you need to copy data from one JIRA instance to another. To create an XML backup:

1. Log into JIRA as a JIRA Administrator.
2. Click on **Administration** from the top menu bar.
3. Click on **Backup Data to XML** from the left hand panel. This will bring up the **Backup JIRA data** page.
4. Specify the name of your exported XML file.
5. Check the **Backup As Zip** option so your exported file will be compressed to save disk space. A `.zip` extension will be added to the file name if the option is checked.

6. Click on the **Backup** button.

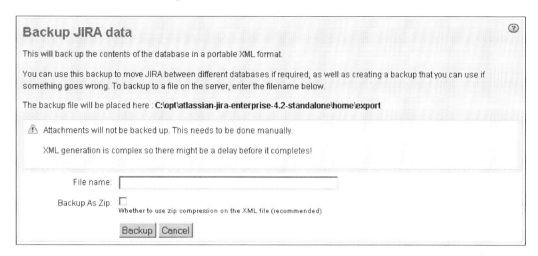

Depending on the size of your JIRA database, the backup process will take some time to complete. Once the backup process completes, JIRA will display the confirmation page with the full path to the exported XML file. If your JIRA's database has too much data, the backup will fail with an error. If this occurs, you will have to back up your data manually from your database.

Restoring from an XML backup

Once you have generated an XML backup, you can use that to restore your JIRA by importing it back in. Please note that when you perform a restore, existing data will be completely wiped. To proceed with a restore:

1. Log into JIRA as a JIRA Administrator.
2. Click on **Administration** from the top menu bar.
3. Click on **Restore Data to XML** from the left-hand panel. This will bring up the **Restore JIRA data from Backup** page.
4. Specify the XML backup file to restore from.
5. Optionally, supply a new JIRA license. You will need to do this if you are restoring from an older version of JIRA (3.x) or the license contained in the backup has expired.

6. Click on the **Restore** button to start the restore process.

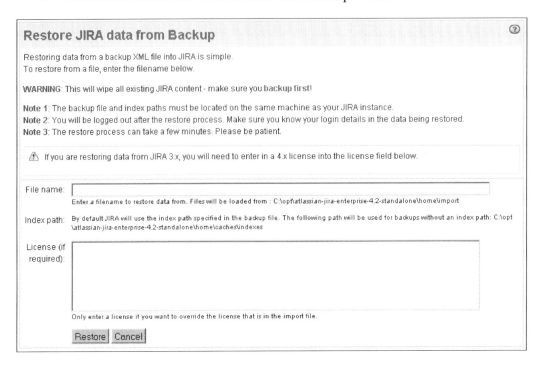

Since attachments are not part of the XML backup, the restore process will not restore the attachments. However, if you are restoring a backup from the same instance, attachments will be automatically located. While JIRA is in the process of restoring from a backup, users will not be able to access JIRA.

You can only restore an export from the same or an older version of JIRA. For example, you cannot restore an export from JIRA 4.2.1 into JIRA 4.1.

Search indexing

In *Chapter 9, Searching, Reporting, and Analysis*, we looked at how you can search for data in JIRA. In order to support large instances with hundreds of thousands of issues, JIRA creates and maintains search indexes on the file system. This index is added and modified automatically in the background whenever issues are created or updates are made. However, sometimes JIRA will require you to perform a manual re-index. This may occur when the index files are corrupted or missing, or changes are made directly in the database causing the index to be out of sync. You will notice this when your searches are constantly returning the wrong set of issues.

When you are re-indexing, you are effectively re-creating the search index on the file system based on the most current data in the database. This ensures the values in both the file system and database are in sync. It is important to note that as the amount of data grows in your database, so will the search index. You will need to allocate enough disk space on the server where you install JIRA. To re-index your JIRA:

1. Log into JIRA as a JIRA Administrator.

2. Click on **Administration** from the top menu bar.

3. Click on **Indexing** from the left-hand panel. This will bring up the **Re-Indexing** page.

4. Click on the **Re-Index** button to start the indexing process.

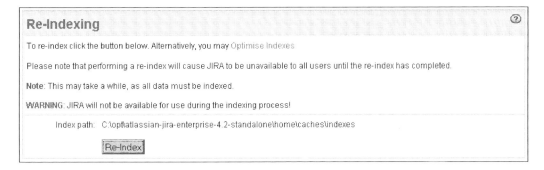

Depending on the size of your JIRA instance, this process can take some time to complete (several hours for some large installations; 300 thousand plus issues). While re-indexing, users will not be able to access JIRA. It is important for you to plan an outage window and make sure users are aware of this.

Services

In *Chapter 7, E-mail and Notification*, we looked at **mail handlers**, which are used by JIRA to periodically poll mailboxes and create issues. Mail handler is an example of a feature in JIRA called **Services**.

A service is something that is run periodically by JIRA, performing a certain function. They are equivalent to that of a cron job in Unix or scheduled job in Windows. A mail handler for example, is a service that creates issues from e-mails pulled from the mail inbox. There are other services used by JIRA, such as the **Mail Queue Service** which flushes out notification e-mails. Services are a great way to set up some automated jobs in JIRA and are often used to integrate JIRA with other systems by constantly polling and sending information between the two.

JIRA comes with a list of useful services that you can install out of the box, but if you want to have services to perform specialized functions, you will need the help of plugins, which will be covered in the next section.

Adding a service

To add a new service in JIRA is a simple process.

1. Log into JIRA as a JIRA Administrator.
2. Click on **Administration** from the top menu bar.
3. Select **Services** from the left panel to bring up the **Services** page.
4. Provide a meaningful name for the service.
5. Specify the full Java class name of the service (you will usually find this in the documentation of the service).
6. Specify the time delay between each service run (in minutes).
7. Click on the **Add Service** button. This will take you to the **Edit Service** page where you can configure the service before it can be run for the first time.
8. Specify the configuration options (defaults are usually found in the service documentation).
9. Click on the **Update** button.

Once you have configured the service, it will be added to JIRA and will automatically be run it as defined in the time delay. Each service run uses system resources, and depending on the complexity of the service, it is recommended that you provide a generous time delay.

Editing a service

You can update the configuration options for existing services. One reason why you might want to do this is to tweak the time delay setting for your service.

1. Browse to the **Services** page.
2. Click on the **Edit** link for the service you wish to update. This will take you to the **Edit Service** page.
3. Update the service configuration options.
4. Click on the **Update** button to apply the change.

Once the changes are applied, they will take affect in the next service run.

Deleting a service

You cannot put a service on hold. If you want it to stop running, you will have to delete it from JIRA.

1. Browse to the **Services** page.

2. Click on the **Delete** link for the service you wish to delete.

There will be no confirmation when you click on the delete link. Once deleted, the job is removed from JIRA immediately and no further service runs will occur (if in the middle of an operation when deleted, the current run will finish).

Plugins

In the previous chapter, we illustrated JIRA's flexibility by allowing you to add new custom fields to capture data, and creating new workflows to model business processes, but it does not stop there. Another powerful feature of JIRA is its built-in plugin system.

Generally, a plugin is a self-contained application with a `.jar` file extension that can be installed into JIRA to add new functionalities or enhance existing features.

1. Log into JIRA as a JIRA Administrator.

2. Click on **Administration** from the top menu bar.

3. Click on **Plugins** from the left-hand panel. This will bring up the **Current Plugins** page.

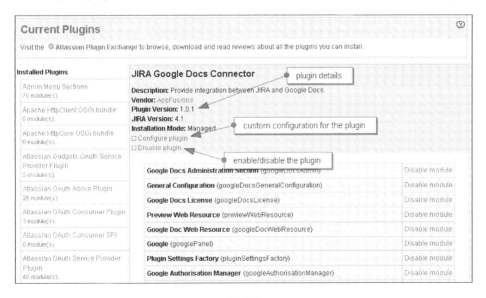

This is where you manage installed plugins. It lists all the plugins that are currently installed and their statuses.

Atlassian plugins type version

This refers to the version of plugins system used by the plugin, not the actual release version of individual plugins.

Starting with JIRA 4.x, Atlassian introduced the **Version 2 Plugins System** (often referred to as V2 Plugins), which supersedes the original **Version 1 Plugins System** (V1 Plugins). For all intents and purposes, the major difference between the two is where the plugins are installed.

- V1 Plugins are installed in the `JIRA_INSTALL/atlassian-jira/WEB-INF/lib` directory.

- V2 Plugins are installed in the `JIRA_HOME/plugins/installed-plugins` directory.

If you install the plugin in the wrong directory, for example, a V1 plugin in the `JIRA_HOME/plugins/installed-plugins` directory, JIRA will not load the plugin and record this in the log file. JIRA will start up as normal.

Plugin Exchange

Atlassian hosts plugins on their Plugin Exchange website. The Plugin Exchange hosts a rich set of plugins from both Atlassian and other third-party vendors for all of Atlassian products such as JIRA. From here, you will be able to search useful plugins, read reviews on plugins you are interested in, and download/buy plugins directly. Plugins hosted on the Plugin Exchange come in two flavors.

- Free/Open source: Created and maintained by the community, and is free to use, usually unsupported and "use at your own risk".

- Commercial: Created and maintained by the plugin vendor. Usually requires a license to be purchased. Often comes with warranty and support.

You can access the Plugin Exchange from `https://plugins.atlassian.com`.

Installing a plugin

Installing a new JIRA plugin will usually require you to restart your JIRA instance. Generally speaking, installing a plugin in JIRA is a straightforward process. However, some complex plugins will require additional steps to set up. It is recommended that you read the installation instruction documentation that comes with the plugin.

1. Shut down your JIRA instance.
2. Copy your plugin file into `JIRA_HOME/plugins/installed-plugins` directory.
3. Start up your JIRA instance.

If the plugin installs successfully, your JIRA should start up without any problems. To verify that the plugin has been successfully installed:

1. Browse to the **Current Plugins** page.
2. Locate and select the plugin that has just been installed.
3. Make sure the plugin is not disabled and all its modules are listed in green.

If the plugin modules are listed in red with error messages, you will need to contact the plugin vendor for further assistance. Usually, in order to assist the plugin vendor to diagnose the problem, you will be asked to send your JIRA log files and provide information on your system, so make sure you have them ready when requesting support.

Configuring a plugin

A simple plugin that adds additional custom field types and workflow post functions can be used straight out of the box after installation. Other plugins that are more complex will require additional configuring, such as licensing information and custom field mappings. Each plugin will have different ways to set configuration options, so you will need to consult the plugin's usage instructions. Generally, if a plugin requires configuration, you will be able to access its configuration page via the plugin's administration page.

1. Browse to the **Current Plugins** page.
2. Locate and click on the plugin you wish to configure.
3. Click on the **Configure** plugin link.

Each plugin will have its own individual configuration page and options, and you will need to refer to the plugin's manual for details.

Enabling/Disabling a plugin

Most plugins developed by third-party vendors can be enabled or disabled. This is particularly useful if you need to urgently stop a plugin to prevent problems but are unable to bring down JIRA due to the restart requirement. You can simply disable it until the system can be brought down to uninstall the plugin.

Disabling a plugin is simple and straightforward.

1. Browse to the **Current Plugins** page.
2. Locate and click on the plugin you wish to disable.
3. Click on the **Disable plugin** link.

Once disabled, the list of plugin modules will turn red. It is important to keep in mind while disabling a plugin is that it will immediately stop most of the functions which it provides, such as new custom field types, but there are some functions which will continue to work. For this reason, if the plugin is causing problems for your JIRA instance, you are advised to uninstall it completely from you system.

Disabled plugins can be re-enabled. To enable a disabled plugin, simply click on the **Enable plugin** link.

Upgrading a plugin

Upgrading an existing plugin follows the same steps as installing a new plugin. The only thing you need to be aware of is that you must first remove the old version from the system.

1. Shut down your JIRA instance.
2. Backup and remove any older versions of the plugin.
3. Copy your plugin file into JIRA.
4. Start up your JIRA instance.

You will also need to read the plugin vendor's installation and upgrade documentation on any special requirements for the upgrade.

Attention needs to be paid when the upgrade involves changing the plugin's type version. For example, if the old plugin uses type **version 1** and the new plugin uses the newer type **version 2**, make sure you remove the old **version 1** plugin from the WEB-INF/lib directory. Failing to do so can lead to unexpected errors.

Uninstalling a plugin

Uninstalling an existing plugin is a simple process. Just remove the plugin file from the `installed-plugins` directory (if the plugin is a V2 plugin), or the `WEB-INF` directory (if the plugin is a V1 plugin). Un-installation requires JIRA to be restarted.

1. Shut down your JIRA instance.
2. Remove the plugin file.
3. Start up your JIRA instance.

Before you uninstall a plugin, you need to first make sure that the plugin does not contain critical functionalities that are currently being used by JIRA. For example, if the plugin has a custom field type that is being used by a workflow condition, uninstalling the plugin may cause the condition to fail. It is best to test this out in a test environment before uninstalling from production, or first disabling the plugin so you can recover from problems quickly by re-enabling the plugin.

Help Desk Project

What we want this time is to set up some automated services to remind our help desk team members about incomplete tasks and escalate them as necessary. As we have seen, while JIRA provides most of the features including letting us to add a variety of automated services, this specific use case is not supported by JIRA out of the box. We will need to to extend JIRA with a custom plugin.

Installing the plugin

The first step is to install the third-party plugin that can be downloaded from the book's website. Remember this process requires us to restart JIRA, so if you are doing this to a production JIRA instance, you might need to let your users know of this disruption. The announcement banner we touched on in this chapter can be used for this purpose.

1. Shut down your JIRA instance.
2. Copy the plugin file (`escalation-lite.jar`) into your `JIRA_HOME/plugins/installed-plugins` directory.
3. Start up your JIRA instance.

Once your JIRA starts up, confirm the plugin is successfully installed by checking it in the **Current Plugins** page.

Configuring the plugin

With the plugin installed, now we just need to set up a few configuration options. The plugin uses the standard plugin configuration:

1. Browse to the **Current Plugins** page.

2. Locate and select **Escalation Lite Plugin**. This will bring up the details page for the plugin.

3. Click on the **Configure plugin** link. This will bring up the custom plugin configuration page.

The custom plugin configuration page shows you a list of priorities available in your JIRA, and lets you specify the time duration for each. If the issue is marked Yes for the Is **Escalation Required** field and is not resolved or has not been updated within the escalation time set for its priority, then the issue will be automatically escalated. You can specify the time duration in the standard JIRA date time format, for example, one day as **1d**, and one week as **1w**.

Setting up the service

We now need to set up the automated service for JIRA to automatically escalate our issues based on our settings.

1. Browse to the **Services** page.
2. Name our new service **Escalation Service**.
3. Specify the full class name of the service: `com.appfusions.jira.plugins.sla.service.EscalationService`.
4. Configure the service by specifying the project key for our Help Desk project, the names of custom fields we have added in *Chapter 4*, a valid user who has access to our project, and the ID for our custom event in *Chapter 7* (you can get the ID by hovering over the **Edit** link in the **View Events** page).
5. Click on the **Add Service** button, this will take you to the **Edit Service** page where you can configure the service before it runs for the first time.

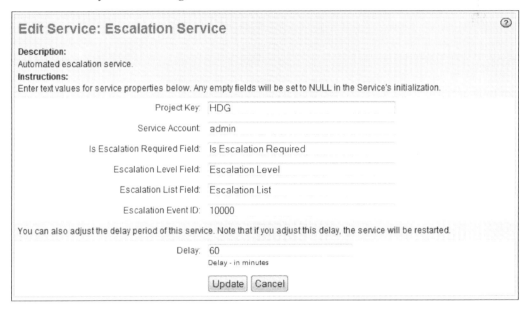

Now that we have our service added, we can let JIRA take care of escalating our issues automatically when they are overdue.

Summary

In this chapter, we rounded up our discussion of JIRA by covering some valuable features such as customization of JIRA's appearance and how to extend JIRA's functionalities through the use of plugins. JIRA is a powerful and flexible product. Best of all, it allows you to make further enhancements with new features through its robust plugin system. Atlassian has a great community and ecosystem with people people who will offer advice and solutions to your problems on the forum, as well as the Plugin Exchange, a place find plugins that will suit your needs.

Index

Thank you for buying
JIRA 4 Essentials

About Packt Publishing

Packt, pronounced 'packed', published its first book "Mastering phpMyAdmin for Effective MySQL Management" in April 2004 and subsequently continued to specialize in publishing highly focused books on specific technologies and solutions.

Our books and publications share the experiences of your fellow IT professionals in adapting and customizing today's systems, applications, and frameworks. Our solution based books give you the knowledge and power to customize the software and technologies you're using to get the job done. Packt books are more specific and less general than the IT books you have seen in the past. Our unique business model allows us to bring you more focused information, giving you more of what you need to know, and less of what you don't.

Packt is a modern, yet unique publishing company, which focuses on producing quality, cutting-edge books for communities of developers, administrators, and newbies alike. For more information, please visit our website: www.packtpub.com.

About Packt Enterprise

In 2010, Packt launched two new brands, Packt Enterprise and Packt Open Source, in order to continue its focus on specialization. This book is part of the Packt Enterprise brand, home to books published on enterprise software – software created by major vendors, including (but not limited to) IBM, Microsoft and Oracle, often for use in other corporations. Its titles will offer information relevant to a range of users of this software, including administrators, developers, architects, and end users.

Writing for Packt

We welcome all inquiries from people who are interested in authoring. Book proposals should be sent to author@packtpub.com. If your book idea is still at an early stage and you would like to discuss it first before writing a formal book proposal, contact us; one of our commissioning editors will get in touch with you.

We're not just looking for published authors; if you have strong technical skills but no writing experience, our experienced editors can help you develop a writing career, or simply get some additional reward for your expertise.

EJB 3.0 Database Persistence with Oracle Fusion Middleware 11*g*

A complete guide to EJB 3.0 database persistence with Oracle Fusion Middleware 11*g*

Deepak Vohra

EJB 3.0 Database Persistence with Oracle Fusion Middleware 11g

ISBN: 978-1-849681-56-8   Paperback: 448 pages

A complete guide to building EJB 3.0 database persistent applications with Oracle Fusion Middleware 11g tools

1. Integrate EJB 3.0 database persistence with Oracle Fusion Middleware tools: WebLogic Server, JDeveloper, and Enterprise Pack for Eclipse

2. Automatically create EJB 3.0 entity beans from database tables

3. Learn to wrap entity beans with session beans and create EJB 3.0 relationships

JDBC 4.0 and Oracle JDeveloper
for J2EE Development

A J2EE developer's guide for using Oracle JDeveloper's integrated database features to build data-driven applications

Deepak Vohra

JDBC 4.0 and Oracle JDeveloper for J2EE Development

ISBN: 978-1-847194-30-5   Paperback: 444 pages

A J2EE developer's guide to using Oracle JDeveloper's integrated database features to build data-driven applications

1. Develop your Java applications using JDBC and Oracle JDeveloper

2. Explore the new features of JDBC 4.0

3. Use JDBC and the data tools in Oracle JDeveloper

4. Configure JDBC with various application servers

Please check **www.PacktPub.com** for information on our titles

Made in the USA
Lexington, KY
15 August 2012